Other titles by Wright Morris
available in Bison Books editions

THE HOME PLACE

PLAINS SONG
FOR FEMALE VOICES

Ceremony in Lone Tree

by Wright Morris

INTRODUCTION TO THE BISON BOOKS EDITION
by Keith Botsford

UNIVERSITY OF NEBRASKA PRESS
LINCOLN AND LONDON

© 1959, 1960 by Wright Morris
Reprinted by arrangement with Josephine Morris
Introduction © 2001 by the University of Nebraska Press
All rights reserved
Manufactured in the United States of America

∞

First Bison Books printing: 1973

Library of Congress Cataloging-in-Publication Data
Morris, Wright, 1910–
Ceremony in Lone Tree / Wright Morris; introduction by
Keith Botsford.
p. cm.
ISBN 0-8032-8276-1 (pbk.: alk. paper)
1. Aged men—Fiction. 2. Nebraska—Fiction. 3. Birth-
days—Fiction. 4. Ghost towns—Fiction. 5. Family
reunions—Fiction. I. Title.
PS3525.07475 C4 2001
813'.52—dc21   2001027957

For Jo

INTRODUCTION
Keith Botsford

The benchmark of any real writer is voice. That voice must be identifiably unique to the writer, so that were you to lay out twenty or thirty pages from as many authors, you should be able to spot that voice. Countless mazurkas exist, but only Chopin's are unique. So it is with writers from America's great center (our Middle Kingdom), many of whom moved East. After Willa Cather, Morris sings truest. Because of his voice.

I'm not sure that this unique voice or its Great Plains context can be pinned down. I fear the professors can't help us; not that there has been an almighty rush to explicate Morris, but even good ones might give us such sensible advice as, "Read him and you'll see." For isn't it a mite obvious to reduce Morris to nostalgia, to the region which is his stage, or to the photography by which many first came to know him? Does it help to pin him with epithets like "Bard of the Prairies"? Readers can figure out that much for themselves. A lot of writers before Morris, and a few that came after him, have attempted the same thing he does, with varying degrees of success. Few, I think, have made so much dance on so little.

Here readers have their chance to work out what is unique about Morris, for *Ceremony in Lone Tree* is quintessential Morris. All the elements of his art are here, pure and concentrated: the basic unities of place and time. Everything tends toward Scanlon's ninetieth birthday in Lone Tree: the way Morris gathers together time in one complex referential bundle, so that past, present, and future all play their roles, bound together like a sheaf of wheat; the awareness of other bounds, of befores and afters, of elsewheres; the magisterial control of detail, in which, in true frugal fashion, nothing is wasted; and the weight and solidity of the prose, its laconicism, its economy, its reverberations.

Morris's books are not long—many are no more than novellas—but they are to be read slowly, even in an age of vanishing spans of attention. In him, this is not shortness of breath but immense concentration. Curiously, this shorter form of fiction has always served particularly well in dealing with characters whose lives are essentially non-verbal, whose field of vision (to use a Morris trope) is so specific to place. They often rely for their effect on their resonance, on what is not said or what did not happen.

Blackbird, the Indian of *A Life*, has little to say and, at the critical moment, nothing at all. But he slices the old man's wrist with the sharp edge of a tin can. Which is exactly what Morris's prose does. In *Ceremony*, a Bomb that doesn't go off is metaphorically present throughout the story. That takes just a few lines:

> "Mr. Boyd," said the woman, "there was no bomb, so I didn't wake you up."
> "Maybe next time," he said.

You can't say how Morris does it, because if it weren't for what went before and comes after, the shaggy-dog Bomb wouldn't matter. It's the weight he applies to everything that counts. *Gravitas*, if you like—though Morris can be terribly funny. Yet who says the comic can't be terrible? Boyd and the waif, Big Daddy and Daughter, are the jokers in this pack, the serious jokers. She's so small ("she used what weight she had to lean on the crank") that when they meet at the one-armed bandit, Boyd is reminded of a bird "in the animal fables, neither young nor old." That's how they begin. She pops out her contact lenses. Together they can joke away the Scanlon clan, the old man ("He was for everybody who hated something or was against something, since that was how he felt himself"), and his offspring in generations.

The realist technique shows people and things as they are. Bits and pieces of something called "reality" are assembled and ordered in a narration. That's Zola, that's John Dos Passos, and that's a big part of Dreiser. But it's not Wright Morris, who is more like an alembic, in whom the vaporous properties of reality are condensed and seen plain.

Something similar happens in Proust: in the madeleine, in Balbec, and in the operations of time. You may remember in Proust Bergotte's rapture, as he dies, at a patch of yellow in Vermeer's *View of Delft*. Same thing: much has been made of very little, but it only makes sense if, when you look at that yellow, or the blood streaming from the old man's wrist, the Bomb, or an old revolver that goes off, you're concerned with ultimates, with essence, with residue.

Unfortunately for Morris and his reputation, we live in a solipsistic age. Who wants to inquire beyond the all-encompassing Self? Ultimates have dropped off the shelf: *Pilgrim's Progress*, all Dante beyond the sexy bits in the *Inferno*, Montaigne—with whom Morris shares so much sangfroid about the real world. What's left is the illusion of reality, what's sexy about it, what the Self can see of it—in Morris's case, ersatz substitutes: the Pretty Horses, Sam Shepherd, the brothers Cohn.

But again, it's too easy to say that Morris's ultimates are those of the desert, those arid places from which our monotheisms arose; that he deals with ultimates because the here and now has nothing to show for its being, just pump handles, worn shoes, dry grass, and a derelict people. I think that's to read Morris as though he were one-dimensional, as though that were *all* he had to say. That's the risk he took as a writer: to make his particular place universal. The lives of Morris's people should be read as what the crowds drawn to the Bomb came to see: "Terrible as it was, it was also a wonderful sight. There was this flash, then this pillar of fire went up and up, like a rabbit's ear." That's what Morris does in *Ceremony*.

> "You better be up for it," she said, and after his name in the register she added:
> WAKE BEFORE BOMB

That's what *Ceremony* is "about."

Writers who look to ultimates—fundamentals—share certain traits. A number of them, for instance, are literary geologists. To us, rocks look alike; to them, not. Consider Charles Dougthy on Arabia, or Euclides da Cunha, who was a surveyor and wrote one of the great unknown texts of the twentieth century, *Os Sertões* (translated in the 1930s by Samuel Putnam as *Rebellion in the Backlands*). Such writers want to know how rocks, or people-as-rocks, were formed. They are writers of the interior of big countries. The interiors, as the French historian Fernand Braudel says, are islands or fastnesses. They are not like the coasts, where everything, races and languages, gets mixed up as the result of commerce. In the great Interior (which is always mysterious, violent, and unadorned), the Henri Taine imperatives—race, milieu, moment—make it possible to "read" people as too humble, too anonymous in their destinies, and too evident. Islands can be studied completely. The story of each individual is the story of all, since all are conditioned by the same "reality."

Morris's Nebraska is an island all right, and if I have any understanding of Morris's work, it is because of two moments in my life: a twenty-four-hour stop my troop train made in the shimmering, dusty heat of July, just outside Parsons, Kansas, and my arrival in Iowa City in the frigid winter of 1949–50. In the first instance, I suspect

I may have asked a question that Morris often asked himself: "Who are these people I see out here, and how do they manage to live?" The second small-time illumination came from the first newspaper I read in Iowa City, the main story of the day being the trial of one Robert Bednacek for the murder of his girlfriend. She had been unfaithful, so he had lapidated her with frozen apples as hard as rocks.

Both the isolation and the cruelty have their roles to play in *Ceremony*. There are ten murders (not so unlike Bednacek's, but even more senseless), and they all come out of nowhere, though they are adumbrated with Morris's painstaking care. Had I not seen Morris country early, traveling his way as he was traveling mine (to Paris and Italy), I don't think he would have the same resonance for me.

I feel strongly about Morris because he wrote about the sort of world many people in America would like to wipe out as anachronistic, outdated, and in the way. Morris people don't read the *New York Times*; they've not heard of international courts of justice or Kosovo. They're stubbornly themselves, and by the standards of the establishment, they're dispensable. How can one equate, the dismissers ask, a vote in Central City to one in New York City, which knows so much better? The fact that Morris's people and Morris are the real America doesn't matter. Those who would wipe them out have long given up on that, and, of course, they've given up on Wright Morris too. If you abolish the literary electoral college, in which each context has its own equal voice, what you have is imaginative miscegenation, literary relativism, and the tyranny of the general.

The word "yarn" occurs to me in this context. Spinning yarn is complex; there are strands and wayward filaments. Used to be when you wanted to know something, you went out and asked an old man. Whatever it was you were facing, he'd been through it—but it took time to get it out of him. With human beings, whose interiors are never evident, you can't flick a switch or turn on a screen and get a "fact." Unlike the old man, the screen hasn't seen for itself. Of course you can't count on the old man for the truth. He could be spitting in the wind. However, you could hold him accountable for what he told you, and you could also see his life and its results.

To the reader unfamiliar with Morris, I can only say this: that any truth in this or any other Morris yarn is a question of accountability. Reading him requires patience because the truth is not an abstract but buried in the perceptions of each character. Since many of these characters—or their fates—spill over from book to book, the truth is not readily observable. The reader will quickly find out in these pages what the major characters *seem* to be, which is what others see them as. McKee has been asleep all his life while his wife Lois has been virginally frozen in her beauty; Etoile is the trapped beauty, and Calvin is the flawed hero. But inside themselves, they are quite other. They have dimensions that can't be contained by the events in which they participate and from which they are in perpetual flight. Bud Momeyer delivers the mail and kills cats with a bow and arrow. His nephew, Lee Roy, is a grease monkey with a religious bent who murders. Boyd is "that rare thing, a completely self-un-made man."

There is no stasis here. Take the matter of violence: the violence of hatred, as in Scanlon; the violence of love, as in Boyd's kissing the exquisite Lois, Scanlon's daughter, who chooses sleep over life; the violence of the child, Gordon, who will do anything to hurt his mother (and surely, she thinks, one day seek to kill her); the violence of the two frustrated killers, so overt, who just want to be seen, to make something of themselves. What boundary can you draw around violence in Morris's work? His characters have it in them to be elusive even to the author's intent.

Every writer is asked at some point, "What is your book about?" The author is always hard pressed to answer. Writers see what they write as a complex web of relationships, of events that precipitate other events and affect people who, though invented, are more real in many ways than the writer's own life.

In *Ceremony*, no straight answer to the question of what the book is about is offered. Interrelated characters and events operate on a series of leitmotifs: one character after another (there are a half-dozen tellers of the tale), enters and sings an aria, his truth, her truth. Among these recurring themes are the nature of violence (Bomb, revolver, anything—including the child's finger that says "Bang! Bang!"); the complex operations of memory and nostalgia for the failed paradise; the nature of failure, of nerve, of the ability to act; and the self-destruction of people (like nature, like civilization).

Action on stage (off-stage is another matter) can be limited—here to the foregathering of the Scanlon brood—but characters must be accountable. They have to be what they are and do what they have to do. Chekhov's axiom is that a gun seen in the first act will go off in the third. If readers know only this book, they will see it as complete in itself; but if they know Morris, they will know that the Scanlons and Boyd come on stage primed: their first act precedes this book—the precarious unity of a ninetieth birthday ceremony.

The identifiable unease at the heart of *Ceremony* is misogyny. The Bomb goes off in the sky, the arrow bites into flesh, and the past penetrates the present. Women both "accepted corruption and savored it." When Boyd brings the girl up to Lone Tree, it's because he wants "to know if it's there, or all in my mind." "I hurt your feelings?" he asks her. "If you're part of this family, you don't have them. You don't show them, that is. It's the law of the land." To their womenfolk, the men are ciphers except in their innate violence. "Darling," says Eileen to Calvin, the runaway who stutters, "your family's not respectable, so don't shoot anybody. Nobody would be at all surprised if you did."

It's feeling that frightens: "the voices of women in the rooms which the voices of men had left." In the confrontation between McKee and Boyd, McKee says, "I hope you didn't come back just to stir up old feelings." Boyd answers that what scares McKee, scares him pissless, "is not the fear of death, but the fear of exposure. The open fly of your feelings. You know why? You might not have any." On the other hand, Boyd starts with a great advantage: "that he *might* do something—or that he might not." This potential is one of Morris's fundamentals. A Bednacek in Iowa just *might* kill his girl with frozen apples. McKee "recognized the nameless face of evil—he recognized it, that is, as stronger than the nameless face of good." His wife, Lois, recognizes that for the murdering young delinquent, Munger, "one way to impress on people how he felt was just to murder them."

I don't think many people have seen the adjacent horrors of what is potential and what is actual as clearly as Wright Morris did. That the Bomb failed to go off doesn't mean that it *won't*.

Contents

The Scene

Come to the window. The one
at the rear of the Lone Tree Hotel. The view is
to the west. There is no obstruction but the sky.
Although there is no one outside to look in, the
yellow blind is drawn low at the window, and between it and the pane a fly is trapped. He has
stopped buzzing. Only the crawling shadow can be
seen. Before the whistle of the train is heard the
loose pane rattles like a simmering pot, then stops,
as if pressed by a hand, as the train goes past. The
blind sucks inward and the dangling cord drags in
the dust on the sill.

At a child's level in the pane there is a flaw that is
round, like an eye in the glass. An eye to that eye, a
scud seems to blow on a sea of grass. Waves of plain
seem to roll up, then break like a surf. Is it a flaw in
the eye, or in the window, that transforms a dry
place into a wet one? Above it towers a sky, like the
sky at sea, a wind blows like the wind at sea, and like
the sea it has no shade: there is no place to hide. One
thing it is that the sea is not: it is dry, not wet.

Drawn up to the window is a horsehair sofa covered with a quilt. On the floor at its side, garlanded
with flowers, is a nightpot full of cigar butts and
ashes. Around it, scattered like seed, are the stubs of
half-burned kitchen matches, the charcoal tips
honed to a point for picking the teeth. They also
serve to aid the digestion and sweeten the breath.

4

The man who smokes the cigars and chews on the matches spends most of the day on the sofa; he is not there now, but the sagging springs hold his shape. He has passed his life, if it can be said he has lived one, in the rooms of the Lone Tree Hotel. His coat hangs in the lobby, his shoes are under the stove, and a runner of ashes marks his trail up and down the halls. His hat, however, never leaves his head. It is the hat, with its wicker sides, the drayman's license at the front, that comes to mind when his children think of him. He has never run a dray, but never mind. The badge is what they see, through the hole where his sleeve has smudged the window, on those rare occasions when they visit him. If the hat is not there, they look for him in the lobby, dozing in one of the hardwood rockers or in one of the beds drawn to a window facing the west. There is little to see, but plenty of room to look.

Scanlon's eyes, a cloudy phlegm color, let in more light than they give out. What he sees are the scenic props of his own mind. His eye to the window, the flaw in the pane, such light as there is illuminates Scanlon, his face like that of a gobbler in the drayman's hat. What he sees is his own business, but the stranger might find the view familiar. A man accustomed to the ruins of war might even feel at home. In the blowouts on the rise are flint arrowheads, and pieces of farm machinery, half buried in sand, resemble nothing so much as artillery equipment, abandoned when the dust began to blow. The tidal shift of the sand reveals one ruin in order to conceal another. It is all there to be seen, but little evidence that Tom Scanlon sees it. Not through the clouded eye he puts to the glass. The emptiness of the plain generates illusions that require little moisture, and grow better, like tall stories, where the mind is dry. The tall corn may flower or burn in the wind, but the plain is a metaphysical landscape and the bumper crop is the one Scanlon sees through the flaw in the glass.

Nothing irked him more than to hear from his children that the place was empty, the town deserted, and that there was nothing to see. He saw plenty. No matter where he looked. Down the tracks to the east, like a headless bird, the bloody neck still raw and dripping, a tub-shaped water tank sits high on stilts. Scanlon once saw a coon crawl out the chute and drink from the spout. Bunches of long-stemmed grass, in this short-grass country, grow where the water drips between the rails, and Scanlon will tell you he has seen a buffalo crop it up. A big bull, of course, high in the shoulders, his short tail like the knot in a whip, walking on the ties like a woman with her skirts tucked up. Another time a wolf, half crazed by the drought, licked the moisture from the rails like ice and chewed on the grass like a dog out of sorts. On occasion stray geese circle the tank like a water hole. All common sights, according to Scanlon, where other men squinted and saw nothing but the waves of heat, as if the cinders of the railbed were still on fire.

It seldom rains in Lone Tree, but he has often seen it raining somewhere else. A blue veil of it will hang like the half-drawn curtain at Scanlon's window. Pillars of cloud loom on the horizon, at night there is much lightning and claps of thunder, and from one window or another rain may be seen falling somewhere. Wind from that direction will smell wet, and Scanlon will complain, if there is someone to listen, about the rheumatic pains in his knees. He suffered greater pains, however, back when he had neighbors who complained, of all things, about the lack of rain.

In the heat of the day, when there is no shadow, the plain seems to be drawn up into the sky, and through the hole in the window it is hard to be sure if the town is still there. It takes on, like a sunning lizard, the colors of the plain. The lines drawn around the weathered buildings smoke and blur. At this time of day Scanlon takes his nap, and by the time he awakes the town is back in its place. The lone tree, a dead cottonwood, can be seen by the shadow it leans to the east, a zigzag line with a fishhook curve at the end. According to Scanlon, Indians once asked permission to bury their dead in the crotch of the tree, and while the body was there the tree had been full of crows. A small boy at the time, Scanlon had shot at them with his father's squirrel gun, using soft lead pellets that he dug out of the trunk of the tree and used over again.

From the highway a half mile to the north, the town sits on the plain as if delivered on a flatcar—as though it were a movie set thrown up during the night. Dry as it is, something about it resembles an ark from which the waters have receded. In the winter it appears to be locked in a sea of ice. In the

summer, like the plain around it, the town seems to
float on a watery surface, stray cattle stand knee-
deep in a blur of reflections, and waves of light and
heat flow across the highway like schools of fish.
Everywhere the tongue is dry, but the mind is wet.
According to his daughters, who should know, the
dirt caked around Tom Scanlon's teeth settled there
in the thirties when the dust began to blow. More of
it can be seen, fine as talcum, on the linoleum floor
in the lobby, where the mice raised in the basement
move to their winter quarters in the cobs behind the
stove.

To the east, relatively speaking, there is much to
see, a lone tree, a water tank, sheets of rain and heat
lightning: to the west a strip of torn screen blurs the
view. The effect is that of now-you-see-it, now-
you-don't. As a rule, there is nothing to see, and if
there is, one doubts it. The pane is smeared where
Scanlon's nose has rubbed the glass. The fact that
there is little to see seems to be what he likes about
it. He can see what he pleases. It need not please
anybody else. Trains come from both directions, but
from the east they come without warning, the
whistle blown away by the wind. From the west,
thin and wild or strumming like a wire fastened to
the building, the sound wakes Scanlon from his
sleep before the building rocks. It gives him time,
that is, to prepare himself. The upgrade freights
rock the building and leave nothing but the noise
in his head, but the downgrade trains leave a vacuum he sometimes raises the window to look at. A

hole? He often thought he might see one there. A cloud of dust would veil the caboose, on the stove one of the pots or the lids would rattle, and if the lamp was lit, the flame would blow as if in a draft.

One day as the dust settled he saw a team of mares, the traces dragging, cantering down the bank where the train had just passed. On the wires above the tracks, dangling like a scarecrow, he saw the body of Emil Bickel, in whose vest pocket the key-wound watch had stopped. At 7:34, proving the train that hit him had been right on time.

To the west the towns are thin and sparse, like the grass, and in a place called Indian Bow the white faces of cattle peer out of the soddies on the slope across the dry bed of the river. They belong to one of Scanlon's grandchildren who married well. On the rise behind the soddies are sunken graves, one of the headstones bearing the name of Will Brady, a railroad man who occasionally stopped off at Lone Tree. Until he married and went east, Scanlon thought him a sensible man.

Down the grade to the east the towns are greener and thicker, like the grass. The town of Polk, the home of Walter McKee, who married Scanlon's eldest daughter, Lois, has elm-shaded streets and a sign on the highway telling you to slow down. There is also a park with a Civil War cannon, the name of Walter McKee carved on the breech and that of his friend, Gordon Boyd, on one of the cannon balls. In the house where Walter McKee was born grass still grows between the slats on the porch, and the neighbor's chickens still lay their eggs under the stoop. At the corner of the porch a tar barrel catches and stores the rain from the roof. At the turn of the century, when McKee was a boy, he buried the white hairs from a mare's tail in the rain barrel, confident they would turn up next as garter snakes. In the middle of the century that isn't done, and a TV aerial, like a giant Martian insect, crouches on the roof as if about to fly off with the house. That is a change, but on its side in the yard is a man's bicycle with the seat missing. The small boy who rides it straddles it through the bars: he never sits down. He mounts it slantwise, like a bareback rider, grease from the chain rubbing off on one leg and soiling the cuff of the pants leg rolled to the knee. Gordon Boyd still bears the scar where the teeth of the sprocket dug into his calf. Bolder than McKee, he liked to ride on the gravel around the patch of grass in the railroad station, leaning forward to hold a strip of berry-box wood against the twirling spokes.

The short cut in the yard, worn there by McKee, still points across the street to a wide vacant lot and to the tree where McKee, taunted by Boyd, climbed to where the sway and the height made him dizzy. He fell on a milk-can lid, breaking his arm. Mrs. Boyd, a white-haired woman, had put his arm to soak in a cold tub of water while Gordon went for the doctor on McKee's new bike. Over that summer Boyd had grown so fast he could pump it from the seat.

The Boyd house, having no basement, had a storm

cave at the back of the yard where McKee smoked corn silk and Boyd smoked Fourth of July punk. The white frame house still has no basement, and the upstairs bedroom, looking out on the porch, is still heated by a pipe that comes up from the stove below. When McKee spent the night with Boyd, Mrs. Boyd would rap a spoon on the pipe to make them quiet, or turn down the damper so the room would get cold. The old coke burner, with the isinglass windows through which Boyd and McKee liked to watch the coke settle, now sits in the woodshed, crowned with the horn of the Victrola. The stove board, however, the floral design worn away where Boyd liked to dress on winter mornings, is now in the corner where the floor boards have sagged, under the new TV. Since the house has no porch high enough to crawl under, Boyd kept his sled and Irish Mail under the porch of a neighbor. Along with Hershey bar tinfoil, several pop bottles, a knife with a woman's leg for a handle, and a tin for condoms, thought to be balloons and blown up till they popped on the Fourth of July, the sled is still there. The boys don't use the ones with wooden runners any more. The chain swing no longer creaks on the porch or spends the winter, cocoonlike, drawn to the ceiling, but the paint still peels where it grazed the clapboards and thumped on the railing warm summer nights. Long after it was gone Mrs. Boyd was kept awake by its creak.

The people change—according to a survey conducted by a new supermarket—but the life in Polk remains much the same. The new trailer park on the east edge of town boasts the latest and best in portable living, but the small fry still fish, like McKee, for crawdads with hunks of liver, and bring them home to mothers who hastily dump them back in the creek. The men live in Polk, where there is plenty of room, and commute to those places where the schools are overcrowded, the rents inflated, but where there is work. At the western edge of town an air-conditioned motel with a stainless-steel diner blinks at night like an airport, just across the street from where McKee chipped his front teeth on the drinking fountain. Once or twice a year on his way to Lone Tree, McKee stops off in Polk for what he calls a real shave, in the shop where he got his haircuts as a boy. The price for a shave and a haircut has changed, but the mirror on the wall is the same. In it, somewhere, is the face McKee had as a boy. Stretched out horizontal, his eyes on the tin ceiling, his lips frothy with the scented lather, he sometimes fancies he hears the mocking voice of Boyd:

Walter McKee,
Button your fly.
Pee in the road
And you'll get a sty.

Although he comes from the south, McKee goes out of his way to enter town from the west, passing the water stack with the word P O L K like a shadow under the new paint. Just beyond the water stack is the grain elevator, the roof flashing like a mirror in the sun, the name T. P. CRETE in black on the fresh coat of aluminum. The same letters were stamped like a legend on McKee's mind. The great man himself was seldom seen in the streets of Polk, or in the rooms of his mansion, but his name, in paint or gold leaf, stared at McKee from walls and windows and the high board fence that went along the lumberyard. T. P. Crete's wife, like a bird in a cage, sometimes went by in her electric car, making no more noise than the strum of the wires on the telephone poles. It was this creature who deprived McKee of his friend Boyd. She sent him, when he proved to be smart, to those high-toned schools in the East that indirectly led to the ruin he made of his life. Destiny manifested itself through the Cretes, and the sight of the name affected McKee like a choir marching in or the sound of his mother humming hymns.

Beyond the grain elevator is the railroad station, the iron wheels of the baggage truck sunk in the gravel, an OUT OF ORDER sign pasted on the face of the penny scales in the lobby. On the east side of the station is a patch of grass. Around it is a fence of heavy wrought iron, the top rail studded to discourage loafers, pigeons and small fry like McKee and Boyd. Polk is full of wide lawns and freshly cropped grass healthy enough for a boy to walk on, but for McKee the greenest grass in the world is the patch inside the wrought-iron fence. He never enters town without a glance at it. If it looks greener than other grass it might be due to the cinder-blackened earth, and the relative sparseness and tenderness of the shoots. But the secret lies in McKee, not in the grass. No man raised on the plains, in the short-grass country, takes a patch of grass for granted, and it is not for nothing they protect it with a fence or iron bars. When McKee thinks of spring, or of his boyhood, or of what the world would be like if men came to their senses, in his mind's eye he sees the patch of green in the cage at Polk. Tall grass now grows between the Burlington tracks that lead south of town to the bottomless sand pit where Boyd, before the eyes of McKee, attempted to walk on water for the first time. But not the last. Nothing seemed to teach him anything.

Southeast of Polk is Lincoln, capital of the state, the present home of McKee and his wife Lois, as well as of Lois's sister Maxine and her family. Tom Scanlon's youngest girl, Edna, married Clyde Ewing, an Oklahoma horse breeder, who found oil on his farm in the Panhandle. The view from their modern air-conditioned house is so much like that around Lone Tree, Edna Ewing felt sure her father would feel right at home in it. Tom Scanlon, however, didn't like the place. For one thing, there were no windows, only those gleaming walls of glass. He had walked from room to room as he did outside, with his head drawn in. Although the floor and walls radiated heat, Scanlon felt cold, since it lacked a stove with an oven door or a rail where he could put his feet. Only in the back door was there something like a window, an opening about the size of a porthole framing the view, with a flaw in the glass to which he could put his eye. Through it he saw, three hundred miles to the north, the forked branches of the lone tree like bleached cattle horns on the railroad embankment that half concealed the town, the false fronts of the buildings like battered remnants of a board fence. Even the hotel, with its MAIL POUCH sign peeling like a circus poster, might be taken for a signboard along an abandoned road. That is how it is, but not how it looks to Scanlon. He stands as if at the screen, gazing down the tracks to where the long-stemmed grass spurts from the cinders like leaks in a garden hose. The mindless wind in his face seems damp with the prospect of rain.

Three stories high, made of the rough-faced brick brought out from Omaha on a flatcar, the Lone Tree Hotel sits where the coaches on the westbound caboose once came to a stop. Eastbound, there were few who troubled to stop. In the westbound caboose were the men who helped Lone Tree to believe in itself. The hotel faces the south, the empty pits that were dug for homes never erected and the shadowy trails, like Inca roads, indicating what were meant to be streets. The door at the front, set in slantwise on the corner, with a floral design in the frosted glass, opens on the prospect of the town. Slabs of imported Italian marble face what was once the bank, the windows boarded like a looted tomb, the vault at the rear once having served as a jail. A sign:

$5. FINE FOR TALKING

TO

PRISONERS

once hung over one of the barred windows, but a brakeman who was something of a card made off with it.

The lobby of the hotel, level with the hitching bar, affords a view of the barbershop interior, the mirror on the wall and whoever might be sitting in the one chair. Only the lower half of the window is curtained, screening off the man who is being shaved but offering him a view of the street and the plain when he sits erect, just his hair being cut. Tucked into the frame of the mirror are the post cards sent back by citizens who left or went traveling to those who were crazy enough to stay on in Lone Tree. The incumbent barber usually doubled as the postmaster. In the glass razor case, laid out on a towel still peppered with his day-old beard, is the razor that shaved William Jennings Bryan. In Lone Tree, at the turn of the century, he pleaded the lost cause of silver, then descended from the platform of the caboose for a shampoo and a shave. On that day a balloon, brought out on a flatcar, reached the altitude of two hundred forty-five feet with Edna Scanlon, who was something of a tomboy, visible in the basket that hung beneath. The century turned that memorable summer, and most of the men in Lone Tree turned with it; like the engines on the roundhouse platform they wheeled from west to east. But neither Scanlon, anchored in the lobby, nor the town of Lone Tree turned with it. The century went its own way after that, and Scanlon went his.

From a rocker in the lobby Scanlon can see the

gap between the barbershop and the building on the west, the yellow blind shadowed with the remaining letters of the word MIL NE Y. On the floor above the millinery is the office of Dr. Twomey, where a cigar-store Indian with human teeth guards the door. He stands grimacing, tomahawk upraised, with what are left of the molars known to drop out when the building is shaken by a downgrade freight. When Twomey set up his practice, the barber chair served very nicely as an operating table, a place for lancing boils, removing adenoids or pulling teeth. A flight of wooden steps without a railing mounted to his office on the second floor, but they collapsed within a week or so after he died. He was a huge man, weighing some three hundred pounds, and it took four men to lower his body to the casket on the wagon in the street. The stairs survived the strain, then collapsed under their own weight.

A hand-cranked gas pump, the crank in a sling, sits several yards in front of the livery stable, as if to disassociate itself from the horses once stabled inside. At the back of the stable, inhabited by bats, is the covered wagon Scanlon was born in, the bottom sloped up at both ends like a river boat. Strips of faded canvas, awning remnants, partially cover the ribs. Until the hotel was built in the eighties, the Scanlon family lived in the rear of the millinery, and the covered wagon, like a gypsy encampment, sat under the lone tree. Before the railroad went through, the pony express stopped in the shade of the tree for water. Scanlon remembers the sweat on the horses, and once being lifted to the pommel of the saddle, but most of the things he remembers took place long before he was born.

In the weeds behind the stable are a rubber-tired fire-hose cart without the hose, two short lengths of ladder and the iron frame for the fire bell. When the water-pressure system proved too expensive, the order for the hose and the fire bell was canceled. On the east side of the stable, the wheels sunk in the sand, a water sprinkler is garlanded with morning glories and painted with the legend VISIT THE LYRIC TONITE. The Lyric, a wooden frame building, has a front of galvanized tin weathered to the leaden color of the drainpipes on the hotel. It stands like a souvenir book end at the east end of the town, holding up the row of false-front stores between it and the bank. Most of the year these shops face the sun, the light glaring on the curtained windows, like a row of blindfolded Confederate soldiers lined up to be shot. A boardwalk, like a fence blown on its side, is half concealed by the tidal drift of the sand—nothing could be drier, but the look of the place is wet. The wash of the sand is rippled as if by the movement of water, and stretches of the walk have the look of a battered pier. The town itself seems to face what is left of a vanished lake. Even the lone tree, stripped of its foliage, rises from the deck of the plain like a mast, and from the highway or the bluffs along the river, the crows'-nest at the top might be that on a ship. The bowl of the sky seems higher, the plain wider, because of it.

A street light still swings at the crossing corner

but in the summer it casts no shadow, glowing like a bolthole in a stove until after nine o'clock. The plain is dark, but the bowl of the sky is full of light. On his horsehair sofa, drawn up to the window, Scanlon can see the hands on his watch until ten o'clock. The light is there after the sun has set and will be. there in the morning before it rises, as if a property of the sky itself. The moon, rather than the sun, might be the source of it. In the summer the bats wing in and out of the stable as if it were dark, their radar clicking, wheel on the sky, then wing into the stable again. At this time of the evening coins come out to be found. The rails gleam like ice in the cinders, and the drayman's badge on Scanlon's hat, bright as a buckle, can be seen through the hole he has rubbed in the glass.

If a grass fire has been smoldering during the day you will see it flicker on the plain at night, and smoke from these fires, like Scanlon himself, has seldom left the rooms of the Lone Tree Hotel. It is there in the curtains like the smell of his cigars. His daughter Lois, the moment she arrives, goes up and down the halls opening the windows, and leaves a bottle of Air Wick in the room where she plans to spend the night. For better or worse—as she often tells McKee—she was born and raised in it.

The last time Lois spent a night in Lone Tree was after her father had been found wrapped up like a mummy, his cold feet in a colder oven, and paraded big as life on the front page of the Omaha *Bee.* The caption of the story read:

MAN WHO KNEW BUFFALO BILL
SPENDS LONELY XMAS

although both his daughter and McKee were out there in time to spend part of Christmas with him. The story brought him many letters and made him famous, and put an end to his Lone Tree hibernation. To keep him entertained, as well as out of mischief, his daughter and her husband took him along the following winter on their trip to Mexico. There he saw a bullfight and met McKee's old friend, Gordon Boyd.

In Claremore, Oklahoma, on their way back, they stopped to see Edna and Clyde Ewing. Clyde claimed to be one fifth Cherokee Indian and an old friend of Will Rogers, whoever that might be. Although they had this new modern home, the Ewings spent most of their time going up and down the country in a house trailer just a few feet shorter than a flatcar. It had two bedrooms, a shower and a bath, with a rumpus room said to be soundproof. In the rumpus room, since they had no children, they kept an English bulldog named Shiloh, whose daddy had been sold for thirty thousand dollars. Scanlon never cared for dogs, and being too old to ride any of the Ewings' prize horses he was put in a buggy, between Ewing and McKee, and allowed to hold the reins while a white mare cantered. It made him hmmmphh. The Ewings were having a family reunion, but Scanlon saw no Cherokees present.

While they were there, they got on the Ewings' TV the report of a tragedy in Lincoln: a high-school boy with a hot-rod had run down and killed two of his classmates. An accident? No, he had run them down as they stood in the street, taunting him. On the TV screen they showed the boy's car, the muffler sticking up beside the windshield like a funnel, the fenders dented where he had smashed into the boys. Then they showed the killer, a boy with glasses, looking like a spaceman in his crash helmet. His name was Lee Roy Momeyer—pronounced *Lee Roy* by his family—the son of a Calloway machine-shop mechanic, and related to Scanlon by marriage. At the time he ran down and killed his classmates, he was working in a grease pit at the gasoline station where Walter McKee had used his influence to get him the job. Eighteen years of age, serious-minded, studious-looking in his thick-lensed glasses, Lee Roy was well intentioned to the point that it hurt—but a little slow. Talking to him, McKee fell into the habit of repeating himself.

"Mr. McKee," Lee Roy would say, "what can I do you for?" and McKee never quite got accustomed to it. And there he was, famous, with his picture on TV. In the morning they had a telegram from Lois's sister, Maxine Momeyer, asking if McKee would go his bail, which he did. Two days later, as they drove into Lincoln, coming in the back way so nobody would see them, there was no mention of Lee Roy Momeyer on the radio. A man and his wife had just been found murdered, but it couldn't have been Lee Roy. They had *him*, as the reporter said, in custody. Before that week was out there had been eight more, shot down like ducks by the mad-dog killer, and then he was captured out in the sand hills not far from Lone Tree. His name was Charlie Munger, and he was well known to Lee Roy Momeyer, who often greased his car. Between them they had killed twelve people in ten days.

Why did they do it?

When they asked Lee Roy Momeyer he replied that he just got tired of being pushed around. Who was pushing *who?* Never mind, that was what he said. The other one, Charlie Munger, said that he wanted to be somebody. Didn't everybody? Almost anybody, that is, but who he happened to be? McKee's little grandson thought he was Davy Crockett, and wore a coonskin hat with a squirrel's tail dangling, and Tom Scanlon, the great-grandfather, seemed to think he was Buffalo Bill. But when McKee read that statement in the paper there was just one person he thought of. His old boyhood chum, Gordon Boyd. Anybody could run over people or shoot them, but so far as McKee knew there was only one other man in history who had tried to walk on water—and He had got away with it.

McKee filed his clippings on these matters in a book entitled THE WALK ON THE WATER, written by Boyd after he had tried it himself. When it came to wanting to be somebody, and wanting, that is, to be it the hard way, there was no one in the same class as Boyd.

The Roundup

Boyd

In Acapulco, where Boyd had gone to sulk, he consumed several cups of the shaved ice doused with sirup from hair-tonic bottles that he knew with reasonable assurance would make him sick. As it did. Deathly sick, but he did not die. The long night of nausea and fever merely stimulated him to remember the details he had come to Acapulco to forget. Running into the McKees at Sanborn's, herding them like goats out to the bullfight where he had acted like a fool, but somehow not quite fool enough. Everything called for talent, and that was one more talent he lacked.

The morning after, McKee had come around and honked his musical horn beneath Boyd's window, not wanting to leave his station wagon parked in front. The car was full of Mexican loot—pottery, baskets and *sarapes*—and he also feared for hubcaps valued at five and a half bucks apiece. In his slippers and soiled bathrobe Boyd had walked down the four flights to the street, to see the face of Lois McKee in the depths of a new straw hat. In the back of the car, like something new in knickknacks, sat the boy with his coonskin hat, and the mad old Scanlon hugging a pair of mounted bull horns.

"Just wanted to tell you," McKee had bawled, "that at least on our side there's no hard feelings," and he had slapped Boyd on the shoulder with his broad hand. Boyd had agreed, then McKee had blurted, "You know you're closer to me than a brother, Gordon," which had left Boyd standing there, speechless, and Mrs. McKee said:

"Why, McKee, what a thing to say to Mr. Boyd," and put one of her gloved hands lightly on Boyd's arm. Hardly a moment, but long enough to finish what the bullfight had started. After thirty years of exile Boyd was back where his life had begun.

So he had gone to Acapulco, to a tourist *posada*, and one of the landlady's numberless offspring was a child named Quirina—Quirina Dolores Lupe Mendoza, as she said. She ran errands, she fanned his sweaty face with a palm-leaf fan. She had, from God knows where, honey-colored hair that hung below her shoulders, with a downlike frost of it along the bony ridges of her spine. Her body was sticklike, the skin along her ribs transparent as vellum, the armpits as smooth as a marble faun's. The doll-like head seemed so large he thought it might break off when she laughed. When she realized it gave him pleasure, she would sit with her hand resting like a bird in one of his own. His hair was sometimes in his eyes or plastered to the film of sweat on his forehead, and she would sit as if daydreaming, running one of her hands through it, as if he were a pet. And when not with him, sitting there on the bed, she would stand in the yard like a flower of evil, growing out of the filth and vileness just for him. Always where he could see her. Oh, she never overlooked that. And puzzling at first, then disturbing, were the large limpid eyes of a kept woman—a well-kept woman—in the face of a child. A woman, that is, who both accepted corruption and savored it.

She seemed incredibly quick to learn all the strange things that he told her, but a day or two later she seemed to have forgotten most of what he said. The same story spread wide the beautiful eyes. The same joke had her laughing again. And then he happened to notice how, hours on end, she would explore her own body like a moneky, not for lice but just as a way of passing the time. She was also very dirty—in the heat he could smell her, although a warm sea lapped the house—and thinking it would please her he gave her his scented shaving soap. The perfume she liked, but not the lather, and would rub it dry on parts of her body. Imperceptibly at first, Boyd began to get well. The pleasures he took in his illness began to wane. He bought a pair of shorts and wandered alone up and down the beach.

He collected shells, driftwood and post-card pictures of himself. In these pictures, taken by boys with antique tripod cameras, he looked for evidence of moral deterioration, but found none. Quite the contrary. He looked reasonably well. He saw himself, sitting or standing, his body several shades darker than his shadow, on the jutting rocks or the salt-white sand, looking much better than he had in years. In one of these pictures a vulture on a post at his back seemed to peer over his shoulder, the bird looking evil indeed, but not Boyd. Knowing how it would shock them, he sent one of these snapshots to the McKees. Nothing surprised him more than the letter he received by return post.

McKee wrote that he was glad to see him looking so well, and that both he and Mrs. McKee wondered if he might be passing through Nebraska toward the end of March. That happened to be the old man's birthday, and they were planning a family reunion —which included him in—at the old man's place in Lone Tree. Nothing would please the whole family more than to see him there. Especially the old man's great-grandson, little Gordon, since he never tired of talking about Boyd, but McKee was thinking in particular of himself. It wouldn't be a family reunion if Boyd wasn't there.

Lone Tree? When Boyd read the name he laughed out loud. Was there a more desolate, more inhuman outpost in the world? Treeless and bleak, home of the Dust Bowl and that eccentric old fool, Scanlon, boarded up in his dilapidated hotel. It made him grateful Acapulco was so far away. And then a week or so later he searched half the day for the letter to see if he still might get to Lone Tree in time.

At sunrise the following morning he hired the boys who spent the day diving for coins to give his '48 Plymouth a push. When it started he just kept going, up the coast route where it was balmy, but when the weather changed at Nogales so did his mind. The idea of going to Lone Tree struck him as mad. The thought of McKee and his wife, of the clan assembled at the dry water hole, led him to wonder if the Acapulco sun had softened his brain. So he went northwest, up through Phoenix to Las Vegas where he looked right at home, in his soiled resort clothes, with the week-end shipment of suckers from Hollywood. A plump matron about his own age, the eastbound side of her face sunburned, nudged his elbow at the bar to ask if he was from Anaheim. She was hopeful. There was something to be said for Anaheim. On the fingers that dunked the ice cubes in her drink were several large stones. Had he ever, she asked him, longed for the unknown? All she wanted before going home was a look at the life south of the border, since she had gone to the trouble of getting the shots, and her arm was sore. Tucking up her sleeve, she showed him her vaccination scars.

Lone Tree, so far away that morning, seemed nearer at hand. On a stool at the bar, the slot machines churning behind him, Boyd recalled that it was in Lone Tree that Walter McKee had taken Lois Scanlon to wife. Did the place show it? Did it have the air of hallowed ground? He left town in the evening, following lights that he thought led him north into Utah, but he had got in with a stream of army-base traffic headed northwest. About midnight, at a place near Beatty, he pulled in for the night, but the motel south of town was full up. He asked the elderly woman who came to the door if the all-night gambling explained it.

"Gambling?" she said, as if it had skipped her mind. "Oh, no, it's the bomb."

The bomb? For a moment Boyd did not reply.

In Mexico he had forgotten about the bomb. It seemed strange to hear about it in a wilderness of slot machines, from an elderly woman who twisted the apron tied at her waist. The radio at her back played old-time hymns. She was white-haired, motherly, and pinned to her dress like a brooch was a piece of metal about the size of a dog tag. But nothing on it. Was that why Boyd stared? "That's to check the fallout," she said when she noticed where he was staring. "Everyone who lives here wears one. After the test they come around and check it. That way they know if the place is safe to live in or not."

Did she smile? Boyd gazed at her as if he failed to grasp what she had said. It led her to feel he was not too bright, and being a motherly sort of person, she opened the screen, asked him to step in. If he didn't mind a room without a bath, she said, and no TV in it, she might put him up.

No, he said, he wouldn't mind, and she showed him the room—one used by her son, but he was making good money helping dude ranchers look for uranium. She wagged her head to indicate what fools she thought they all were. She would let it lie. It didn't poison people in the rocks where they found it or make the dust hot. As Boyd signed the register she added: Did he want to be up for the bomb?

For the bomb? He saw that it was a routine question.

Just before dawn, she replied. That was when the breeze died, and they did it. When he didn't reply she said if he hadn't seen a bomb go off, he should.

He owed it to himself. Terrible as it was, it was also a wonderful sight. There was this flash, then this pillar of fire went up and up, like a rabbit's ear.

Boyd turned as if he saw it.

"You better be up for it," she said, and after his name in the register she added:

WAKE BEFORE BOMB

then added an exclamation point.

Boyd had gone to bed soon enough, but not to sleep. Neon signs at the gambling halls made a pattern of lights on the ceiling, and he could hear gusts of jukebox music when the doors opened. It seemed an odd place to be having a hell of a time. He got up, built a fire in the stove out of the shingles in the wood box, then sat there, the lights off, warming his hands. The sound of the draft in the chimney made him think of the house he was born in, he and McKee lying awake in the cold room upstairs. His mother would pound on the pipe with the poker to shut them up. Later, standing at the top of the stairs with her lamp, her shadow looming on the wall like a monster, she would hold it out before her and ask, "Gordon, you two awake or asleep?" They had to stuff the corners of their pillows in their mouths to keep from laughing out loud. Why was it so funny? Had it seemed—to kids as smart as themselves—a strange question to ask anybody? Awake or asleep? But if that voice now spoke to him from the pipe—what would he say? What would Mc-Kee? In Boyd's estimation, McKee had been asleep most of his life. He had curled up snugly in the cocoon God's Loveliest Creature had spun for him. What sort of bomb would wake him up? Back in Polk and Lone Tree no bomb was expected, no matron stopped the stranger to put to him the question, wearing the dog tag that bore, like a headstone, his invisible number. No one cried out back there, because everybody slept. The old man in the past, the young ones in the future, McKee in his cocoon, and Lois, the ever-patient, ever-chaste Penelope, busy at her looming. WAKE BEFORE BOMB? How did one do it? Was it even advisable? The past, whether one liked it or not, was all that one actually possessed: the green stuff, the gilt-edge securities. The present was that moment of exchange—when all might be lost. Why risk it? Why not sleep on the money in the bank? To wake before the bomb was to risk losing all to gain what might be so little—a brief moment in the present, that one moment later joined the past. Nevertheless, as the lady said, it was a wonderful sight. There was this flash, then the pillar of fire went up and up as if to heaven, and the heat and the light of that moment illuminated for a fraction the flesh and bones of the present. Did these bones live? At that moment they did. The meeting point, the melting point of the past confronting the present. Where no heat was thrown off, there was no light—where it failed to ignite the present, it was dead. The phoenix, that strange bird of ashes, rose each day from the embers where the past had died and the future was at stake. To wake before bomb was tricky business. What if it scared you to sleep?

When that pillar of fire went up and up, what

would be revealed? He raised the window as if he might see. Down the road where the signs were blinking a small one read BREAKFAST AT ALL HOURS. It made him hungry. He dressed and walked down the road to the restaurant. Through the window he could see the ranks of slot machines. Under a hooded lamp at the rear men with their shirt sleeves rolled, ties dangling, stood around a table like a pit exhibiting snakes. One with a rake, his eyes shaded, leaned forward to drag in the dice. The bar looked empty, the fellow behind it with a visor shading his face, one of the metal tags like a campaign button clipped to his shirt. Boyd had stepped inside before he saw the girl on the stool at the end. She faced a slot machine, her sweater sleeve pushed to the elbow on the arm she rested on the crank. Did she need the stool to reach it? She looked that small. She dipped her hand into the bag that hung from her shoulder, the mouth gaping, then used what weight she had to lean on the crank. Boyd could hear the cylinders spin, click to a stop. In the dim light she leaned forward to read them, said aloud:

"Two friggin oranges and one pineapple. Sweet Jesus, what would he make of that."

"What's he like?" said the barman, giving Boyd a wink. "Vodka or gin?"

Her hand clawed around in the bag for matches. The flame lit up a face that Boyd had seen on the sly birds in the animal fables, neither young nor old. She blew out a cloud of smoke, then turned and said, "Big Daddy, you got change for a dollar?" and held up a crumpled bill.

"She means you," said the barman. "I'm her Baby Doll."

Boyd walked down the counter and made change for the dollar. The hand into which he dropped the coins snapped shut on them like a trap. The small fist shook at him, and she said, "That's the last of his friggin money."

"You better keep a dime for carfare," said the barman.

"A friggin buffalo nickel," she said, sorting the coins, "don't that mean luck?" The skin across her nose was so tight Boyd could see the dimple in the sharp tip. Something about her eyes made him stare. Birdlike, she cocked her head to one side.

"You see something funny?" Before he replied she tipped her head to the bar, and put her fingers to one eye as if to pop it. Something dropped on the bar. One eye lidded, she looked back at him. "How you like that? Better?"

"She pullin' that eye business on you?" said the barman. "Thought I'd lose my lunch when she pulled it on me."

She tipped her head to the bar, covered one eye, then felt around till she found what she wanted. On the tip of her finger Boyd could see it. Like a tiddly-wink.

"You ever see such a friggin silly thing in your life?"

His mouth a little dry, Boyd said, "Does it work?"

"Glasses got me Irwin. I'm for anything but glasses. He took me for a friggin intellectual type."

"I'd like to see this guy," said the barman.

"What type are you?" said Boyd.

Both eyes open, she looked at Boyd's face, a piece at a time. On the glassy pupil of one eye he could see the reflection of the pressed-tin ceiling.

"What type am I? Big Daddy, what type you like?"

"Say she was the shy type myself," said the barman, "wouldn't you?"

"What a friggin bore it is to get to know people. Don't you think they're nicer before you know them?"

"How you like that for an approach?" said the barman.

"At thirty-two," she said, "he'd put it all behind him. Imagine that?"

"Who?" said Boyd.

"Irwin. Sweet Jesus."

"If I was thirty-two—" said Boyd.

"You know what? You probably sounded just like him. The friggin good old days. How it was in college. How all that jazz in the old cars was so different. Sure it's different. It's gone."

"I take it you didn't like him?" said Boyd.

"How the hell you like life insurance? He was a friggin computer. He computed his love life. He had it all computed when it would be over. Sweet Jesus, that's one thing I'm not computing, are you?"

"Not at my age," said Boyd.

"I got news for you," she said. "You're just like him. The friggin brainy type." She turned on the stool to give the crank a jerk, then wheeled and said, "You think we meet the same person over and over?

He's so friggin scared of everything, like you are."

"What makes you think I'm so friggin scared?" He hadn't meant to say friggin. It had just slipped out.

"Big Daddy, let's not get personal. It louses up everything when you get personal. I don't mind your bein scared. I'm no goddam Joan of Arc."

"How you like that?" said the barman. "Now I ask you."

In the bag where she had spilled the coins she clawed around for one, turned to the room. Three men and a woman sat at a green-covered table, playing cards. No one moved. Smoke rose into the hooded lamp as if the woman's hair were on fire.

"Let's get some friggin life in this joint," she said, and stepped down from the stool into her sandals, then shuffled through the sawdust to the jukebox in the corner. She wore new Levis, and crossing the room, slipped her hands into the tight front pockets. "Big Daddy," she called, reading the labels, "what sort of music you like?" Before he answered she said, "Don't bother. Sweet Jesus, I can hear it. One of those great old tunes you used to sing in college. One of those friggin classics that went along with the good old cars, and the good old lays. I don't dig that jazz." She dropped a coin into the machine. "If you're like Irwin you met the only real friggin woman of your life back in high school. That's all, you just met her. Lucky for you she married somebody else." The music started and she came back to the bar, her arms raised as if she wanted a lift to the stool. "This is on my money, Big Daddy, let's dance."

Boyd slipped an arm around her. In the corner of the bar, like an eye, the TV screened flickered at them. Her head flat on his chest, she said, "You coming or going to Reno, Big Daddy?"

"Daughter," he said, "I'm like Irwin. The only real friggin woman of my life got away."

She stopped dancing and said, "You kidding?"

"Lucky for me, as you say, she married somebody else."

"I only said that. Sweet Jesus. I never thought it really happened."

"That's what's good about the good old days. The other fellow got the girl."

The music stopped, but she didn't seem to take note of it. At the front of her mouth, pushed back into service, was a piece of gum she had forgotten.

"You like another dime?" he said. "The music's stopped."

What little weight she had hung on him, as if she had fainted.

"She pass out on you?" the barman said.

Boyd eased her over to the counter and hoisted her, gently, to one of the stools. He hadn't noticed at the part in her dark hair the blonde roots coming in. "Give her a shot of this," the barman said, and slid a short one down the counter. When he held it to her lips, she sniffed it like a cat, turned away.

"You all right, Daughter?"

"The friggin music's stopped. You think a dime will start it?"

"First she says let's not get personal, then she faints and lets you have it."

"When Irwin's feelings were hurt, he would get

out of bed and go sleep in his Eames chair. That hurt him worse than I did. When my feelings were hurt, he would say, 'Go buy yourself something.' Sweet Jesus."

"Pretty goddam decent of him, I'd say," said the barman.

"Why didn't she marry you, Big Daddy?"

"For one thing, I didn't ask her."

Did she hear that?

"First sensible thing I've heard a man say in thirty-two years," the barman said.

She put the heels of her hands to her eyes. The stool she sat on started rocking. "You hear anything?" she said. Boyd listened. At the gaming table he could hear the rake drag in the dice. "You don't hear it?" He shook his head. "You think if I gave you a dime you could hear it? You think if you gave *her* a dime she could hear it?"

"I have it on good authority," said Boyd, "she doesn't need the dime. She makes her own music."

"Sweet Jesus, would I like to hear it."

"You would? Maybe we can arrange it."

She spread her fingers so her eyes could peer at his face.

"How you like that one," said the barman. "How you like that on a bar stool?"

She dropped her hands, and Boyd said, "She's throwing a little party, old friends of the family." He smiled. "Like me to introduce you? I'm your Daddy. You're my Daughter."

"Why you say that?"

"For a long time, Daughter, she's expected the worst. Maybe this is the time to let her have it."

She struck at him, the cigarettes in the pack fanning out on the floor and on the bar at his back. "I'd hate to be the only friggin woman in your life! You know why? I wouldn't be in it. Any more than she's been in it. You're too friggin scared to play *any* music!"

The street door swung open and a woman in slacks, blowing on her hands, a man's hat pulled down on her head, came in and said, "Any coffee? Guess they called it off. Goddam place looks about the same."

"The bomb?" the girl yelled. "You mean they didn't do it?" She hopped off the stool and ran through the door. At the curb she looked around as if surprised to find the town was still there. Boyd left money on the bar and walked out and stood beside her. In the green light of dawn her painted toenails looked black; some chain she had stopped wearing had left its shadow on her neck.

"You going my way?" he said. "The good old days are gone, as you say, but I've still got one of the cars."

Her bag hung gaping, stuffed like a bureau drawer, and she put a hand into it as he walked away. "Sweet Jesus!" she said, just before sneezing, then blew her nose. He left her there and walked up the grade to the motel where the office door stood open.

"Mr. Boyd," said the woman, "there was no bomb, so I didn't wake you up."

"Maybe next time," he said.

"Oh, there'll be a next time all right," she replied. "Maybe tonight. Where'll you be tonight?"

"If I don't see it, maybe I'll hear it," he said.

He put his bag in the car, then spread the map out on the hood where the morning light fell on it. Where was he going? Lone Tree was not on the map. "If you're driving," McKee had written, "just ask anybody in Calloway. They all know the old man. They'll tell you where to turn off." He folded up the map, then turned to see her at the front of the drive. Her handbag was still gaping, and she had a canvas bag with a fresh flight sticker.

"A friggin Plymouth?" she said. "That's what Irwin was driving." Boyd stood there, silent, and she said, "I thought you might need a push. Didn't everybody need one in the good old days?"

During the day she slept like a kid, curled in the seat. Boyd covered her with his raincoat, seeing no more of her than the green circle around her neck, one of her earrings and the hand that clutched the pack of filter-tip cigarettes. From one finger the ring was missing; on another a school ring with red stones was caked with the soap she had used in the washroom. By dark they were over in Wyoming and stopped near Evanston for the night. She didn't seem surprised to see where she was. "My brother was here in the war," she said, and looked around as if she might see other members of her family. In his raincoat, the sleeves rolled up, one side of her face patterned with the seat cover, she looked like a teenage schoolgirl. The night cook in the diner assumed Boyd was her father. "Let me bring the kid a hot chocolate," he said. Boyd let him. She drank it, leaving her plum-colored lipstick on the rim of the cup. He took a room with two beds, stepped out for a smoke, and when he came back she was facing the wall, asleep. On the floor were her sandals. Had she gone to bed in her clothes? On the shelf in the bathroom she had left her piece of chlorophyll gum, as if she meant to chew it later, and in an aspirin tin her contact lenses. He took a shower, lit a cigarette, then dropped off to sleep before he had smoked it.

Toward morning she woke him up. She was there above him, his raincoat around her shoulders, an arm raised to twist a strand of her hair.

"What's that friggin noise?"

He sat up to listen for it. The bomb? Neon lights blinked on the diner and a trailer flicked by, the tires whining.

"What noise?" and he leaned forward to see if somebody might be fooling with the car.

"*That* noise." She pointed toward the back. Behind them in a gully a train was passing. Boyd knew the sound of it so well he hadn't heard it.

"You mean the train?"

"That friggin awful rumble."

"That's just a train, a freight train." He sat up to find a cigarette for her, light it. "If you live out here, you get used to it."

"Who the hell would live out *here?*"

"They do," he said; then: "She does," and he pushed up the blind so that the moonlight spilled into the room. A strip of snow fence, rippling like surf, lay on its side near the cut where the train passed. Reflected in the window Boyd could see her

face, owl-eyed, the chapped lips slightly parted. At
her side, a few inches from his head, she clicked
her nails like a metal cricket.

"What do you see?"

"Me?" she said. "Moonshine."

He raised his head from the pillow to look at it
with her. All moonshine, he thought. Is it all in your
mind? The friggin good old songs, the gold old
cars, the gold old bags, the whole friggin business?
Where else? Through the fence the lights of the caboose flicked by, and he said, "Now you see it, now
you don't, eh?"

"I didn't see it at all. What was it?"

She took one of the bobby pins from her hair
and bit down on the tip in a way that made him
shudder.

"Daughter, when you go home, how do you
feel?"

"Third Avenue? You think I'm crazy?"

"Just supposing you did."

She thought a moment, said, "Awful. Sweet
Jesus."

"Daughter, you express my own feelings."

"Then why you going back?"

"I want to know if it's there, or all in my mind."

She said nothing. In the yard at the front, like
dozing pachyderms, he could hear the purr of the
idling Diesels.

"I don't care if it's there or not, Big Daddy. You
need me for that?"

"They take me for a clown. We're going to clown
it up."

She dropped down on the bed at his side. "You scared of your own friggin kind? Is that it?"

"Daughter, I'm scared they might be real—I mean realer than I am."

She didn't seem to question it. "You think they know you as well as I do?"

"Nope. They're not friggin perfect strangers."

She got up from his side and crossed to her bed. His coat dropped in a puddle at her feet, and he could see the gold chains on her sandals. "I hurt your feelings?" he said. "If you're part of this family, you don't have them. You don't show them, that is. It's the law of the land."

After some time she said, "You ever feel you're in a friggin movie? You ever stand up in a movie and tell the friggin hero which way to run?"

"That's right, Daughter, and this is the movie."

"The friggin moonlight made me think of it," she said. And that was all.

In the morning she waited for him in the seat of the car. She wore a pair of dark glasses and a straw hat with a visor that she had bought in the gasoline station. Instead of Levis she wore corduroy pants that fit snugly around her ankles. Her face showed a little windburn from the day before.

"I look more like your daughter?" When he nodded she said, "It's the friggin dark glasses." She didn't explain. At the highway in front of the diner she took his hand and let him lead her across it. She waited to see what he ordered for breakfast, ordered the same. The idea of being a daughter appealed to her. When he spread a map out on the counter, she leaned toward him, her head on his shoulder, her arm around his back in a daughterly way. He pointed out where they were in Wyoming, and where they were going, over in Nebraska. "Where's Duluth?" she said. "Irwin's from there." He explained it was not on this map. He saw that a map without Duluth held little interest for her. He bought her cigarettes and chlorophyll gum when he paid the bill.

Near Cheyenne he had a little trouble with the car. He thought it might be the head wind, but near Laramie, with the wind at the back, they almost stopped on a grade. The motor ran fine but seemed to be disconnected from the wheels. In Laramie a mechanic explained the clutch was shot. But since it was downgrade from Cheyenne he might nurse it along to where he was going. Boyd nursed it along in the wind stream of the big trucks. The girl slept, her head on his shoulder, the brown hand with the high-school ring resting on his pants leg, gripping the pack of cigarettes. In Nebraska they picked up a tail breeze and cruised along like a prairie schooner until a freight train blocked the road on a detour near Cozad. Boyd had to bring the car to a stop on an incline; it began to drift backward while still in gear. To keep from blocking the road he let it slide into the ditch. He sat there, the motor idling, the clutch spinning as if disengaged, and watched one of the brakemen go along the cars toward the caboose. Seeing Boyd in the ditch, he waved his stick, hollered, "Next time, take the train!" Down the tracks, no more than five or six cars, Boyd could see the caboose.

He gave the girl a shake to wake her. He took her bag from the rear, went around the car to pull her into the open and tugging her by the hand, went along the waist-high weeds in the ditch toward the caboose. He fell on the embankment, tearing the knee of his pants, and the girl stood and laughed at him until he brought the soft side of the bag flat against her bottom. The brakeman was there on the caboose platform, and put his hand down for the girl. As Boyd gave her a push from behind she said, "Sweet Jesus. It *is* a friggin movie!"

Before he reached the platform he felt the car jolt. The brakeman pushed the bag into the aisle, then slipped off his glove to take from his bib a silver watch with a snap-lid case. He wore one of the high-crowned striped denim hats Boyd had often seen on McKee's father, a railroad man retired to the swing on the porch.

"You stop at Lone Tree?" Boyd asked.

"Lone Tree?" he said, and took a moment to look at the girl, her face flushed from running, then at Boyd, with the knee showing through the hole in his pants. He snapped the lid on his watch, then turned to wag his head at the door of the caboose. Down the aisle, facing the door, sat a big fellow with his hat tipped over his face. One of his feet stood in the aisle, the pants leg tucked up, and Boyd could see the sock bulge where the underwear was folded. "He's getting off at Lone Tree, too," said the brakeman. "What's going on at Lone Tree?"

The cab jolted again, and the creaking of the wheels sounded like a carful of squealing pigs. The brakeman dropped down the steps to wave his flag. At the detour crossing Boyd saw the Plymouth and wondered why it was that the windshield seemed to be vibrating.

"Sweet Jesus," said the girl, "you leave the friggin motor running?" He had. In the ignition were his keys, a tab with his initials and a charm guaranteed to bring luck to the bearer. Perhaps it had. He gripped the rail, his eyes on the tracks that drew the two halves of the plain together, like a zipper, joining at the rear what it had just divided at the front. Why, he wondered, reaching toward the girl, did things coming toward him seem to break into pieces, and things that receded into the past seem to make sense?

"It makes me dizzy," she said, gripping his arm, and over her head Boyd winked at the brakeman who doubtless was also a father, and knew he had a problem on his hands.

McKee

McKee had dropped the letter into the box, then he had raised the flap and peered into the chute in the hope that it might have stuck. But when he wanted one to stick, it never did. Although Boyd was several thousand miles away, and in an out-of-the-way place where it would probably never reach him, McKee felt the same panic as if he had seen Boyd coming down the street. And yet it hadn't crossed his mind that Boyd would come until the lid snapped down on the box. Right at that moment he knew that he would. Boyd always managed to do what nobody in his right mind would ever do.

An impulse? McKee had impulses like everybody. That wasn't new. What was new was that he had given in to it. That is to say that McKee, like everybody in the family, was jittery. The Lincoln boy who had run around shooting people as though they were no more than signs on the highway had not shot at McKee, but McKee might have felt better if he had. The boy was now in jail. That should have settled that. Half a dozen times a day Mrs. McKee would say, "If a boy like that can run around shooting people. . . ," leaving McKee to finish the sentence. When little Gordon would fire off his cap gun, McKee would jump. "Bang, bang," he would yell, "you're dead!" and there were times when McKee didn't doubt it. But what troubled McKee, more than the threat to his life and the murders, were the few words the boy had said. "I want to be somebody." That was what he had said.

When McKee read that in the paper he had hoisted the sheet to hide behind it. There was just one person in the world who came to mind when he read that statement, and it was not young Munger, the murderer. Not on your life. It was McKee's old boyhood chum, Gordon Boyd.

It had given Mrs. McKee such a fright she didn't think of Boyd, nor even of Munger. What she thought of mostly was herself. In the new split-level house they had built in the suburbs, with the glass on three sides of it, the lights were kept burning most of the night. The house was set off by itself, which was what they had wanted, but with the lights lit up it looked like a factory and attracted more attention than if they had been out. But you couldn't tell that to Mrs. McKee. "If I'm going to be shot, I want to know who it is," she said. McKee didn't. No, he would prefer being shot in the dark. What the devil good would it do, knowing, and being dead?

But what surprised him the most in a person like Lois was how scared she seemed to be about her own life. She had always been a woman who gave little thought to herself. On her mind, in case he happened to ask her, was always somebody else. Not that McKee didn't value his life, but at sixty-one he felt he had lived it, and it was other lives he worried about. Boyd's, for instance, if you could call it a life, and now that they were growing up, his grand-children. He had just assumed it was the same with Mrs. McKee, only more so since she was a woman. But when the heating system would come on, as it sometimes did, with a snap, she would grab McKee and lie almost rigid half the night. Nothing would calm her down except daylight. And in the room across the hall, where he slept most of the day and stayed awake most of the night, they could hear old Scanlon muttering away and cackling to himself. The very thing that scared the wits out of other people had given him a new lease on life. Those fool pistols he had from his father, that hadn't been fired for half a century, he oiled and polished, and carried one in a holster at his hip. When he went off for a walk, the kids followed him around the streets. Everybody knew the old man was crazy, but they liked to listen to his stories, half of which, McKee was sure, were about how badly the McKees were treating him, since they did have to lock him in the place at night.

When McKee had appeared for consultation to speak on behalf of Lee Roy Momeyer, he had been careful not to mention what he had once seen happen. He had driven the car over the pit and walked out in front while the car was greased. Out of the corner of his eye he had seen Lee Roy aim his grease gun, like it was a pistol, and spray the pants and shoes of a college boy who stood at the front. Deliberate. But he claimed it was an accident. He didn't know the young man from Adam, but he resented his shoes and the sports car he was down there working beneath. Out in front of the station was a sign that said:

HAVE GUNS—WILL LUBRICATE

which gave McKee the willies the first time he set eyes on it. That was four months before Charlie Munger started shooting them down. What had Lee Roy said? "I just got tired of bein' pushed around." But who was pushing who? McKee would like to know. The day he bought his new station wagon and drove it home like he had it loaded with eggs, four or five of these hoodlums in a souped-up Ford swooped out of nowhere right up beside him, guffawed like hyenas, then leaned far out to scratch their matches on the paint on his hood. McKee didn't shout. No, he didn't even whimper. He just slowed down and watched them roar away. As men come and go, he was not easily frightened—in case he was, he could make a show of nerve—but the grinning faces of those young hoodlums scared him worse than he dared to admit. McKee had recognized the nameless face of evil—he recognized it, that is, as stronger than the nameless face of good. Everybody talked about Good, but had McKee ever set eyes on it? Had he ever felt pure Good? No, but he had come face to face with evil. He had seen the underside of the rock. What troubled him was not what he saw, but the nameless appetite behind it, the lust for evil in the faces of the beardless boys. McKee felt more life in their life than in himself. He didn't want a showdown. He felt himself beaten at the start. If McKee represented Good, like the Gray Ladies on the war posters, then the forces of Evil would carry the day.

"McKeeeee!" Lois called. Through the kitchen window McKee could see her hugging little Gordon like he was a baby and couldn't walk. "McKee," she called, "you want to help father?" as if McKee had a choice in the matter. The old man was spry as a goat till he thought he was doing you a favor, like being present at a family reunion to honor him. On the other hand the old man knew, even better than McKee did, that this get-together wasn't with him in mind at all. His ninetieth birthday was just an excuse to let the women get together and connive about Etoile's and Calvin's marriage. McKee found it hard to believe he had a grandson old enough to marry into his own family, which was what stirred up this thing between Lois and the boy's mother Eileen. Eileen *McKee*—McKee could never believe that was her name, although she had been his daughter-in-law for twenty years. After bucking the marriage of those kids for almost two years on the grounds that the blood of first cousins didn't mix, Lois had resigned herself, as she said, to letting nature take its course. As Eileen said, what other course was there for nature to take?

"McKee, father is waiting," she called, and McKee could see him, in the chair on the sun porch, sunning himself with his hook-and-eye shoes on but unlaced. He could lace those shoes as well as anybody, but nothing pleased him more than to see

McKee do it, since McKee always had trouble tying the bow. He couldn't seem to do it like they did in the shoe stores, so it would pull loose without knotting. McKee was sure the old man tangled it purposely. "Can't you tie a bow yet!" he would bark, which riled McKee a little, since the old man had not learned anything else in ninety years.

"McKee—" Lois called, but McKee timed it so the garage door closed on the rest of it. Overhead he heard the hiss of the ventilating fan. The new garage had electric doors for McKee, who thought he might drop dead lifting the old ones, and a fan for Mrs. McKee, who thought he'd kill himself with carbon monoxide gas. The big surprise was that with the fan turned on McKee couldn't hear through the intercom system, so he could fool with the car or sit and read the paper more or less undisturbed. What he liked about the house—like the upstairs bathroom with a view across the fields he could sit and look at—was like the coin pocket in his suit coat, something extra he hadn't expected. After more than forty years of backing up to the heat or sitting with his feet over it, radiant heat was like a cup of coffee right after he had had a front tooth filled, and the painkiller took the heat and flavor out of it. He enjoyed heat most if he was cold in spots.

In the front seat of the car where he had left it was yesterday's evening paper. There were days he simply lacked the nerve to look at it. The way the paper was folded he could make out the headlines—GIRLS KIDNAP HUMBOLDT FARMER—so he

naturally turned it over to see who did it. Two
girls, if that was what you could call them, the face
of one almost lopsided, had hitched a ride from a
farmer, then put a gun to his head and told him to
hit for Texas. Why Texas? One of them had heard
there were "soldiers in Texas." In Kansas somewhere the car had run out of gas. Gazing at their
blank, lopsided faces, McKee felt a familiar disquiet.
Where did they come from? Were they born the
way normal children were born? What troubled
McKee was not their trouble, but the knowledge
that nothing he could say or do would ever change
their belief that he was their mortal enemy. Every
time McKee entered a corner drugstore or blinked
his eyes in a movie lobby he saw these youngsters
gazing at him with their sightless eyes. McKee had
once, to spare its suffering, tried to drown a bird
that had flown into a window and broken its neck.
When the small body had resisted drowning, he had
lost his nerve. He had thought it lifeless, but when
its life was threatened, it had stiffened like a steel
spring, hissed like a dragon and looked at him with
such hate he had dropped it in the weeds and run for
his life. Where did it get such courage? Could it be
found in that small battered head or that tiny heart?
Had McKee, in threatening a bird, threatened life
itself? Did those two girls from the reformatory feel
threatened by something the same way, so that they
fought back blindly and put a pistol to a farmer's
head? In McKee's mind, like one of those disks little
Gordon let spin on his record player, he could hear
the flat voice of Lee Roy Momeyer speaking from

the hollow of his crash helmet. "I guess I just got tired of bein' pushed around."

But who the devil was pushing *who?*

McKee raised the door as if for air.

"McKee!" Lois called. "You want him *that way* before the day starts?"

Want who? McKee wheeled to see which one she meant. She was holding little Gordon, so the one she meant was the old man. It wasn't like him at all, but he said, "Didn't that boy come with his legs, Lois?" She carried him around so much it was one of the things that upset his stomach, the way a puppy would get upset if you handled him.

She said, "On the table you'll find a carton of sheets." Just the night before she had told him that Maxine would bring the sheets, since they had only new expensive percale ones in the McKees' new house. She saw what he was thinking and said, "You think I'm going to have the Ewings thinking that when we go to Lone Tree we use only the old ones?" Before McKee reached the door she called, "Father! Will you put that down!" and McKee knew what to expect. There he was, with his laces flapping, out on the stoop with the carton of sheets, knowing very well he was scaring the daylights out of all of them. All he had to do was step on those laces and he'd fall down the steps.

"Now you let me do that!" said McKee, and cut across the grass to head him off.

"If you don't want him doing it," she called, "you can always do it yourself."

He took the carton of sheets from the old man,

and while he had his feet there on the stoop, he laced up his shoes. He had managed to slip on one blue sock and one black. He was never fool enough to mix them so that you knew he did it on purpose. No, he would always claim he couldn't see the color because the windows let in too much light, there being nothing but windows in the new house.

"You think you're shoein' a horse?" he said, by which he meant McKee had laced him too tight.

"You shoe a mule different than a horse," said McKee, and left him to think that over. Which he would do. Like an elephant, he never forgot an injury.

"McKee," said Lois, when he came up with the sheets, "I told Maxine she and Etoile could ride along with us. You just can't ask them to ride all the way in that Hupmobile."

She didn't say Bud—no, just Maxine and Etoile —knowing just so long as she didn't say it McKee didn't have to rear up and put his foot down, although it was understood Bud would be there. One day he would say, "How's tricks, McKee?" and McKee would put his hand on his head and squash that mailman's hat like a pot down over his ears. If peace in the family meant that McKee had to put up with a mailman who liked to play Indian, then peace, as he told Mrs. McKee, was not worth the price.

"McKee—" she called, as he headed for the garage. "Don't be surprised if the children ask you to borrow the car. It's been discussed."

What the devil led it to pop into his mind? That a

man ended up doing all the crazy things he had done as a kid—like Boyd ending up squirting pop at a bull. The idea didn't seem to apply to McKee, since as a kid he had done very little. Back inside the garage where it was cool and dark, he tried to think. He had neither squirted pop, tried to walk on water, nor distinguished himself in any special manner. What had he done? He pushed the button to raise the doors, and as they went up, letting in the light, it wouldn't have surprised him to see Boyd walking up the drive. Watching Boyd, after all, was what he'd been doing all his life.

Lois

Lifting his arms to her shoulders, she said, "Now hug your Grandma," and drew his body to her, her hands on his hips, feeling the tight grip of his strong little legs. Hot with sleep, the wrinkled side of his face lay on her neck. From the sound of his breathing she knew that he had drooled on her dress. An acrid smell, sweet to her, of the milk that had staled in his mouth made her want to kiss him, to lick him like a bitch licked her pups. Somewhere she had read of Eskimo women who cleaned their children like animals, and the thought had first sickened her. Then her grandchildren came along and shamelessly, knowing what she was doing, she would sometimes almost eat little Gordon alive.

In Kansas City, where Lois had gone with her daughter-in-law Eileen when these spells began to come on her, they had sat in a small, neat room waiting her turn. Through the ventilator right over their heads the voice had said, "Mrs. Logsdon, the bitch in you is something to be proud of, treat it with more respect." The consultation Lois had had proved nothing, but that overheard remark was worth the one hundred dollars. The bitch in herself she was treating with more respect. Her own children might have been somebody else's, slipped into her bed during an illness, but the grandchildren she could hug, lick and love, and if necessary eat.

Gordon was no child, he was a boy, ashamed to
let her hug and kiss him in public, but if she got him
sleepy he loved it. Sleep did for him what drinking
seemed to do for men. He lost his sense of shame.
Hugging her like a baby, he would nuzzle like a
puppy at her breasts.

"Hug Grandmother tight," she said, and when
he did she noticed that his hair smelled of the fertilizer in the back of McKee's car. He liked to sprawl
there with his grandfather on the pads from the
summer furniture, firing his water pistol at the cars
that passed. If she could have one wish in the world
it would be to live where there were no guns, nor
anything that you could point at anyone. She was
as troubled when he spied on her and suddenly said,
"Bang, you're dead, Grandma," as if the madman
who had killed all those people had cornered her.
How could you play at killing people without
sooner or later killing them? The pointed finger,
like the water gun, could kill something in a person
that would never recover, and in some cases they
might as well be dead.

She stopped in the door to peer down the hall at
her father's room, with the ox shoe that somebody
had given him nailed to it. If they let him out of the
house Scanlon would wander the streets and come
home with such things; if they didn't, he slept all
day and drove them crazy all night with his muttering, cackling and all-night radio programs. He didn't
care for music or entertainment at all, but he seemed
to think the men who talked all night, against the
Jews or the liberals or something, had stayed up

until that hour just to talk to *him*. He would shout at them, agree with them, argue at length with them, but at least he had the sense, as McKee had pointed out, not to send them the money they asked for. No, he was shrewd. He knew better than that, but he was for everybody who hated something or was against something, since that was how he felt himself. Toward morning he was as worn out as people she had seen at political rallies, and thank God for that, since it gave them a chance to sleep. The new home they had built, which was such a showplace people drove by on Sunday to look at it, seemed to amplify every voice except the one in the room with her, so when McKee spoke to her she always had to ask him to say it again. But she could hear her father, clear down the hall, cock the trigger of the pistol he had with him, and when he snapped it shut, she invariably jumped.

It had seemed such a godsend to think of McKee in another bed, with the bathroom between them, until she found she couldn't bear him that far away. Another single bed had to be bought and placed beside her own. On the pretext that her father couldn't live without him she could borrow little Gordon, his mother being sickly, and he slept in a playpen crib at the foot of her bed. He began in the crib, but once he was asleep she could pick him up like he was under ether and curl him up beside her. Awake, he would have one of his tantrums and hold his breath till his lips and ears were blue, since he hated women like every male member of the family. At Christmas, when the family got together,

he had bellowed, "*I don't want to play with girls!*"
For all her love and need of him she could have put
his head into a bowl and held it under. There she
had it. There every living woman had it. All these
blessed little boys who were born girl haters would
grow up and have to have one around the house to
play with. After toads and snakes to play with came
little girls.

In the bathroom she had put in with the child in
mind, with Mother Goose rhymes on the wall and
ceiling, she lowered him to the stool but he slipped
right off like it was hot. He gave her one of his
looks, then turned to face the toilet like a man. What
did she think *he* was? Since she had let McKee take
him into the men's room in the hotel in Mexico City,
he would no longer let her take him to the ladies'
room. He knew the difference now, and the *difference* was what he wanted. He refused to wear his
snow suit because it didn't have a fly.

"Where's it go?" he said, and watched the water
swirl and flush away.

"Into the ground," she said. "It goes down the
pipes into the ground." Although she had no way of
knowing whether it did or not. Where it *all* went
in a city like Lincoln often troubled her. Just a year
ago he would have asked her why, then where, then
how and what, but now he said nothing, and she
realized that he knew she didn't know. How did he
know? She only knew that he did. The thousand
things they had shared between them and found the
day too short to discuss had narrowed down to just
a handful of things he would bring up—then sud-

denly drop. With the first answer she gave him he knew that she didn't know. That made her foolish, and she would say:

"What do you think Grandma has in her pocket?" Or in her drawer, in her purse, in her cupboard, but no longer in her mind, nor in her heart, where she had once kept it. But when she had nothing—and he *knew* it—that made her panicky.

"Grandma's going shopping," she would say, "you want to come along and help her shop?" But he had learned about that, and knew very well that she went shopping just to entertain him, so he made her shopping miserable. He filled his pockets with gum, candy bars, razor blades or anything he found down on his level, not to mention all he could swallow or stuff into his mouth. Going through his pockets was such an ordeal—never knowing what might turn up there—shopping had been one thing more crossed off their list. What was left?

"You want to watch TV while Grandma makes us brownies?" and he did, he almost said yes, then he realized that that was what *she* wanted, and slowly wagged his head. What little monster in him made him want that? Once he was awake and *knew* what he wanted, what he wanted the most was to deprive her of something. That was not something she could blame on her father, who had no interest in what somebody else wanted; it was something new, and when she could bear to think about it at all, it frightened her worse than the young man who might shoot at her like a clay pigeon. That was horrible, but it made sense. Little boys who walked along knocking the heads off flowers were in the same class. But if little Gordon knew how much she loved his hair, he would cut it off. If he could grasp what a glance from his eyes meant to her, he would seal them. And if he knew what she sometimes felt when she scooped him into her arms, he would take his life rather than give her such a moment of pleasure. He was, as anybody would tell you, one of the most lovable children imaginable, but he was also this little monster that made her blood run cold.

She had known that for months, but she would not admit it until in Mexico, in that hotel in Cuernavaca where they had sat one afternoon having tea. McKee had taken little Gordon to the men's room, and she had sat there at the table, her father dozing, facing the most beautiful view imaginable, a paradise of birds and flowers, as the guidebook said. At a table nearby a very pretty young Mexican woman sat with her two children, a little girl about five and a boy about little Gordon's age. He had an air gun, which she thought was odd, and after he had finished eating he stood at the wall and fired at the pigeons on the roofs below. That, as McKee would tell her, was Mexico, but she had been relieved to see that his mother had no intention of tolerating it. She spoke to him, several times, and when he shot it off once more, she saw her walk over, take hold of his ear and without moving her elbow from her side, give him a slap across the face like a board had cracked. Then she came back to the table, sat down, and was pouring herself more of her coffee when Lois, watching the boy, saw him put his eye to the barrel as if to see if it was loaded, and with complete deliberation pull the trigger of the gun. She had cried out "Ohhhhh!" and got to her feet, but his mother had heard the gun go off, and she knew—Lois sensed that she knew—exactly what had happened, since she did not scream, nor throw her arms around him, but took him by the hand, as though by a leash, and forgetting the other child, walked through the lobby to where cars were parked at the front. The boy made no sound, he stood at her side, one hand clamped over his eyes, and she had pulled him into the cab at the curb and they had driven off.

A nightmare? She did not mention it to McKee. When he sensed that something was wrong, she said it was something she must have eaten, which was often true, and they had left. Back in Mexico City she had pulled the blinds and gone to bed as if she were sick, and she had been. What food she had eaten she threw up. Part of it was the shock—she couldn't get over seeing the mother and the child walk off—but what made her ill was what she refused to admit. It had been no accident. The child had deprived itself of one eye because of the pain it would give the mother. A loss that neither of them would ever, for one moment, forget. What she couldn't stomach had not been the sight, terrible as it was, but that human beings found pleasure in torturing each other. Not only that Mexican child, who would now look at the world through one dark eye, but the pretty blue-eyed boy that McKee had happily taken off to the men's room. How well he would have understood a shot like that! Men who went around shooting others were just stupid, frustrated children, compared with these little monsters who had learned to shoot themselves. Knowing *that* hurt those who loved them worse than anything else.

Gordon's mother, Eileen, had simply not been able to stand it, which was why it was possible for Lois to borrow the child from time to time. The doctor in Kansas City had told Eileen that this was a phase, and wouldn't last once he found something he wanted worse than tormenting her. Wasn't that just a way of saying he would begin to torment somebody else? Always a woman, of course, and always one who couldn't help but be mad about him. He had the same good looks as his brother Calvin, but without any of Calvin's shyness, and he didn't mind at all having women around to wait on him. It was Lois, not his great-grandfather, nor McKee, nor his own father, who supplied him with the things he wanted, such as the coonskin hats and all those guns. After the nightmare of the bullfight she was sure he would scream until he had a sword and one of those silly outfits, but what he suddenly wanted, even before they left, was a glove and a baseball, which McKee had been able to find for him at Sears. When he found that suits went along with it, why of course he had to have a suit, which she was only too glad to buy for him. McKee had hinted darkly that this baseball business wasn't so simple as she seemed to think, but she would rather see him hurt, with his fingers banged or a black eye from a batted ball, than forever shooting something dead from a closet door or the basement.

"I suppose you're Davy Crockett today," she said, since she had learned to be clever. He waited to see if she meant it, taking the suit from the closet before he denied it. "You certainly don't want a baseball suit where there's no place to play it, and I'm not so sure what your Grandpa would think." (McKee was actually the child's grandfather, but he just refused to admit it.) She found if hard to believe that the child was drifting away from Grandpa Scanlon—he would just as soon *not* please him as anyone else. "Since this is Grandpa's birthday party ——" she went on, but McKee called from the kitchen.

"Lois," he said, "I'm setting the timer at four minutes."

Nothing had given McKee so much pleasure as the self-timer he had given her for Christmas, which he could set like a dial telephone. Once he had set it, and the bell rang, he would go ahead and eat his own breakfast of oatmeal and peanut butter on raisin toast.

"You want to go tell your Grandpa breakfast is ready?" As a rule she just asked him out of habit; naturally he didn't want to.

"Whose birthday is it?" he asked.

"Your grandfather is ninety years old tomorrow."

He sucked air through his teeth the way he had learned from McKee. An observant person could see the bad habits of the whole family by just spending an hour with her grandson. He snuffled like his father, twitched his eyes and face like his mother, sucked air into his mouth like McKee, screwed his fingers in his ears and sniffed the wax like his grandfather, and the face he made like a sick chipmunk was said to be hers.

"When will you be ninety?"

"I just hope I'm never ninety."

"Why not?"

"You—" she began, and realized this was one thing they had never discussed. Had she ever talked about *anything* dying with him? "All sorts of people just don't live to be that old."

"Somebody shoots them?"

Keeping her voice calm, she said, "Most of them just die because their time has come."

"Grandpa's time hasn't come?"

She slowly wagged her head. "No, and you should be thankful." That was a slip. She could just as well have said, and *we* should be thankful. To take his mind off that she said, "One thing nobody in the world knows is when his time has come. That is God's secret."

He had taken from his pocket the baseball she had bought him, and he turned it slowly, reading the label. It was the way he acted when she had drifted out of her depth. When he knew there was little point in listening to what she said. His arrogance came so naturally that it was a moment before she felt the impact. Death. What did the little monster think he knew about death?

"A penny for your thoughts, or do you think

your grandmother wouldn't understand them?"

"But what if it *is*-unt a secret?" and he gave her such a straight, searching look she felt that her own time was no secret, at least to him.

"If it isn't a secret, I'll know who it is that let it out," and she scooped him up before he could object and walked through the house to the kitchen, where McKee, as if he still sat at the table where there wasn't room for his knees, straddled the corner, his legs spread, scooping oatmeal into his mouth with one of her sugar spoons.

"Bell rang about two minutes ago," he said, wagging the spoon in the direction of the timer, "poured the water off your eggs and left them in the pan."

She let little Gordon slide down her body to the floor. McKee had put out for him the crunchy cereal that crackled when he poured his milk on it and came in the cartons that he made into guns, hats, houses and flags. She watched him scoot to the icebox, ferret out his milk, then come back to take the place across from McKee, like an old hog and a small suckling pig in the same trough. Once they reached the kitchen they were both the same. Fifty years from now, the same age as McKee, she could see him in whatever they had for a kitchen, snorfeling through his nose because his mouth was full, dipping his cereal spoon into the sugar, then idly stirring his coffee while he ran his tongue around his gums.

"I don't suppose either of you—" she began, but the sentence remained unfinished when her father, in his carpet slippers and a robe of McKee's with the sleeves half rolled, shuffled in from the hall without a word and took his place. On the corner of the table spread he wiped the knife and the spoon, the fork usually having egg on it, as he had done for the seventeen years her mother had turned from the stove to feed him. What would he eat? Two eggs fried so hard only a sharp knife would cut them, and if one of them ran, ever so slightly, he would push it toward her and say, "Chicken in it." Then his coffee, her Silex coffee, into which he would pour four teaspoons of sugar and Carnation canned milk until he was sure it was cool. The odor of it at breakfast almost made her sick. Orange juice gave him, he said, acid stomach, but there were times she could persuade him to eat peaches under a gravy of canned cream. Then he would sit picking his teeth with the matches he had sucked the heads off, the sulphur being, as he never failed to say, good for the blood.

For this she had asked McKee to build her a new house? The kitchen walls were of glass, so the first thing she had to do was pull the drapes lest someone passing might see the characters inside. Neither her father nor McKee could get it through their heads that the cupboards were all at eye level, since they had always stooped for anything in the way of food. In the thirteen months they had been in the house the dining room had been used three times, twice at Christmas and once at Thanksgiving; all the other meals she had to serve in the kitchen, where the coffeepot sat on the table and McKee felt, as he said, it was all right to push back his chair.

The way her father blinked at the light she could tell he had sat up most of the night or padded in his slippers around the halls. It had been such a triumph to get him to come to the table without his hat, she had not pushed the problem of getting him to wash or shave. The top of his head, the hair matted since he never used a comb, was like the root-covered bottom side of a rock—and as hard, she always reminded herself, to penetrate. Nothing new had entered it through any opening for almost all of the ninety years. It had come sealed, like the motor in her appliances, and would go on working until the day it stopped. She had never heard him once speak of her mother, who had borne and raised his four daughters, one of whom had taken him, by force, into her home. He was more like a piece of nature than a man. A withered slab of cactus, more dead than alive, that resisted every well-intentioned effort to save it and left prickly needles in friend and foe alike. She looked at him, and on the rim of his glass he rapped his spoon.

"Sounds like one of the paying guests would like a little service," said McKee, rising, and she smiled and said, "Happy birthday, Father," and turned to fry his eggs.

Maxine

Her face to the screen, she peered slantwise down the driveway to her lilac bush. Buds on it. But she didn't know whether she liked it or not. It had been such a terrible winter Maxine was not at all ready for spring. She was cold down where it would take some time to thaw her out. Beyond the lilac bush, down the gravel road, she could see the house, and the sheds beside it, where the first two murdered bodies had been found. She didn't know the people personally, except to wave when they drove by in the summer, but they had been on her husband's mail route for twenty-seven years. It was Bud who came and told her there was something funny going on at the Bartletts', but no one in his right mind, and that included his wife Maxine, paid attention to what Bud Momeyer said. That was two months ago, almost three, but Bud was still telling people how he just knew that something was funny when he walked into the yard. It never crossed his mind, then or later, to fear for his own life or anybody else's—what impressed him was that he felt something funny, and he did.

"I just knew something was funny," he would say, "and dang if it didn't prove to be right." Since he was the kindest person in the world and would walk around ants he saw on the sidewalk, the way he felt about murders, earthquakes and atomic bombs was hard to understand. He didn't mean it personally any more than little Gordon meant to shoot her dead with his cap pistol, but Maxine felt he enjoyed it the same way. One of the big days of the year for Bud was the Labor Day week end, when he waited to see if there were more dead on the highways than the year before.

Was it rain she smelled? Her nose to the screen, she could hear the groaning of the faucet at the side of the house and the sprinkler raining on the front walk. "Oh, Etoile!" she cried, since it would be Etoile, crazy for water, who had turned on the sprinkler just to stand in it. "Eeeee-toal!" she repeated like a hog caller, and regretted for the thousandth time giving the girl a name, however nice it looked, that sounded like that. "How you spell that, Missus Momeyer?" people would ask her, and she would reply, "E-t-o-i-l-e, same as toilet," which meant they wouldn't trouble to ask her what it meant.

The sprinkling stopped, but right before her eyes a jet of water rose to the level of the window, which meant that the girl had made a fold in the hose. Another minute and it would blow off the nozzle or spring a new leak. It had been happening for years, first Etoile, then Lee Roy, but only now did Maxine see it for what it was. That piece of garden hose, kinks and all, through which flowed more than she could keep under control, was her life. When she tried to shut if off at one end, it just broke out somewhere else. Pretty much the same way, people would tell you, that the Munger boy broke out of the traces, and whipped around like a fire hose when the men let it get out of hand.

So she said nothing, she waited for whatever it was to happen; but nothing happened, the sprinkler rained again on the walk. The hot bricks steamed a little the way they did in the summertime. Leaning back from the sink—holding on as if the sink might get away from her—Maxine looked through the screen at the girl who stood under the sprinkler as if under a shower. She looked like one of those statues she had seen in a Kansas City park. Any day now, as other mothers said, she would come down with something or break out with something, but up to now she hadn't, and when she got wet or did anything to make her flushed, Maxine sometimes felt she would like to bite into her, like a peach. What little there was to be said against her she had ferreted out. Her eyes, for instance, beautiful as they were, seemed to be wider apart then they should be, and Maxine had stretched a celluloid ruler across her nose to make sure of that. Only to find they were no wider than her own, just how they looked. It had been a relief when the dentist found her teeth were going to need braces, since it gave Maxine something to complain about. Her sister Lois was glad to pay for them since it was *her* teeth Etoile had, as well as her long, flipperlike flat feet. They called for the special orthopedic shoes that she could have had, hand-me-down, from Lois, but that was where Maxine called a halt. The child was growing too fast as it was. Already the college boys were whistling at her. Up through last summer

Maxine had been able to dress her in middy blouses and tunics, with bows in her hair to match the tennis sneakers on her long feet. With her pencil box labeled SCHOOL DAZE, and her notebook with the pyramid on the cover, she actually *looked* younger, with her books hugged to her front, than some of the smart little girls wearing pumps and make-up. Etoile didn't need it. She came with her own make-up, as Mrs. Olmsted said. But in the pocket of her notebook, along with Marlon Brando, Maxine found a ten-page article, clipped from a magazine called *Erotica*. There were pictures of the busts of famous beauties, beginning with the Venus de Milo, down to Jayne Mansfield and Christine Jorgensen, who had started out as a man and ended up as a woman. Under Jayne Mansfield, Etoile had written, *Not so hot*. The article recommended massage with the bare hand and a daily application of cracked ice for firmness. Maxine had almost panicked. She had gone through the drawers of Etoile's bureau as if she might find something like cracked ice, and read two months of the diary she kept on the back of her telephone pad. On Tuesday, November 8, she had written, *Ran down the stairs just to feel my breasts bobbing. Poor Lillian Strauss!* In her pencil box she found a secret compartment, with mascara for her eyes, and Tabu, a perfume no man could resist. Pinned to the lid was a snapshot of a boy without a stitch on, his back turned to the camera, that Maxine recognized as Etoile's cousin Calvin because he was wearing his stirrup boots. Etoile had taken that picture herself since no boy in his right mind would have given it to her, the light being particularly strong between his legs.

When Bud's nephew Lee Roy made a visit to Lincoln he naturally stayed the week at their house, sleeping on the bed under the basement stairs Bud had once used. Like all the Momeyers, he was small, but different from most of them in that he was quiet, kept to himself and had no interest in inventing anything. His mother wrote to Maxine that he was of a religious turn of mind. His interest was auto mechanics, which they didn't offer in Calloway, and he hoped to enter high school in Lincoln, where they did. He came up in the strangest-looking car that Maxine had ever set eyes on, but he got up at eight Sunday morning and took Maxine and Etoile to church. After that they walked or let Bud drive them, but Maxine was impressed with Lee Roy's habits and felt it would be a good thing for Etoile to have him around the house. If he wanted to pay for his board, she said, and if he didn't mind sleeping down in the basement, where the oil burner smelled, he was free to stay with them. Thanks to McKee, Lee Roy found work in the O Street Texaco station, where he was small enough to work without stooping in the grease pit.

Maxine had thought it would be good for Etoile, since he would take her to and from school, but his car was so peculiar she refused to ride with him. The first week of school, seeing them together, some smart aleck referred to them as Mutt and Jeff, since Etoile was about a head taller than Lee Roy. After that he sort of avoided her. It was not Etoile's fault he was so short, but even when they were at home and there was no one to see them, Lee Roy would sit down if Etoile happened to be standing up. People new to the neighborhood thought Maxine had first been married to somebody else and that Lee Roy was Bud's child and Etoile hers. Lee Roy had the short, bowed Momeyer legs, the head a little too big for the shoulders, but he would never make a mailman since he hated to walk anywhere.

At fifty-three Bud had more spark than Etoile and Lee Roy put together. After working all day he would come home and pick and dress half a dozen chickens, then go off with his bow and arrow until it was dark. He was like a spring-wind toy that never unwound. He actually seemed to get younger as the people around him died off or got older. When the new *Popular Mechanics* arrived, he would sit up and read half the night. If anyone should ask Maxine—and pray God they wouldn't—why it was that Bud Momeyer never grew old, she would have to reply that first he would have to grow up. But he hadn't. No, he hadn't and he never would.

She would never forget, nor tell anybody about, the honeymoon in the Ozarks she had spent with Bud Momeyer helping him put together a telescope kit. Night after night in this ramshackle cabin all she did was heat smelly glue in a pot and hold her finger till it was numb on joints being glued. When she got to bed, there were maps on the ceiling they had to memorize by flashlight. He had to have a telescope when he read somewhere that there was more to see than met the eye, and they had gone to the Ozarks in order to be closer to the heavens. Before Maxine had given it any thought, he had his mind set on calling their first-born Luna if it was a girl, or Pluto if it happened to be a boy, and only by the grace of God would he settle for Etoile since that meant a star. Then he turned to harnessing the power from the sun, the wobbling of the globe and what it might lead to, a match that would strike forever, buttons small children could eat, the self-filling fountain pen, and finally the bow and arrow. When he came home with *that* and all those cruel-looking arrows, Maxine had thrown her apron over her head. It was on her mind every time she hung clothes out in the yard. Was it the walking around? The quiver like a mailbag on his back? She couldn't believe he ever hurt anything with it except himself. When he did, he would say, "Criminenty," or "Dang!" It made her lid her eyes to remember when she thought his absolute refusal to swear was so wonderful. Never did she hear from him anything worse than Gee Whiz, What the Deuce, and Dang. He never seemed to feel anything those words didn't cover. The Russians were those dang rooshuns, and a young hoodlum who shot ten people was some darn kid. But time and again she told herself that she could forgive him all that, even love him for it, if she could ever see him without that mailman's hat on his head. He wore it at meals, he wore it reading the paper, and when he did take it off, in church or at the movies, all she seemed to see was the ridge it had worn into his head. Then she could hardly wait to see him with it back on.

* * *

The screen door slammed. Maxine raised her eyes to the pocket mirror, placed on the sill, to watch Etoile make wet tracks on the clean linoleum floor. Just her back, the panties of her sunsuit so tight across her bottom the pattern of anchors seemed to be part of her skin. Nor did covering up her bottom cover up such a girl. Soon now, as Lois hinted, those dark cars parked along the side roads would be on her mind so long as Etoile was not home in bed. She wouldn't be able to let Bud drive past one of them. "Eeee-toal," she would call, "is that you?"—not really of course, but the way the mothers did who turned up at the hairdressers with red eyes and their lips chewed raw.

Was there anything so bad some good didn't come of it? Her sister Lois had been so upset by the murders and what it might do to a boy like Calvin that she would rather let Etoile have him than the police. That was not what she said, but what she meant. After talking her head off about baby monsters and how early marriages stunted certain people, especially cousins, she now wanted to see them married by June. But now that that was what Lois wanted, you could be sure that Etoile would be against it or that Calvin, just to make her more nervous, would take a shot at someone. It was not enough that Calvin stuttered, but Etoile, to show how smart she was, would take the words right off his lips like a parakeet. If he didn't know what was on his mind till Etoile told him, as Eileen said, why should he complain about that? He hadn't used his head, up till then, for more than his hat.

* * *

A honk—only it wasn't a honk, but a rasp, like a doorbell—led Maxine to purse her lips, lid her eyes. "One day I got to fix that dang horn, Maxine," Bud had said the summer they got it, and that was now fourteen, no, fifteen summers ago. The Hupmobile, ten years old at the time, had been part of the Aurora Fire Department before they raised the funds for a new building and a new fire truck. On its roof, like the new police cars, was a big red light that never worked but glowed like fire when the sun fell on it. If they happened to pull up behind somebody at a time of day when the sun struck it, the driver would sometimes pull off the road and stop. They took Bud for a state patrolman in his uniform and mailman's hat. People new to Lincoln or boys who had just grown up would sometimes stick notes on the windshield offering to buy it since they thought it was an antique. When he discovered that was what it was, he refused to sell. The top leaked so bad Maxine had to sit with a piece of bread paper over her hat when it rained, and when the windows were down, she couldn't hear herself think. The spokes were loose, and every wheel had a "frog" in it. It had become such a showpiece Maxine would get out two blocks before she needed to, and walk, rather than have the galoots all come up and stare at her when they parked. They seemed to think she should wear the clothes that went along with it, and the truth was, she did.

Through the slit in the curtains over the sink she watched Bud back away from the car, the seat of his uniform shiny, then lean back in to take his

quiver of arrows from the seat. He took them somewhere to have the points sharpened on an emery
wheel. At the sight of him, looking like a little Indian, she knew why it was that her mother, faced
with her father, would gather up her apron and
throw it over her head. Maxine had been such a
baby at the time she had never heard of the ostrich,
but her mother's gesture seemed more expressive
and full of despair. There she would stand, looking
almost headless, facing the kitchen wall with the
calendars on it, while her father would make lead
bullets that he had no gun to fire. A man like that
had worn her mother out, just the way kinks made
in the garden hose made leaks elsewhere, and one
day, one kink too many, would blow its top.

"Maxine?" Bud called. "You people ready?"

How many years had his wife and daughter been
people he drove around like a chauffeur in the
Hupmobile, squeezed into the front seat since the
rear seat had been taken out? With the windows
up they would almost die from the smell of cracked
and bad eggs and wet chicken feathers that remained in the car after his week-end deliveries. The
trouble with her back dated from the summer she
had to ride with her legs stiff since Bud had spilled a
full can of cracked eggs over the seat. "Dang it,
Maxine," he said, when she almost fainted, "don't
you worry. I've seen a leather Buick seat that'll fit
it," as if she could replace her own worn-out parts
the same way. He couldn't seem to get it through
his head that people wore out. At times like that,
shamelessly, Maxine would like to sell Etoile to the

highest bidder rather than see her end up with legs she couldn't cross, her hair like a bird's nest, her legs lumpy with veins, and with ankles that folded over her shoes like spats. Self-pity wagged her head from side to side, and her eyes watered as if she were peeling onions. She gulped a breath of fresh air through the window at the sink. In a year Calvin McKee would be worth a fortune, but it would never cross his mind, any more than Etoile's, to get her off her feet and get that Hupmobile out of her life. No, they would expect her, once a month, to ask them over so she could cook for them or to ride in the Hupmobile the three hundred and twenty miles to the ranch, where she could do the same. Only Mr. Ludlow, of the Woodmen of the World, who stopped by now and then to talk about her insurance, realized what was missing from *her* life. "Mrs. Momeyer," he said "*I'd* like to see you and your family in Coronado Arms," the new development that was run like a first-class hotel. He mentioned it in connection with insurance that would make it possible in fifteen years—or maybe five or six months if a girl like Etoile was persuaded to marry him. Mr. Ludlow was frank. He was thirty-two, and that probably would seem outrageous to Etoile at the moment, but in a few years she would be twenty and he would only be thirty-five. That's how strange such things were.

When he first brought the matter up, Maxine could only wag her head and smile, since that was in the spring and nature was taking its course. But not Calvin's nature. No, right at that point he had to run off. There was something missing in a boy his age who would give a girl like Etoile a gift certificate to the Rod & Reel, a fisherman's store. A stutter was no excuse for something like that. But Mr. Ludlow and all the rest would have to wait until Calvin shot at somebody or until Etoile read his mind and asked him to marry her, which she just might. In the corner of her mirror, with other signs, was one that said:

JUST MARRIED

dim lights

If *that* was on her mind, Etoile wouldn't trouble to dim the lights.

"Hi!" said Bud, letting the screen door slam; then he opened the door to the icebox and while it hung open, helped himself to a long drink of milk. Out of the bottle. It was just too much trouble to reach for a glass. So the neck of the bottle and the lip would be dirty, and unless Maxine remembered to clean it, Etoile would refuse to touch a drop of it.

"Bud—" she said, just as he closed the door with a bang. In the pantry she could hear him unscrewing the lid to the cookie jar. She couldn't hear that sound without thinking of poor little Lee Roy, with his greasy ears, who couldn't keep his dirty little hand out of the cookie jar.

"Magzeen," Bud said, "you about ready?" and hearing him munch on the cookies she turned, without a word, from the sink. Her hands left a trail of water from the sink to her room. In the mirror on

the dresser—in it with everything else: the unmade bed, the curtain looped around the bedpost,
the cup on the sill that she put her teeth in—in the
mirror this woman, her bust worn slantwise due to
the rip in her corset, on her face a comically
startled expression, like people you laugh at in the
movies because they have unimportant roles.
Around her middle this tire, as her daughter called
it, like the inner tubes she liked to take swimming,
the sidewalls stained and dirty where she leaned on
the sink. Was there any resemblance to that beauty,
Lois Scanlon McKee, her sister? The ears. The only
thing she couldn't dip into the sink. The small,
pink ears that Bud Momeyer considered something
of a blemish. "Dang it, Maxine, how you hear so
much with pigeon ears like that?"

Hearing the drip of water in the bathroom, she
said, "Your mother has a headache. You want to
bring her two aspirin?"

On Etoile's face, when she appeared in the door,
was the expression she wore when she broke a bad
egg in the morning.

"You know what, Mother?" she said, and Maxine
did; if nothing else she knew that. If something
didn't happen over the week end—if Calvin didn't
speak, or Etoile didn't speak for him, or Eileen or
Lois didn't shoot somebody, or McKee or her father
do something crazy—if something didn't happen to
change the world, she would do it herself. The
shapeless body in the mirror seemed to have two
heads. Her own, and there beside it, like the sweet-
hearts on candy boxes, the girl with lips like a cherry
and skin like a peach.

Etoile

Her dark side to the mirror, the morning light behind her, rising on her toes to make her long legs longer, the light like sugar candy in her just-washed hair, she looked like the eclipse of the moon on page 58 in her atlas. A moon goddess, the faucet dribbling in the sink, she sang:

> *What should I wear,*
> *What should I wear?*
> *Although I look*
> *Much better bare.*

Turning off the water, she switched on the overhead light. Blonde all over, all she needed was a fence rail to lean on like the girls in the folded pages of *Playboy* or in the picture pinned to the telephone booth in Laughlin's drugstore. Wheeling slowly, like the new Dodge on the platform in the Cornhusker lobby, she saw the raspberry lipstick painted on her lips, and the welt where Calvin had snapped her fanny with a towel. The shower raining in the tub, she sang:

> *Ashes to ashes,*
> *Dust to dust.*
> *I'd rather have a baby*
> *Than a rubber bust.*

She sang it like a cheer, her breasts bobbing, gazing over her shoulder at the cabinet mirror until the hot water steamed the glass. In Miss Baum's nasal voice, she said:

In many women the brown discoloration of the nip-puls betrays the advent of pregnancy.

Had Etoile been betrayed? No, alas. Nor had Miss Baum, who told them all that in the third-period gym class, wearing her bloomers, tapping with her pointer on the swollen belly in the diagram. Lola Burkin was pregnant at the time, and Etoile could see her squirm as though she was having breast pains, and five weeks later she just dropped out of school. Peggy Rooney said she saw her in McCrory's basement in Omaha selling make-up she put on her face and wiped off. Etoile was not swollen, nor were her nipples brown, but on evidence she found more convincing she had not been a virgin for ten months and thirteen days. She kept count just in case something unusual turned up. Eileen would take her word for it since Eileen knew something had happened, brown nipples or not, the night of June 17 in their place in Estes Park. Eileen had asked her out to spend the summer, naturally hoping something *would* happen, and waiting for it to happen, Etoile could baby-sit on their night-out nights. That afternoon they had all gone swimming at the new pool over in Greeley, except for Calvin, who couldn't swim a stroke. He had sat in the car making nooses for gopher traps. When the time came to go, Etoile called him over to pull her out of the water, and when he put down his hand, she had braced herself on the wall and pulled him in. He was wearing his blue jeans and stirrup boots. He might have drowned. He actually hollered for help, as though his speech was normal, and when they pulled him out of the water, it poured from his pants like a drainpipe, and there was a quart or more in each of his boots. She had almost had hysterics when she saw his hat, the one he was so proud of, floating on the pool like a bird with its head tucked under its wing. He had this crazy idea swimming pools were dirty because people took baths in them, and the moment he got home he took a hot shower.

What got into her? She was home alone with Calvin and little Gordon since Eileen and big Gordon had gone to a movie, and when she heard the water drumming in the shower, she took off her clothes, put on her shower cap and stepped in at his back. He couldn't believe it. He put his fists into his eyes like they were full of soap. When he reached to turn off the warm water she grabbed him by the hair, the way she did in the pool. Maybe he thought he would drown in the shower. He scooped her up, banged her head on the nozzle, and she had a grip on the shower curtain when they fell over backward, Calvin on top of her. She saw stars, just as she had read in books. That was all she saw or remembered until she woke up, the water drumming on her feet, her head pillowed on a wet towel on the bathroom floor.

What had happened? Since the skin on her back was sore, she had hoped for the worst. On her thigh was a bruise that looked like a man's hand if she rubbed it, and when she sat down, there was

something like blood on the sheet of her bunk. Nowhere could she find the skin broken. She had gone
back in the shower, turning on the warm water,
remembering what she knew about pregnancy, but
it wasn't much. When she came out of the shower,
she found little Gordon hugging the stuffed bear he
liked to sleep with, his eyes wide, but smart enough
to keep his mouth shut.

"Calvin's gone," he said, and so he was. Nor did
he show up in the morning for breakfast, the meal
that he liked the most. Calvin often went off to
sulk, but he always took his horse or his gun with
him, but not this time. When Eileen asked her if anything unusual had happened, Etoile had been ob-
liged to say that it might have, but she wouldn't
really know until about the twenty-seventh of the
month. Eileen said, "Darling, if it stutters I'll take
it off your hands."

While she waited for a post card from Calvin,
Etoile waited for morning nausea and breast pains,
but all the pains she had were somewhere else. Then
they stopped when Calvin wrote from Utah that
they shouldn't worry about him. With Eileen and
his father, who was just like him except for
the fact he didn't stutter, they made two trips as
far as Salt Lake, looking for him. Eileen was so
high-strung all the time Etoile could hardly tell if
it was Calvin missing or her husband being along
that made her worse. She had to take pills to sleep,
then pills to wake her up so she could drive. Etoile
liked the Mormon Tabernacle and kept a diary on
the back of post cards which she mailed to herself

at the ranch. On July 19 she wrote from Provo, *Feel in my bones something is about to happen*. But she didn't get the card mailed until they were in Colorado somewhere, and it was three days before it turned up at home. She got it in the morning on the twenty-fourth, and in the afternoon while she was exercising Pablo, Calvin called up from Lone Tree, and Eileen said, "My darling, his voice has changed, but nothing else." She meant that he still couldn't say a word with it. That was the week end Lois told her mother that cousins shouldn't marry or their babies would turn up with too many fingers, and all in all it had been the most exciting summer of her life.

On her birthday, in October, Calvin gave her toilet water that smelled like leather, with a picture of his horse Pablo in one of his horseshoes made of bronze. She had often seen the toilet water in the men's shop at Miller & Paine's. Three bars of soap went along with it which he kept himself, since she recognized the smell. There was always a little dried soap lather in his ears. On his birthday, in November, she gave him an album of records, *Come On, Let's Dance*, with diagrams on the back of the box to teach him the steps. But after two sides of one record she gave up. He wore stirrup boots with silver rowels, and nothing would persuade him to take them off. It had made her so mad she had gone into the bathroom and doused herself with the leather-smelling water, but it was lost on him since he liked the smell of it. But later, cleaning up the dishes, she knew there was something on his mind.

She had turned off the water, thinking he was going to propose. In the quiet she could hear the soapsuds drying on her arms. But that was all, not a gibber, and if it had not been for the girls waiting to grab him, she would have given up. Then she got a letter:

DEAR ETOILE,

Thank you very much for Come On Lets Dance. Its a honey. Mother says you might like to go to the Old Timers dance in Ogallala. Before you wonder why Ogallala dont forget its Grandfathers birthday on the 31st of March. Mother says we'll all be together out in Lone Tree, which is near Ogallala. You can go as the Girl of the Golden West and I can go as I am.

Sincerely

CALVIN

On the map in her atlas Ogallala looked close to Cheyenne, where people eloped and got married, but Calvin, as his mother always said, was *not* people. If *people* did it, Calvin would have nothing to do with it. She would have to find a place nobody ever heard of, like Olney or Minden, and just trust to luck there would be a justice of the peace. On the stationery Eileen had given her, with the vanilla-flavored mucilage and her name under a star, she got as far as the date and the place and the street, but she couldn't bring herself to say *Calvin Doll* and risk wasting one sheet. In a paperback book she was reading in installments while she was having her braces fitted, the girl wrote to the boy she really liked, *Gregory Doll*. It made her almost crazy to write like that to somebody besides Mildred Lorbeer, who was anything but. But the moment she wrote *Calvin Doll* on her blotter, it looked strange. It was Calvin. How could someone be Calvin Doll?

That was over New Year's, and before she got any farther, her cousin Lee Roy, who wasn't overly bright, had run his crazy hot-rod into two boys who were bullying him. Etoile had seen him, in his crash helmet, looking like one of the peewee football players who used the gymnasium in the wintertime. Tuesday and Wednesday she stayed out of school, and on Thursday they found the bodies of Mr. and Mrs. Bartlett in the shed beside their house. Then a girl who had once loaned Etoile her bathing suit, parked along a dark road along with her boy friend, necking, but not one of the papers mentioned *that*. No, they just said that she had been molested so people like her Aunt Lois, who was dying to be molested, would leave the lights on in her house all night. That was the truth. Did anybody mention it? Half the people she knew read the paper hoping somebody they knew had been shot or molested, and Etoile was like most people in that respect.

"Eeeee-toal!" her mother called.

"Yes, Muh-thurrrrr!"

"You know how your Uncle Walter feels about waiting."

"He feels it's what he's supposed to be doing," she said, since that was all Etoile ever saw him doing. She often saw him, holding pennies in his hand, peering at the needle in the parking meters or circling the block in front of Miller & Paine's, waiting for Aunt Lois to come out. Uncle Walter took a morning off from his work to drive her around, since walking on the concrete sidewalks hurt her feet. She had Etoile's feet, without any arches, the toes so long they were almost fingers, and the boys used to say she could shoot marbles with them.

"Your mother has a headache. You want to bring her two aspirin?"

When her mother was near the end of her rope, she referred to herself as her mother. Etoile raised the window to air out the steam, and wiped the film from the face of the mirror. Using one hand, she pushed up her hair and with the other held the towel to her breasts. What did Eileen say to her mother over the phone? "I know they're spoiled, my dear, but it makes me giddy just to think of those babies!" The *worst* that could happen would be that they would have *her* feet, and *his* stutter. From the bottle on the cabinet shelf she shook out several aspirins, had one herself. If the ride didn't give her a headache, Aunt Lois would. She filled the toothbrush glass with water, then stepped into the bedroom where her mother faced the mirror, looking the same from the front as from the rear. In the cafeteria line at school the boys called the woman who ladled out the soup, "Bessie, the unborn pig." She had no chin. The steam from the soup made her rosy pink. What would they call her mother besides an old bag?

"You know what, Mother?" she said, and watched her drink most of the water, then dissolve the aspirin in what was left. She had read somewhere that they burned a hole, like a match head, in the walls of the stomach.

Her mother swallowed, grimaced, said, "Know what?"

Etoile had no idea. Had she forgotten?

"Sometimes I think we're all stark mad," her mother said. She put her arms back to unbutton her dress, but since just before Christmas her arms wouldn't reach. Etoile had to button and unbutton her. She moved around behind her, and over her mother's shoulder she saw their two heads in the mirror.

"What should I wear, Mother?" she said, and waited for her to say, as she always did, that she might wear something to please her Aunt Lois. Her mother didn't, however, so she said, "Why can't I just go as I am?" and stuck her bare bottom out from the towel. The shoulders with the dark welts worn there by the bra straps heaved and shook. Was it so funny? Etoile lidded her eyes as if ashamed at what she saw in the mirror. Her mother had placed one hand on the dresser, and the way the mirror vibrated, it was hard for Etoile to see her face. She let the towel she was holding drop and reached both arms as far as they would go around what had once been her mother's waist. Her face she buried in the folds of her mother's neck. There they were, bawling together, when Uncle Walter gave a toot on the horn that played four musical notes.

"Here they are, you people," her father called,

and there he was in the door, wearing his red hunter's cap, his bow in his hand and the quiver of arrows at his back.

Her mother raised her apron, blew her nose in it, then said, "Tell your father to knock, Etoile. It's time he got it through his head you're a big girl now."

Calvin

Nineteen years of age, wearing a wide-brimmed hat and stirrup boots like his father, Calvin had walked out on the highway south of Greeley the summer before with nothing but the ten dollars he had borrowed from Mr. Lyons at the Texaco station. He walked unless somebody asked him to ride, but nearly everybody asked him. He was wearing boots with spurs and walked like a man accustomed to horseback. Nor was anyone put out when he proved to be the silent type. He nodded in agreement or sat reflecting, his ice-blue eyes looking out the window, the finger of one hand lightly brushing the edge of the lower lip that gave him trouble when he talked. Facing the mirror where he sometimes practiced, he could see it vibrating like the throat of a gobbler. He slipped the finger up as if he might conceal that or pin it down. A tendency to gibber, as his mother said, had got so bad he had to drop out of high school and spend the morning with a tutor on the ranch. A college student from Colorado Springs gave him books on sex hygiene and said that in love it was action that counted, not words. Calvin's gibber did not improve. It symptomized— she finally told him—his silly rebellion against a world where he couldn't ride horses, shoot guns and live just as he pleased. Maybe it did. If to live as he

pleased meant he had to gibber, then Calvin would
gibber. But preferably alone.

From Greeley a fisherman with trout flies in
his hat took him over the mountains to Steam-
boat Springs, where five men in a trailer, out hunting, rode him over to Craig. Nobody questioned
that he knew his own business or what it was. They
offered to take him all the way to Provo—which
was right on the edge of his grandfather's country—
but at Jensen City, on the Green River, they had to
wait a day for the bridge to be repaired. The water
was running high with the melting snow and Calvin
sat on the bridge, looking at it. The bank along the
east side of the river was smooth, with a few
ashpits where fires had been built, and near the foot
of the bridge, in its shadow, three hairy burros were
tethered. Calvin had raised a pair of them on his
father's ranch. He had learned to ride them Mexican
fashion, seated far back on the haunch, his legs dangling so that his boots grazed the ground. Two of
the burros had packsaddles, with flannel-wrapped
canteens strapped to the saddle horns and two small
picks and one shovel crossed at the rear. An enamel
wash pan like a dented helmet was at the top of one
pack. Nothing was missing, it seemed to Calvin, but
the figure of his Grandfather Scanlon, a squirrel
gun in his hand, a Davy Crockett coonskin hat on
his head. So many times that Calvin would recognize
the trail—if he came upon it—the old man had taken
him across the desert into the hell-hole of Death
Valley where he had stumbled on this man who had
been dead for some time. His grandfather had the

feeling he had seen him somewhere, since the crisp yellow beard was his own, and a familiar faraway music came out of his mouth. And he had. The way he told the story the dead man was himself.

Calvin had never been in doubt about what he meant. In every man there was one man who died if the other one was to go on living, and the old man who lived in Lone Tree was the one who had died. The one who lived took his hat, his squirrel gun, and slipped off.

In the early afternoon, the sun moving over, Calvin took the liberty of pulling the stake and tethering the burros where they could crop the sparse grass. With the enamel pan he brought them some river water to drink. Not much bigger than Saint Bernards, they had gray-bearded faces, jack-rabbit ears, and drank with the sound of water sluicing down a drain.

An hour before sunset, from the west, a heavy-set man walking a packed burro came across the river and down the slope to where Calvin sat. He wore a brimless hat, the crown almost black where his head sweated through it. The leather ends of his suspenders were sewn to his pants. When he stooped, his shirt was gray where the webbing crossed at the back, blue under the armpits and brown at the tails, where he wiped his hands. His shoes were new; he kicked them off because they hurt his feet. The burro was loaded with flour, salt, a slab of bacon and a sack of beans, and a pan so new it gleamed like a mirror with the sky. He seemed neither friendly nor unfriendly. Nodding at Calvin, he grunted. At times he talked to the burros, at times to himself. Calvin recognized the sounds as those spoken by the German janitor in his high school, and like that man he had wrinkles at the back of his neck. He scrubbed the old pan with sand, in the river, then made, with river water, salt and flour, a flat pancake with strips of bacon across the top. Did Calvin look hungry? He turned from the fire and with a motion of the pan included him in. In the new pan he prepared his own and ate it with a knife, giving Calvin the fork. The spoon was buried in the coffee grounds he added water to. After eating he smoked a pipe, belching like the man Calvin had once seen swallow fifty goldfish, then by magic whoop them all up. Now and then he grunted. He did not seem to expect Calvin to speak. For a young man whose lower lip gibbered because he liked horses better than people, it seemed he had found the heaven that his Grandfather Scanlon talked about. You got there by going through hell, and he had done that. Without comment, except to show him how to roll his pack and sleep in it, the prospector bedded down with him for the night. Overhead were the stars, at his feet running water that would soon be in the Grand Canyon, and the glow of a dying fire, like cracks in the earth. Nothing seemed finer to him than the sound of a burro staling during the night.

The man's name was Fischer or Visscher or something like that. He referred to Calvin as Poy. "Poy —" he would say, then indicate what he wanted done. In the early morning while it was cool, they walked the twenty-some miles back to Vernal, where Calvin bought a blanket, suspenders for his pants and a corncob pipe. He wrote his mother a post card telling her not to worry, since he planned to do a little prospecting, and in the evening, with Mr. Fischer, he smoked his new pipe.

They spent five days going down the river, swollen and moiling with the melting snow water, moving along as idly, it seemed to Calvin, as some of the drift timber on the stream going downstream merely because it was easier than going up.

Mr. Fischer talked a good deal now, sometimes in a language that Calvin did not understand, sometimes to the burros, but most of the time to himself. Calvin picked up what he knew by eavesdropping. There was no mention of where they were going, but a good deal of talk about what he called "bockets." Calvin at first thought he meant buckets, for which he could see a certain amount of use, but he meant pockets, although not like the ones they had in their pants. These were pockets they would find, if they were lucky, up along the ridges where he always seemed to be squinting, and he would sometimes take his pick and hack away at a piece of it. In a pan he kept cleaner than the ones they ate out of he would dip in the hollows and look for *colors*, which seemed to tell him where they were going, as if the pan served him as a map.

Except for the water, which never seemed to flow through the deserts of his grandfather's talk, Calvin had never been in a world where he felt so much at home. In every detail it seemed to be the world his grandfather had described, and pretty much as he had left it. Men with burros had gone up this canyon before them, sometimes leaving in the ledges scooped-out little pockets or a piece of metal where they had built a fire. Some of these men fished and left the bones at the campsite, and one man had shot a deer; the bones had been scattered by the *kyotes*, as Mr. Fischer called them. Why, Calvin wondered, didn't Mr. Fischer hunt and fish? He seemed to be content to eat beans and biscuits and nothing else. Calvin was not content, it made him constipated, and one morning, standing in the shallows, he dipped his hat into the stream and scooped out a trout. Mr. Fischer wouldn't touch it. He couldn't stand the smell it left in the pan. Calvin learned to broil the trout on the end of his fork, the fire flaring under the drippings, and he found he could eat them almost raw.

The first panned gold Calvin ever saw made him think of what he saw in the dentist's office when a tooth with a gold filling had been drilled. When he spit into the bowl it gleamed, and the dentist had said, "There goes good money!" This dust Mr. Fischer let him have when he panned it out. They were looking for the pocket that it had washed out of when Calvin saw on the ridge above him what he thought must be a Martian or a space man, as if he and Mr. Fischer had come to the end of the world. He stood above them, in his pith helmet, wearing a harness that was hung with gadgets, and when he caught Calvin's eye, he waved the tool he held in his hand. Calvin waved in return. They were too far apart to speak. Mr. Fischer, at his side, did not wave; he took the pipe from his mouth and spit out the juice, then he glanced around the country as if he hated it all and said, "U-ranyum kyotes."

Where had he come from? How had he got there? Like Mr. Fischer, whose face had gone bitter, Calvin felt the man was cheating. Where were his burros, his tin pans and his pick? What sort of mining was it to go around with this machine in your hand? Mr. Fischer said no more, but the way he swung the pick and dug into the shale and gravel, Calvin knew what he saw at the end of it. Without having seen the face of this man he hated him. If he had had his gun along he might have taken a few pot shots at him. This was his grandfather's country, Mr. Fischer's country, and it was now Calvin McKee's country, to be defended from these cheaters the way you'd scare off cattle thieves.

What pockets they found were mostly empty, but the more Calvin dug and felt discouraged, the less Mr. Fischer really seemed to mind. What he had read and seen on TV had led Calvin to feel that sooner or later, never so very much later, people like Mr. Fischer stumbled on a Comstock Lode. The problem was mostly how to keep it hidden while you packed it out. After more than three weeks all of Calvin's gold dust was less than what it took to fill a cigarette paper or weight the corner of the Bull Durham bag he kept it in. His boots were worn out, one stirrup torn away, and his knee showed through the hole in his pants, but he could sit for hours crouched on his heels and sleep on the ground without stiffness in the morning. Like Fischer, in the morning and evening he wet his face and neck in the river and forgot about such things as a bath. His teeth and gums he rubbed hard with a strip of bacon rind.

In July, running short of flour, they moved up the stream to the bridge at Jensen, and in the cool of the evening tethered the burros and walked into town. A movie, closed during the winter months, had opened up. He had not known Mr. Fischer was near-sighted until he stepped into the movie, leading Calvin to the second row of seats at the front. The picture was about cattle rustling, but Mr. Fischer seldom noticed the people. Out loud he would say, "Mormon country," pointing at the landscape behind the people or naming the peaks he saw and the mountain ranges. Calvin, however, kept his eyes on the girl who wore pants, rode a horse like a man, with her long blonde hair streaming in the wind. Her skin was white, and when she swung her long leg over the horse, Calvin felt it in his thighs the way he did looking down from a height. Why was that? It was what his cousin Etoile did when she crawled into her bunk at night after taking a shower, smell-ing strongly of soap. She would put one long foot on his berth, and when Calvin opened his eyes, he would see it like a marble column to where it forked at the crotch. Then he would lie there, smelling her soap, smelling the orange Lifesavers or the banana candy she always took to bed.

When they came out of the movie, they walked out of town to where they had set up camp in a meadow, and could hear the mountain water coursing in the ditch all night. Calvin didn't sleep, and early in the morning, when the cattle came in close to look at them, he got up quietly and walked into town. A gasoline truck, headed east toward Craig, stopped, and the fellow asked him where he'd left his horse. He was a local boy, and knew what it was like to walk in stirrup boots.

He was clear over to Craig in the afternoon, and the next morning, before daylight, he was in the ice hatch of an eastbound freight out of Laramie. He had every intention of getting off at North Platte and hitching a ride north to Chadron, getting in just in time to surprise his dear, sweet, silly mother. In the yards at North Platte a westbound train had stopped long enough to let the passengers eat, and some of them were out on the platform as he walked past. They stopped eating or talking to turn and look at him. In the window of the baggage department he caught a look at himself. He knew that there was a hole in one knee of his pants and that the toes and heels of his boots were scuffed through, but he had no idea what the rest of him was like. He hadn't troubled to look. The night in the ice hatch of the freight had almost blackened his face with soot, so that his eyes seem to peer out from a black mask. His clothes, since he hadn't changed them, were shaped to his body like buckskin and he looked like the rustler he had seen in that movie who had hidden in the mountains till the posse had flushed him out. What he saw scared him, as it did everybody else. He kept going, waiting for someone to shout or whistle at him, and when the freight came in and began to move, he climbed back on. He couldn't go home, even to his mother, looking as he did. He rode on a flatcar loaded with tractors down the long dry slope of the plain, through towns where the cattle barns were printed with his father's name, G. P. McKEE. What a story it would be if they picked up his son, looking like a bum, with two ounces of gold dust in a Bull Durham pack. Who would ever believe he had panned it out himself? Who? Why, Grandfather Scanlon, of course. He would not only believe it, but if Calvin walked in on him looking like he did, it would be no more than the old man would expect. If he hadn't died, which he might have, or if the family hadn't taken him to Lincoln, he would be holed up where he always was, in Lone Tree.

Calvin left the flatcar and moved to the back out of the smoke and cinders, to look ahead for it. Freights, he seemed to remember, sometimes stopped there for water. But this one, rolling downgrade like a flyer, went through Lone Tree without a whistle; he had just time enough to recognize it. There was no sign of anybody being there. But half an hour east the freight began to brake and pulled on a siding to let a flyer pass. Calvin climbed off. He could see traffic on the highway a mile to the north, but he stayed along the tracks. On the highway one of the police cars might pick him up. He walked all day, twice drinking water lying in shallow pools under the culverts and once eating grain he found under the chute of an elevator. He got into Lone Tree just about sunset, the sun on the windows of the vacant buildings, the door to the back of the hotel open, but the screen latched. His nose to the screen, he rapped. On the sofa over near the window he saw the old man slowly push up, showing his back. His coat was off, and his suspenders were like a strap around a hobo's bundle, his head tipped over so low it was out of sight. He turned so slowly Calvin feared to see his face.

"Samuels," he said. "That you, Samuels?" his glasses dangling from his shirt pocket, his eyes almost closed against the bright light. All Calvin could do was gibber like a monkey, his finger to his lip. He had to stand there, his legs trembling, until the old man shuffled over to open the screen.

"The wagon," he cried. "You come with the wagon?" and threw his arms around him, almost bawling; then he leaned back and squinted at his face. Calvin felt his lip trembling like he had a tic, but no sound came out.

"But Miss Samantha," the old man shouted, grabbing him by the shoulders, "Miss Samantha's all right?" Up and down, slowly, Calvin pumped his head. As if the excitement had been too much for him, the old man rocked on his heels, then dropped on the sofa. All Calvin wanted to do at the time was cheer him up. Seated there on the sofa, his hands propped on his knees, the old man put his head out like a viper, sang:

> *I've travelled the mountains all over*
> *And now to the valleys I'll go*
> *And live like a pip in the clover*
> *In sight of huge mountains of snow.*

Calvin had never before heard the old man sing, if that was the word. He stopped there, said, "Boy, you hear that?" Calvin could hear the whine of a truck on the highway. "Hear that?" he repeated. "That's the wind flappin' the canvas like a sail." He turned to look through the window at his back. "We was strung out in a line, maybe fifty, sixty wagons, looking like so many caterpillars with their fuzz burned off. Along about now the fireflies would come out, and Miss Samantha kept them in a bottle where they glowed at night. When she shook the bottle and they buzzed, I could see her face. Her hair was black as it is where the harness cuffs a mule's hide and her skin was fair and flecked with gold like buttermilk. She had a nose in her face like mine, she had ears and fuzz on her cheeks like mine, but I couldn't tell you if Miss Samantha had eyes or not. I knew she had 'em, but I couldn't tell you——"

There he stopped, feeling in the floor the rumble of a train before they heard it, and through the screen they watched the downgrade cars flick past. When the caboose went by it seemed to take a piece of the plain along with it. A wall of light rose from the track bed to the sky. Calvin waited for the old man to go on, then turned to see that he had dozed off. His head lolled forward on his chest, and in the band of his drayman's hat were the burned matches he had sucked to a fine point.

Calvin left him dozing on the sofa and walked over to the diner on the highway where the cook knew him and let him call his mother collect. Hearing him, she cried, "My darling! You've made your fortune?"

He could see her face, with the staring eyes, the mouth in the wide silly smile that led people to doubt they had heard what she said.

"Etoile is here, darling. A foot taller. You should see her in your hat and boots riding Pablo. He loves it. I just hope she doesn't read *his* mind."

So did Calvin. Seeing her on Pablo, riding western style in his stirrup boots like the girl in the movie, it crossed his mind how much like Samantha Etoile must be. Her hair was brown, not black like a mule's hide, but would the old man know the difference by the light from a jar of fireflies? And her eyes? Calvin still didn't know the color of her eyes. But how explain all that to a girl who told him what he was thinking the moment he stammered, and if she didn't like what he was thinking, told him off?

Over Christmas when he heard his mother talking of what they should do for Grandfather on his birthday, Calvin knew what it should be, but it was nothing he could talk about. He would get a wagon or a buggy, and with a team of mules, if he could find them, he would drive up to the window where the old man slept, and crack his whip. When he cried out, "That you, Samuels?" that's who it would be. And Miss Samantha would be there on the buckboard if he could just get it through Etoile's head who Samantha was and how much they looked alike. To get it through her head he wrote a long letter, then he thought better of it and wrote a short one, not mentioning the details it would take a little doing to work out. Like the mules. Nobody in the county had a team of mules. A man in North Platte had a team of oxen he yoked to a wagon over the summer, but all they did was stand there while tourists took pictures of them. He almost died laughing when Calvin suggested hitching them up. Then he found the mules over near Liggett, but before anything at all had been settled a man was shot and killed as he slept in his car just a few miles north. Calvin didn't know till later, since he didn't read the papers, that this was the tenth murder in about eight days, the first nine having been in Lincoln where Etoile lived. Everybody in the state but Calvin got pretty upset. The Liggett fellow wouldn't rent him the mules, and somebody who had seen him with his rifle turned his name in to the state police. They stopped him at a road block near Chadron, and when all Calvin could do was stutter, drove him clear to Grand Island with an armed guard in the seat. His mother had to drive over from the ranch and talk for him.

"My darling," she said, putting her finger to his lips, "don't shoot a dozen people unless they're policemen." She kissed him, then added, "It's not worth the trouble, sweetheart. It's been done."

Bud

On the occasion of his twenty-fifth year of service, during which neither wind nor rain, sleet nor snow, heat nor cold had stopped him, some of Bud's customers, as he called them, pooled their offerings and bought him a cart for toting his mailbag. Made of aluminum and stainless steel, with two wire wheels the size of those on a baby carriage, it resembled something new in a shopping cart or a golf-bag tote for the fairway. The three weeks Bud Momeyer used it the soreness in his left side was relieved, but blisters developed on both hands. The mail service itself almost ground to a halt the week Bud explained what a lifesaver it was and wondered how he had managed to do without it for twenty-five years. The rubber-tired wheel was a wonderful invention, but as Bud was the first to say, if God had thought they were better than legs, it would be wheels, not legs, that he put on mailmen. The cart had to be left at the curb like a horse, but, unlike a horse on a dairy wagon, when you whistled farther down the line, it stayed right where it was. Until he got the cart Bud would have said a man could learn to carry the mail in an hour, which he could, but that was not *delivering* it. Like kids learn the short cuts across a yard, he had puzzled out the shortest possible way between two porches. It was never the way he could take that cart. He liked to sort out the mail as he went along, glancing at the post cards or the handwriting, so that he was prepared to discuss the matter if and when it came up. The cart put an end to all that; it gave him no time to read more than the address and turned him into a sort of special-delivery errand boy. It took him forty minutes longer, working fast, than just going along at his usual pace. Stranger yet, he missed the weight of the bag, held like a baby while he was talking, and always there to slap or pull something out of if he had to get on or if the conversation lagged. But the telling point was that the cart made him feel like a fool. Dogs that never barked, barked. Some of the younger hoodlums whistled or jeered. That might happen only once in four or five days, but it was on his mind until it happened, then it was on his mind, as he peered over his shoulder, because it had. Beginning Monday, the fourth week, he left it home. He got up early that morning to wrap his right hand in a wad of gauze, just the fingers showing, and starting with Maxine, he told the deliberate lie that his blisters had broken and become infected. He had to be careful since a mailman had only one right hand.

That Bud Momeyer might lie, deliberately or otherwise, crossed the mind of only one person who knew him, and Maxine Momeyer got her mail on a different route. People who had promoted the cart felt guilty, and the others were glad to see it condemned. No one in his right mind expected Bud to risk his hand again, and he didn't. When the bandage came off, the cart did not come back. It could be seen in the Momeyer yard, converted into a fertilizer spreader in the spring or used as a shopping cart when the car broke down. The pain came back in Bud's left side, but not so bad it kept him awake, the dogs stopped barking, the kids stopped whistling, and he had time to catch up on the news that for two weeks had almost got away from him. What cortisone was doing to Agnes Lorbeer or the latest drug for Mr. Avery, who kept himself alive by walking almost twenty miles a day. Mr. Avery, who was Bud's own age, but looked old enough to be his grandfather, left the house when Bud appeared in the morning, walked a mile or so with him, like the dogs, then usually reappeared, five hours later, just in time for the afternoon delivery, so tired he looked dead, but still alive.

Had he died? Or didn't he like walking with the cart? That was the sort of thing Bud didn't know until his route got back to normal, and Mrs. Milton Ashley had the time to bring him up to date on her son Milton, who was busy making a name for himself in the world. At the end of the war Standard Oil had sent him to the Far East with his family. Before the piece appeared in the Lincoln *Courier*, most of the people on Bud Momeyer's route knew that Milton Ashley had received the Order of the Siam Crown, Fourth Class, pinned on him in Bangkok by the Ambassador himself. If the letter was from Milton, with one of those foreign stamps, Mrs. Ashley would open it there on the porch or ask Bud to step into the hallway while she read it to him. Bud had been a classmate of Milton's at Roosevelt High. Milton came to school in his mother's electric car just before the bell rang, ate apples during recess, and once a year had a birthday party to which Bud, being in his class, was invited to come. As far as Bud could recall, Milton had never actually spoken to him. He had carried Milton's mail for more than ten years before the article appeared in the Omaha *World-Herald* citing Milton's achievements and listing his old Lincoln school friends who would remember him. Bud Momeyer's name had appeared in that list. Several people remarked on that and often asked Bud what was new about Milton, as if he might know, and thanks to Mrs. Ashley keeping him posted, he usually did. His children were Wendy, Judy and Ronald; they had already flown more than sixty thousand miles, which was the equal of flying around the world two and a half times. Mrs. Ashley flew the children home to Lincoln for Christmas every two or three years. Bud had met the children, always surprised to see how pale they looked from such a hot country, and Mrs. Ashley had referred to him as their father's old friend. Their mother was usually in bed when he came by with the mail. When she and one of the children were lost at sea, Bud Momeyer was invited to the memorial service, for which he had to go out and buy another blue suit. His name appeared in the paper as an old close friend. None of this was important or changed his life or made him swell-headed or the like, but it was the sort of thing he couldn't explain to Maxine. Why he would rather work than take a vacation, that is.

The Ashley family was just one of many that Bud

Momeyer, in no way related, had somehow got to be part of. Take the coffee he had on cold winter mornings with Mrs. Rossiter. A woman of eighty now, almost blind, with one hip so bad she could hardly walk, yet as bright and independent as any person he knew. While she had her sight TV was a help, and in her seventies she had taken to watching baseball, soon knowing more about the game than most men ever did. All summer long he had to give her time to keep him up to date. When Milwaukee won the Series, she had him in to eat a dish of prune whip in celebration.

Although he was married and the father of a daughter, which were things he had in common with so many people, Bud had more in common with their families than he did with his own. His opinion was asked. Was it the uniform? It helped. When they saw him without it, they never asked him any questions.

When he didn't show up, there were people who phoned. He certainly knew their kids better than his own kid, especially the ones who liked to walk along with him, or those whose stories he got in detail from their worried parents. Maxine hardly ever said a word to him. When the mail cart came into his life and changed his old habits, Bud had lain awake nights like some of the people who talked to him. He wasn't losing his life or his kid, but he was losing everybody else's, and in some strange way these other families were his own. Their problems seemed to be the ones he could help. When he told Mrs. Clayton she was looking better, as she often was at nine twenty in the morning, he didn't have to be around at suppertime when she looked much worse. The secret was in the mail pouch. He had to move on. Only when the last letter was delivered did he have to come home. The strangest feeling Bud had had in all his life was when it occurred to him that Maxine might be telling Mr. Pollard, their mailman, what she told nobody else. A bigger fool than Leo Pollard, Bud Momeyer had seldom seen.

Which was why Bud Momeyer, underpaid and overworked, still liked his work better than his vacations, like that motorman in the joke who took a trolley ride on his day off. Saturday and Sunday, weather permitting, Bud dressed and delivered frying chickens, the Hupmobile followed by a sniffing mongrel pack of idle dogs. The rear of the car smelled of dressed poultry, wet chicken feathers and cracked eggs which he sold in bulk to the women who still made angel-food cakes. Being the sort of person women could talk to the way they could to their pets, without interruption, he would sometimes sit in the kitchen while the cake was baked. No man was upset when he stepped into the kitchen and saw Bud Momeyer sampling a pie or being asked his opinion about grades of linoleum. He could fix shade rollers, salvage the irons and cords he sometimes saw in the cans at the curbing, and on his way in with the mail he would return them to the owner, to be picked up and repaired later. Vacuum cleaners, slipping egg beaters, knives that needed sharpening, a cuckoo clock that had stopped cuckooing, radios and phonograph turntables, anything that ran that had stopped running—all were offered to Bud to see what he could do. If he couldn't fix it, why then just throw it away. Twenty years of what he couldn't fix but had never managed to throw away filled the garage and the basement and his basement room.

In a collection of stuff from Mrs. Crawford's attic he found a quiver with five arrows and a five-foot bow missing only the cord. It was bound with green cord where you gripped it, and the twenty-some years in the attic had done little more than age the grain of the wood. The arrows had been made and feathered by Mr. Crawford himself. A taxidermist, in his spare time he did a little hunting with the bow and arrow, since he held the opinion that it gave the bird a fighting chance. The gun did not. Not to mention what it did to the bird. After his passing Mrs. Crawford had put the bow and arrows, with dozens of stuffed birds, into the attic, since she couldn't bear to throw them away. After the war, however, with the need for housing, she had been able to rent the attic, and most of the stuff had been piled at the curb. If he had not been on duty that particular morning Bud would have lost it to the Goodwill people, who claimed that he cost them several hundred dollars a year, at least. What Bud salvaged was never put back on the curb again.

The bow and arrow put an end to Bud's work on the self-filling fountain pen. The patent had been filed at great expense, and all that remained for Bud to do was sell the idea to an interested party. Once the bow was strung, there was no more of that.

Over the winter he turned, tipped and feathered arrows, and spring and summer, on daylight-saving time, he shot them into the mattress at the back of his sheds or at the scarecrow made of straw that hung from the tree at the rear of his lot.

At that time Bud had the run of the sixty-five acres that soon was turned into a new shopping center. When that happened, he felt hemmed in and took to the open country. Until then he had never intended to hunt. But in the open country there was very little to shoot *at*. So he began on the rabbits, without much luck since they could hop off to a fair distance, and unless it was winter he found it hard to see the arrow again.

Quite by accident he got around to cats. The number of kittens Bud Momeyer had saved in his twenty-five years as a mailman probably ran to several hundred, and that, in time, was thousands of cats. But kittens, as anyone would tell you, were different from cats. One of his neighbors, Mr. Lyle, paid a bounty of fifty cents a head for the cats that molested his hamster farm. They did crazy things. They would climb wire fences and swim across small dams. Wires put up to electrocute cats merely killed dogs. A stream ran along at the back of his farm, and one day Bud, walking along it, saw a wild-looking tom eying him from the roof of a shed. More to frighten him off than hit him, Bud aimed at the wall just beneath. The weight of the arrow turned the tom half way around. Bud could see the arrow on one side of him and the feathers on the other, just before he stepped off the roof and dropped to the ground.

Not a sound. Not a whimper. Nor was it in any way messy. Bud did not feel bad. He did not feel much of anything. He didn't mention the shooting to Maxine or collect the fifty cents from Mr. Lyle, but over the summer he bagged another four cats. They were accustomed to boys with rifles and air guns and wouldn't move from their tracks at the twang of his bow.

The only persons he mentioned this to were Mr. Lyle, who was glad to hear about it, and his brother's boy Lee Roy, who was boarding with them. He was a quiet, studious boy who liked to help Bud feather his arrows in return for what Bud could do for him. That was quite a bit, up through Christmas, since he seemed a little slow at mathematics and what the numbers meant on the ratchet of Bud's micrometer. According to Maxine, he took a lot of kidding because of his car, which Etoile wouldn't ride in, since it was worse than sitting under a hairdryer. Bud was over on P Street, south of the high school, talking with Mr. Ewell who was out chipping ice, when he heard the siren go south on Twenty-first. A moment later they saw the blinker on the ambulance. Mr. Ewell commented that they ought to keep cars off the streets in the winter and Bud didn't hear what the trouble was until he got home. Maxine had locked herself in the bathroom, which she did when she smelled trouble, but Etoile was in the kitchen with the radio on.

"Where's Lee Roy?" Bud had asked, since his car wasn't in the driveway.

"He ran over two bullies, and I don't blame him," she had replied.

Hearing it like that before the details, Bud had been more shocked by what she said than by what Lee Roy had done. He figured he had run into two boys because it couldn't be helped. But Lee Roy had run them down right there in the schoolyard with everybody watching, and had nothing whatsoever to say for himself. Then, before they even had a letter from his people, Mr. and Mrs. Bartlett over on J Street were found dead in the shed alongside their house. When they had mail, which wasn't often, Bud had delivered it. Mrs. Bartlett canned cherries and gave him a jar at Christmastime.

A day later they found two more, then three of them, and before it was over Bud had been shot at by one of the old ladies who liked him most. Lincoln was like a town hit by the pest, with everybody secretly scared of everybody else. He could hear bolts click when he walked up to a house. Wouldn't it be the last person you might suspect—that is to say, Bud Momeyer? Some people thought so.

The day the news came over the radio that the killer had been captured somewhere out in the sandhills, they were seated at the table, about to eat. Nobody took a breath till they heard the name announced.

Maxine said, "I swear to God it's the bomb or something, everybody's crazy!"

And Etoile had said, "You want to know somethin'?" but before she had managed to say it, Maxine had almost screamed at her. "No! You hear me, Etoile, I don't!" and she got up from the table, as though she was sick, and went and locked herself in the bathroom.

"Why you want to make your mother upset?" Bud had said, so upset himself he couldn't swallow. As a rule a family quarrel made him hungry, not sick, but he had sat there at the table, the meat and biscuits cooling, the announcer going over the list of the murders, and Etoile sitting beside him white as a sheet. When the announcer said nobody knew why in the world Munger did it, she had blurted out *Ha!*

"If you're so smart, young lady," Bud said, "I suppose you know why?"

"You want to know why?" she yelled. "It's because nobody wants to know why. It's because nobody wants to know *any-thing!* Everybody hates everybody, but nobody knows why anybody gets shot. You want to know somethin'? I'd like to shoot a few dozen people myself!"

She had bounced her napkin ring on the table, and her chair fell over when she pushed it back. The cold food spread before him, the coffee perking black in the percolator, Bud had said, "You want to pour your daddy's coffee, Etoile?" and she had. After all that had happened, it was a comfort to him to know she was right.

Lee Roy

In the Texaco station near the college Lee Roy Momeyer spent most of his time in the cool of the grease pit, hot-rods and small foreign cars being his specialty. As the boss liked to say, he was small enough to get under them. He could move around without straining his neck or bumping his head. To keep the grease out of his hair he wore caps made from the bottoms of paper bags. It gave him the look, from above, of a Chinaman. He could have worked on the level at one of the pumps, but being down in the pit was cool in the summer, and the college boys didn't honk their horns and yell, "Hey there, big boy!" One from the East, with a white Porsche, always tipped Lee Roy after a grease job with lead quarters he got from a guy who serviced slot machines. He would flip him the coin, then say, "Big Boy, go have yourself a ball."

Lee Roy spent the quarters at the Sugar Bowl, where they had a jukebox that would take them. They also had a cigarette machine but he didn't smoke.

Lee Roy's hot-rod, a '37 Ford coupe with Graham wheels, the top shaved off, sat at the side of the building where he could keep his eye on it. There were all sorts of hot-rods, but only Lee Roy had one with the mufflers alongside the windshield—a little hot in the summer, but in the winter it melted the snow and ice. Without a top, it still kept him warm as toast. The idea had been Lee Roy's own, but his father, a mechanic, had curved the pipes and electrically welded the joints. At considerable expense Lee Roy had chrome-plated the mufflers. The motor burned a lot of oil, but it hardly mattered since he got most of it for nothing, using the high-class oil he drained from the foreign cars. All he had to do when he needed oil was tell the college boy his oil looked dirty, and he would have it changed. Lee Roy would let it drain into a can he kept handy in the grease pit, then fill his car with stuff worth sixty-five cents a quart. He liked the smell of good British oil in the exhaust.

Lee Roy's home was in Calloway, where, to please his mother, he had planned to study for the ministry until the summer he helped his father repair a few cars. There was no explaining, as his father said, his aptitude. A man in North Platte had spent eleven hundred dollars for a motor analyzer that Lee Roy had put to shame with a screw driver. In three or four minutes, with the motor idling, Lee Roy could tune up carburetor systems that had his father, a specialist, almost bug-eyed. A man from Omaha drove his Jaguar out to Calloway once a month just to let Lee Roy listen to it idle and set the points. The way certain doctors could look at a patient and know the trouble was in his liver, Lee Roy could listen to a motor and put his finger on the spot. But that was all. He didn't really grasp how a motor ran. The cutaway charts in his father's shop showing the principle and parts of a gasoline engine were as much a mystery to Lee Roy as algebra. Algebra kept him out of the Calloway high school, and to get away from algebra he had come to Lincoln where he could take physical ed and shop. In shop they took apart and reassembled a motor like the one in Lee Roy's hot-rod, and if he did this often enough he might grasp the principle. If he didn't grasp the principle, he could always go back to the ministry.

In Lincoln he stayed with his father's brother and his family. They let him have a room in the basement that was meant to be temporary, but Lee Roy liked being next to the furnace in the wintertime. He was free, if he wanted, to sit and work at the table in the kitchen or listen to the radio in the living room. He was the least nuisance, Maxine told his mother, of any member of the family, by which she meant he closed the icebox door without banging it. He liked a cold glass of milk about bedtime, but he never drank out of the bottle or left the glass, the way Etoile did, dirty in the sink. His mother had been strict in the way she brought him up.

There were times when Lee Roy would have liked a game of rummy if there had been boys in the family or if the girl, Etoile, had been friendlier. She kept to herself in the room right above him where he could hear her dress and undress, or listen to the radio she sometimes left on all night. Part of the unfriendliness was due to the fact she was the same age as Lee Roy, but grew more than five inches the year he grew less than one. Because of her he took a shower at the Y, since she never left any hot water, or if he was in the tub, she would come by and holler, "Just don't wade in over your head, Mr. Momeyer."

Her mother, on the other hand, treated Lee Roy just like one of the family, mending his clothes and whenever he would beat it, making him fudge. Mr. Momeyer asked Lee Roy to just call him Bud. He was like an older brother in most respects and helped Lee Roy with the decimal system, metric weights and measures and how to use a micrometer. Mr. Momeyer liked to hunt with a bow and arrow, and Lee Roy would help him sort feathers for the arrows or on Sunday mornings work on his Hupmobile. Mr. Momeyer liked to hunt more than he liked to kill things, but with a bow and arrow the rabbit had the same chance Lee Roy had when he crossed O Street against the lights. Mr. Momeyer's car was even older than Lee Roy's and should have been simpler in principle, but the only way to start it in cold weather was with a push.

If Lee Roy could have stayed in the basement, where they couldn't come and find him, or down in the grease pit, where they couldn't come and see him, he would have liked Lincoln better than Calloway. But every morning he had to drive his car to school. They were always there, all three of them, either out in front, blocking the driveway, or out in back where he had to park. They pretended not to hear him when he honked, and they pretended not to see him if he didn't. Bobo Lamkin was six feet four inches tall, his face so pimpled it was lumpy.

He never took his hands out of his pockets except to play basketball. Andy Larsen had a duck's-ass hairdo and put a wave in it with a home-Toni. Stu Smiley owned the Chevvy they rode around in. Bobo was the leader. They did what he said. If he said lie down and get run over, that's what they did.

The one little thing Lee Roy could do for Mr. Momeyer was take Etoile to school in the morning, but the second week of school they blocked the driveway with their car. When Lee Roy climbed out, Bobo hollered, "See you keep that pet on a leash, girlie," and the next morning she refused to ride in his car. When he asked her why, she said the smell from the mufflers made her sick.

If she felt sick—and maybe she did—Lee Roy had a better idea why. That summer she had gone to Colorado to spend her vacation with her cousin Calvin, and either Calvin or somebody else had you-know-what. Not that Lee Roy had anything against Calvin unless it was his luck. What was a little thing like a stutter if you were six foot two and looked like Gary Cooper? When he came to Lincoln in the family car, he brought it to Lee Roy for a grease job and sat in the car oiling the rifle he kept in the seat. He looked so much like a state trooper people coming up behind him were afraid to go by him. Maybe he knew horses, but he didn't know beans about cars. "Lee-lee-lee—" he would stutter, and Lee Roy would say, "Yes sir," and look under the hood. People sold him new plugs four or five times a year by pulling off a wire while the motor idled, but Lee Roy didn't do any more than drain his oil. All he really had against Calvin was his luck.

Both Etoile's room and the bathroom were right over Lee Roy's head, and he could hear her clothes drop on the floor when she took them off. She took enough baths, as her mother said, to irrigate the two acres that were dry most of the summer. If the bathroom door was locked, it was usually Etoile. She had ruined the hairbrush by hammering on the bolt to unlock it, as it was sometimes hard to get it open. Lee Roy could tell by the creak in the boards just where she was standing, but not what she was doing, since she would let the water run. When her mother said, "For heaven's sake, E-toal!" Etoile would say she was washing her hair. A towel around her head, her bathing suit on, she would go out in back and sit in the sand pile where Lee Roy could see her through the slats on the back steps. When she came back from Colorado, she had scratches on her back she said she got when she slipped and fell down a slope, and when her long hair dried, it covered most of them. She liked to sit with her halter down so the tan wouldn't leave a line, and when she raised her arms, Lee Roy could see her breasts. They weren't like walnuts, lemons or melons but almost flat with big nipples. Above her left breast, almost at her armpit, she had a bruise that looked like a birthmark or the bites Lee Roy used to give himself. But it was out of the question, being where it was, that she had bitten herself.

That was the summer Calvin just walked off and his family ran ads in the paper for him until he turned up about six weeks later, looking like a bum. Nobody talked about it. Lee Roy got the details listening to Maxine on the telephone, since she nearly always repeated what she found hard to believe. The way Lee Roy saw it, Calvin did it and then ran off. When Etoile got home she spent most of her time taking baths and fooling around in the tub to keep from having a baby, which had worked. She had probably used one of the machines he saw in drugstore windows along with pills that gave a girl the cramps. In about half the cars Lee Roy greased he found hairpins, lipsticks and you-know-whats, and sometimes girls' panties tucked into the glove compartment or the pocket on the door. Not that Lee Roy minded. All he had against *them* was their luck.

When business got heavy on holidays and week ends, he had a boy named Charlie to help him in the pit. He was no bigger than Lee Roy, maybe smaller, since he wore shoes to make him look taller. He couldn't be left alone with a car or he might forget to put the oil back in it, but one thing he knew was how to cut the big boys down to size. Down there in the grease pit he would let them have a squirt from the spring oilcan. A big guy with light flannels or white buck shoes would have to drop them off at the nearest cleaner. If they let out a yell, he could always say it was an accident. If there were no college boys around he would take the grease gun, aim it like a rifle, then pin the flies to the wall of the garage with a gob of grease. "F——k the bastards," he would say, and he didn't mean the flies. He seemed to think some of these big guys were out to get him, and he would hide in the men's room when he heard a car honk, or lie on the floor of the pit like he was scared to death. Lee Roy had never seen anybody so scared act so tough. One day he drove in and asked Lee Roy to put his Ford on the hoist or he'd blow his brains out, and Lee Roy did, since he had a rifle beside him on the seat. Up on the hoist Lee Roy could see him peering out the windows, just his hair showing, as if the place was crowded with white-shoed college boys. Not that Lee Roy minded—he felt the same way when Bobo Lamkin pulled in for gas and whistled the way he did with one finger in his mouth. "F——k the bastards!" Lee Roy would say, and with his head ducked down in the pit, spray the bottom of whatever car he had on the rack.

Then this happened. The day before Thanksgiving Andy Larsen, wearing one roller skate and his little brother's knee pants, blocked the driveway beside the school, hooting at Lee Roy and his car and yelling, "That's my skate!" Lee Roy pushed him with the bumper into the street, where he fell forward and scraped his knees. Mr. Colfax, the football coach, kept Bobo Lamkin from beating Lee Roy up. The principal of the school, Mr. Devoe, asked Lee Roy to leave his car at home till after Christmas.

In December, three days before Christmas, while Lee Roy was in the pit with the doors closed, someone poured liquid detergent into both his mufflers and painted *Chinese Junk* on the rear with a spray gun. When Lee Roy drove home both mufflers blew bubbles, and they tagged along behind him with the horn blowing. People coming toward him pulled off the road until he passed.

After Christmas he drove back to school and everything was all right, nothing happened all morning. His car started all right when it was time to leave. But when he headed down the driveway he could see them, Bobo Lamkin wearing a girl's gym bloomers, the other two with old ladies' hats on their heads. When Lee Roy gave a toot on his horn, they all looked at the sky. Where the walks had been shoveled, half the student body waited to see what Lee Roy would do, and he could see their faces in the laboratory windows on the second floor. He saw Etoile, taller than Mrs. Ansley, on the steps of the library, wearing the rubber boots that gave her blisters on both feet. "F——k the bastards," Lee Roy said, gripped the wheel like he did the oilcan and heard the gas hiss in the carburetors as he gave it the gun. Allowing for the fact that the drive was slippery, it did pretty well. Two of them didn't budge, but Stu Smiley, hearing his kid sister scream at him, got one leg into the snowdrift, and the fender caught him just right to spin him around. Lee Roy felt the weight of the other two as if he had thumped into a snowbank, and Bobo Lamkin stayed on the hood till Lee Roy came to a stop. In his rearview mirror the kids standing on the steps looked the way they did in the class picture, not one of them moving, only one of them making sound. Stu Smiley lay with his head pushed in the snowbank, whimpering like a dog.

Lee Roy was the first to move. He got out of his car. When he turned to face the school, one of the girls screamed and ran. Mr. Colfax had stopped shoveling snow and with Mr. Gunther, the janitor, cut across the yard to where the drive was cleared, then stopped. "Lee Roy," Mr. Gunther said, "Lee Roy, you all right?" From an upstairs window Mrs. Lawson cried, "For heaven's sake, somebody call the police." Somebody called the police, and Lee Roy was still there, his feet cold in the gym shoes he was wearing, when he heard the sirens come out from town and saw the blinker on the roof. The cops drove in, then they had to back out to let the ambulance in.

"Lost control of it, eh?" one of them said, but Lee Roy shook his head. No, he hadn't lost control. He had been in control for once in his life. "F——k the bastards," he had said, and that was just what he had done. Nobody asked him, or he could have told them who was shooting down people like pigeons and had half the people in Lincoln scared to death. Not that he minded since it wasn't likely he would shoot Lee Roy. They had him in a safer place than the grease pit or his room in the Momeyer basement, and neither Bobo Lamkin nor anybody else was pushing him around.

Jennings

At the end of March on the slow freight that made even the stops without a whistle, Jennings sat in the caboose with a family going down the line for a funeral. A man and his wife, his wife's younger sister and five evenly spaced children, the three smaller boys dressed in what survived of what the oldest boy had worn, so that the youngest boy of the lot wore the oldest clothes. Jennings could make out in their mended folds almost every shape but that of the boy who wore them. The biggest lad wore his own new suit of that pale-blue color popular with farm boys, but from the way the collar hung loose on his neck the striped shirt had belonged to his father. How old was he? Just old enough for a death in the family. Someone he hardly knew. His scrubbed expectant face troubled Jennings like the wail of a newborn infant and the wearisome prospect of what would prove to be its life. One day this boy would have children of his own, the eldest son wearing one of his shirts, and that boy would turn on his elders the gaze of those who inherit the earth. It made him weary. He turned to the window and stared at the plain.

A man in his fifties, part-time newspaperman, author of adventure stories for boys of all ages, there was something in the way Jennings wore his clothes or, as women said, the way he didn't wear them, that gave him the air of being dated, whatever his age. Although he had never mounted a horse, he wrote of men who lived in the saddle, their trigger fingers hairless from the heat of their shooting irons. These stories sold well, and most of them could be found under the name of W. B. Jennings in the Cheyenne drugstores where he soaked up his atmosphere. The West was in his blood, as one critic said, since his father had been born in a soddy and both his parents lay buried in a place called Indian Bow. These were facts; they bore out the impression Jennings made on both friends and strangers, a big soft-spoken man with the sad-eyed gaze of a Saint Bernard. He was not only big but also slow, and the trust that strangers vested in him was the mindless faith people seemed to have in anything huge. Like the rock on the insurance posters, he seemed to represent something: something good. When a big dog is friendly, he just naturally seems friendlier than a small dog.

In the middle of the summer he wore a blue serge suit with the print of bench slats across the back and a sprinkling of grass in the frayed cuffs of the pants. The tie with the pearl pin he slipped on and off by loosening the bow, which had faded to a lighter color than the rest of it. During his brief marriage he had tried to wear Oxfords—the way a small fry would try his first shoes—but the sight of his ankles made him uneasy and with the death of his wife he went back to hook-and-eye shoes. When he crossed his legs, winter or summer, a fold of underwear could be seen bulging his socks: heat and cold, that is, were treated impartially. A black fedora, with a wide brim, he wore pulled down low on his head in the winter, but in the summer tipped back to expose his curly hair. He had tried many dressings, without success, to take the curl out of it. The West was in his blood if anything was, and he saw little reason to mention the fact that his father had spent his last years in Chicago employed as a department-store Santa Claus. In the Santa suit, with the balloons in his pocket, he had died. Not that Jennings took pains to conceal this fact—he merely wanted time to understand it. Understand what? That he was the son of a man who thought he was Santa Claus.

He tipped the hat from his face to look at the woman across the aisle. The high caboose seat kept her feet from the floor. It gave her, it seemed to Jennings, something of the detachment she radiated, serene and intact with her responsibility, if not her grief. The train in which she rode was no eastbound freight but an instrument of God's will and man's destiny—from this ceremony of death she would salvage something for the living. She would return, that is, with more than she had left. Not so, however, the man at her side. He was held upright by the press of his coat, but he knew that from today life would be different. Something familiar was gone forever. Well, never mind. Approaching Cozad he rose from the seat to step out on the platform and gaze at the landscape, then return to reassure them all that it looked about the same. That much, at least, had not changed. At the station they were met by a man who would not break his silence till the body was buried and he had hung up on old hooks his funeral clothes. Jennings watched them all take seats in the pick-up, the man and his wife in the cab, the children on the boards in the rear where the floor was still yellow with corn. They rode north to where a row of poplars sat on the rise. There he saw the hearse, three or four cars, and the fresh mound of earth partially concealed by pads of bright-green undertaker's grass. The male members of the party, in dark suits, stood around a coffin strewn with flowers, their bared heads shiny as eggs in the shimmering March light..

That morning, thinking there might be a story in the strange case of Lee Roy Momeyer, Jennings had taken a train to Calloway. He had followed closely the case of Charlie Munger, the most celebrated gunman since Billy the Kid, but Lee Roy Momeyer, the Bible student, seemed to be an outlaw of greater interest. He thought there might be a moral in the life of a boy who used his homemade hot-rod as a weapon, but the family had not been of much help. The Momeyer house at the edge of town sat at the front of a field of wrecked cars, the back yard serving as a used-car parking lot. The front yard, strewn with secondhand parts, was fenced in from the road by a chain of old tires, only those with white sidewalls used across the front. A wagon sideboard propped against the house was painted with the sign:

MACHINERY OF ALL KIND FIXT

The yard was shadeless, the blinds drawn on the side of the house exposed to the sun, and something about the scene—the white-walled tires or the swing drawn up to the ceiling of the porch for the winter —depressed Jennings so much he had walked up, then turned to leave. Mrs. Momeyer, spying at a window, had stepped out to ask him what he wanted. She had been only too glad, she said, to talk about Lee Roy and relieve her feelings. She led him inside to see the copy of his Bible with the words that puzzled him underlined, and the religious mottoes and pictures on the walls of his room. While she talked, a radio in the kitchen played a program of hymns. Now and then her husband, sick with a cold, put in a word from the top of the stairs. "You want to know about Lee Roy," he said, saying *Leeee*-roy, "you go speak to Maxine."

Who was Maxine? That was the wife of Mr. Momeyer's brother, a well-known Lincoln mailman. Lee Roy had been living with them at the time. "They're right over in Lone Tree," Mr. Momeyer added, "if you'd like to stop in on your way back." Maxine's father, a pioneer, had lived in his family's hotel in Lone Tree all of his ninety years, even after the town was deserted. The family would gather there on his ninetieth birthday, which was tomorrow.

Jennings had thanked them, although he had no intention of stopping by. He was not driving, and only an occasional freight made the stop. In the diner near the railroad station he had a cup of coffee while waiting for his train. On the subject of Lee Roy the cook had little to add. In his opinion, the world had not suffered much of a loss. Lee Roy's hot-rod, parked in front of the diner, sometimes threw up gravel against the windows. He liked to wash down jelly doughnuts with a cold glass of milk.

While the cook swabbed the counter Jennings had turned to the morning paper. The mad-dog killer, Charlie Munger, was coming up for trial. The article reviewed the hysteria that had seized the people of Lincoln while the unknown assassin roamed the streets. Hardware stores had sold out their stock of rifles and shells. A woman sixty years of age, alone in the house, had shot at the milkman with a gun that exploded, blinding her in one eye. A choral group had got together and walked around the streets singing hymns. Prayers had been read in all the churches, and mail service had to be postponed after a postman had been fired on by mistake. Jennings read these reports with an eye for the details, then stepped outside to find an eastbound freight, the caboose near the station, on the siding waiting for the flyer to go by.

The brakeman stood out on the platform, and Jennings walked over to ask him, just in passing, if they made a stop at Lone Tree. They did, if he didn't mind a half-mile walk into town. Jennings minded very much, but nevertheless he bought a ticket and joined the family bound for the funeral.

In a coach that was part of a mail car, the seat within a few yards of his father's coffin, Jennings had once made a funeral trip himself. He had come all the way from Chicago by night, and from Omaha west he had sat wide awake by the window. It had dawned on him, young as he was, that in traveling from east to west his father's life was rolling up on itself like a scroll. The names of the towns— Omaha, Murdock, Calloway and Indian Bow—had been stages in the life of a man who thought he was Santa Claus. With what remained Jennings had returned to the barren slope behind the soddy where Mexican track hands who spoke no English used their picks to break the sod for his coffin.

To get to Menomonee Street in Chicago you take a Clark Street car in the Loop and ride north to where it skirts the edge of Lincoln Park. A statue of Lincoln, weathered to the same green as the copper gutters on the homes of the rich, can be seen from Clark Street whenever the trees are bare. A boy of seventeen at the time, Jennings rode up front behind the motorman, since he had been told to keep his eye out for Lincoln as a landmark. Just a block or two farther north he was to get off. It was a sleety winter day, and the cab of the streetcar had been full of the smell of wet clothes and the flinty smell of the sand crushed on the tracks. The bell seemed to be clanging most of the time. Another smell, like a burning wire, came from the box that supported the crank, and at one point a flash from the box filled the cab with light. Where the car made stops, Jennings would sometimes see down the narrow streets to where the world ended, nothing there but the gray wall of the sky. Once in his life Jennings made this trip, a ride of twenty or twenty-five minutes, but no other journey had so impressed itself on his mind. At its end, luminous in the hall-way, was the green runner of rat poison that led up the stairs to the room above the delicatessen store.

The room his father had lived in had windows overlooking the street where Jennings had seen boys seated on the curb, eating snails. It contained a table, two chairs, an armless rocker, an imitation fireplace, a marble slab with a gas burner and an iron frame bed with a sag like a spout at one side. His father's good shoes sat there, as if his feet poured into them. On the table, the cloth turned back to keep it from getting dirty, was a can of Carnation milk with a large hole and a small one, and beside it a fork with a bent green prong, used to keep the large hole open. On the mantelpiece over the fireplace was a shaving mug with the word *Sweetheart* on it, and in the mug were buttons, a streetcar token, a roller-skate key with a twist in it and a bronze medallion given to the buyer of Buster Brown shoes. God knows why, but Jennings went off with the medal and the roller-skate key. After all, they had been his. In the brown suit coat his father took off to put on the Santa suit he had found the post card, stamped and addressed to Jennings but never mailed. Food stains had spotted the picture on the front of it. A saucer ring made it hard to read the message on the back.

DEAR SON

Have moved. Have nice little place of our own now, two-plate gas. Warm sun in windows every morning, nice view of park. Plan to get new console radio soon now, let you pick it out. Plan to pick up car so we can drive out in country, get out in air. Turning over in my mind plan to send you to Harvard, send you to Yale. Saw robin in yard this morning. Saw him catch worm.

It had his father's style, one that was formed when he had been a station agent and words cost money. Was it the inside story of the men who thought they were Santa Claus? Jennings had seen them on wintry corners with bits of beard frozen to their faces, ringing a bell with the mittened hand missing the thumb. Waiting for his father's landlady to bring him some food, he had stood at the window white with frost and let the tears run down his face into his open mouth. Through a hole his breath melted in the frost he could see the street, black with slush, and the sooty yard where his father saw the robin catch the worm.

Near Cozad, Jennings stepped out on the platform for a breath of fresh air. As a boy, had his father had too much of it? There was little but fresh air at Indian Bow where white-faced Herefords now peered from the windows of the soddy in which the man who thought he was Santa Claus was born. Where the crossing bell once clanged, the last man in town, a hobo, lived in what remained of a truck struck by a train. Jennings would sometimes exchange a few words with him. He didn't seem to find it strange that a man like Jennings would walk

along the tracks, using the ties, to where he could
see the props of a windmill on the rise across the
river. That was all. The wind wheel was gone.
Between the legs, like a bell clapper, the man Jennings would have called Grandfather had hung
head down, swinging on a length of baling wire.
Had he leaped or fallen? Had he, too, dreamed of
Santa Claus? What led a boy, born and raised in
this soddy, to roll down the plain like a pebble to
where men were paid to be Santa Claus? And another, a few years later, to leave at home his well-
thumbed Bible; and another to take up his gun like
Billy the Kid? In some way left to Jennings to dis-
cover, these lives seemed to be related, not merely
to each other but to the man on the platform of
the caboose. Local boys. Local boys who made—
or unmade—good.

As the freight braked to a stop Jennings thought
he would step off and stretch his legs, but when he
leaned from the steps he saw this car up ahead at
the crossing drift slowly backward into the ditch.
The fellow at the wheel leaped out of the seat as if
it were hot. He hustled to the rear, grabbed a bag,
then pulled a youngster from the seat at the front
and dragged her behind him as they ran along the
ditch. The man wore the sort of clothes Jennings
had seen in the old days on carnival barkers, good-
looking in a way he associated with confidence men.
He couldn't tell if the kid behind was a boy or a girl,
since it was not so unusual any more for a girl to
wear pants. Jennings figured the pair of them, the
kid as a stooge, had swiped that car across the line

somewhere and had picked this moment to make their getaway. When it was clear they were headed for the caboose he left the platform and went back to his seat, tipping his hat over his face as if asleep. He heard them come up the bank, the man wheezing, then he heard the youngster say, "Sweet Jesus, it's like a friggin movie!" That's what he heard if he could believe his ears. "Lone Tree?" the man inquired, and the brakeman, nodding his head at Jennings, replied, "He's gettin' off at Lone Tree too. What's goin' on in Lone Tree?" The caboose jolted, and through lidded eyes Jennings saw the pair of them out on the platform. The youngster with him, a slip of a girl, wore sandals with gold chains, her toenails the color of the bubble gum the boys in the caboose had been chewing. Jennings never saw a kid like that without being thankful he didn't have one, and he felt a certain pity for the poor devil who did. He wore no hat. There was a tear in the knee of his pants. Jennings couldn't help but wonder where such a character might be from.

The Ceremony

Boyd

"You wait till we pull out," the brakeman said, "and you can walk on the ties. She might like it better."

He wagged his flagstick at the girl, who stood on one of the tarred ties in the cinder bed. The train ride had made her sullen. Her hair was stringy with soot and one strand of it hung separated from the rest, twisted like a piece of rope. She did not look pretty. The wind had chapped her lips. In his rain-coat, the hat bulging the pocket, her hands slipped into the sleeves like a muff, she looked like a tired kid coming home from summer camp. His daughter? The taste of the joke had gone flat. Like so many of his bright ideas it was better in theory than in practice. If the stranger had not been there on the platform he would have put her back on the caboose. Duluth. She was also dying to see Duluth.

"The feet I got now," the big fellow said, looking down at them on the caboose platform, "I know better than walk along the ties. I'm going to ride along and break a leg dropping off." His shoulders shook with what Boyd recognized as a laugh.

From the east, like a car with a flat wheel approaching, the claps came down the line and jolted the caboose. The girl leaped back; the caboose stopped and then without a jolt slowly moved away as if by itself. Boyd had the sensation of being deprived not merely of his own kind but of life itself. The last particle of it burned dimly in the caboose lights. He seemed to be the only object between the plain and the sky. A tidal shadow of silence seemed to rise from the tracks, as if the plain were the sinking roof of the world. A wide ditch with waist-high weeds humming faintly with the first insects stood between them and the dirt road south of the tracks. The fence along the road was clogged with tumbleweed.

"Let's go," he said, and stooped for her bag. He took a step or two on the ties, then turned to see if she was coming. She stood huddled on the tie, as if he had left her on an island. Dark against the light, he couldn't see her face. "What's the trouble?"

"You don't want me. You think I don't know?"

He started back toward her, and like a squirrel she hopped away, the gold chains glinting on her sandals.

"Now look—" he said.

"Look, look, look, look," she echoed. "I'm not a friggin look."

Silhouetted on the sky between the shining rails, she looked as if she were waiting for a train to hit her. His raincoat hung, like the topcoat of a hobo, to within a few inches of the track bed.

"Daughter, you should know me better. I'm just scared."

"You're scared of what they'll think of me. I know."

"That's right. Are you scared worse than I am?"

He thought she was. That is, he hoped she was.

A half mile to the north was the east-west highway, and down the highway to the east diner lights flickered. One of them could hitch a ride to the east, one to the west. But perhaps that scared her worse. She came along the ties and took a grip on his hand.

"Walk on the rail," he said. "Put your hand on my shoulder."

"Big Daddy," she said, giving it a try, "this something you did as a friggin kid?" Her shadow went ahead of them, the arm flapping like a wing. When he glanced at her he saw the tongue between her chapped lips.

"Daughter, suck it in or you'll bite it off."

She made no comment, concentrating on the rails, and they went along the tracks to the cattle loader, where sparrows sat along the wires like clothespins. Down the tracks the last of the light burned like a fire in the top windows. The bare branches of the lone tree seemed to rise from a dark lake. Two cars were parked at the back of the hotel, and Boyd recognized McKee's station wagon. Beside it, looking like a toy, a small wire-wheeled sports car. Along the wall, beneath the MAIL POUCH sign, was what looked to be a stainless-steel diner. At one end lights were burning. A TV aerial perched on the roof.

"Looks like the place is picking up," he said, and the girl replied, "What a pad. There a bar in it?"

Beyond the cattle loader the track bed widened and they could walk along the cinders. The diner turned out to be a house trailer, and one of the doors on the side stood open. A dog whimpered, and a voice said, "Clyde, don't you feed him that steak till we see what *we're* eating. You remember last night?"

Passing by, Boyd could see the Oklahoma license and, through the window where the light was burning, the head of a man running a comb through his beard.

"That them?" she said. "Sweet Jesus."

The blinds were drawn at the back windows of the hotel. They could hear voices, a radio was playing, and in the shadow of the trailer he put down the bag he was carrying. Was the place full of people he didn't know? McKee had never mentioned a member of the family who lived in a trailer the size of a freight car, or one who ran around the state in a lemon-colored sports car with wire wheels. In the seat of the car he saw a pair of dark glasses and leather driving gloves. His foot resting on the bag, Boyd checked the tear in his pants. Through the hole he could feel the clot on his knee. The girl watched him without comment as he buttoned the collar of his shirt. He ran a comb through his hair, hoping she would do the same. She did nothing. The night was warm, almost balmy, but she looked cold.

"Daughter, you forget I'm the one who's scared?"

"I don't claim to be from here. Wherever it is. Where is it?"

She looked around as if she found the place hard to see. At the top of the lone tree, as if nailed there, a crow perched in the last of the sunlight. At the base of the tree, on a buggy seat that had served as a bench in what had once been shade, the big fellow they had seen on the caboose sat smoking a cigar. His legs were crossed. Light from the sky glowed on his face. Had he sat himself there in the hope that Boyd and the girl would come along and make some sort of scene? Boyd felt no impulse to make one, however. Not here. Miles to the west an airplane beacon flicked on the sky like summer lightning: on the face of the moon the vapor trail of a jet slowly dissolved. As if he had beheld it with his own eyes Boyd saw the pillar of fire, like a rabbit's ear, and the message printed after his name in the registry.

"Daughter, you like to wake me before the bomb?"

"How long we known each other? It been too friggin long?"

"In the middle of life, Morgenstern Boyd had everything to live for, everything worth living for having eluded him. He was that rare thing, a completely self-unmade man."

"You forget something, Big Daddy. Whoever Morgenstern was, he's a friggin bore."

"Daughter, say we make it just Daddy? Whoever Morgenstern was, he still is. At least, I think he is."

She turned—was it to leave?—took four or five steps toward the trailer, then tripped on something that almost sent her sprawling, and blinked the trailer lights. Inside, the dog lunged for the door, hoarsely barked.

"Clyde," cried a voice, "that your razor again?"

Boyd didn't catch his reply. The dog bayed; the girl was back at his side, gripping his arm. When the

door to the hotel popped open an oblong patch of
light fell on the yard, showing the girl's sandals, her
dirty feet and the tear in the knee of his pants.
Against the light he could see the figure of a girl.
She said, "Hi."

"Hi!" replied the one at his side.

The one in the door turned and called, "Uncle
Walter, here's some more people," and her face,
seen in profile, looked familiar. Was it that of the
only friggin woman in Boyd's life?

"For heaven's sake, Etoile, who is it?"

"For cryin' out loud," she replied, "how would I
know?" Then she stepped from the door as the
shadow coming up behind her filled it. The solid
lump of McKee, his hand checking his fly, blocked
off the light so that they stood in his shadow.

"Boyd?" he said, peering toward them. "That
you, Boyd?" And making out the figure that stood
beside him, he removed his hat, patted down his
cowlick.

Boyd waited till he stepped from the light, then
said, "How are you, McKee?"

"Mother!" cried the girl. "It's Mr. Boyd and Mrs.
Boyd!"

"Will you let them in!" she called. "Will you
open the screen and let them in!"

It was McKee who did it, shifting his hat to his
left hand.

"Won't you folks step in," he said, and Boyd
stepped back to let the girl go in before him. A dim
bulb, pulled off center by a string, dangled from the
ceiling on a lumpy cord. All four corners of the

room looked dark. In one a stove, a Home Comfort range, with a heavy-bodied woman who stood holding a stove lid; in another a sofa on which two people sat erect, as if for their portrait. Was it powder that made the face of the woman look like a mask? She held one hand in the palm of the other, and by pressure of the thumb methodically cracked her knuckles. The young man at her side gazed at Boyd like the young men on the Navy posters, one of those youths the combined armed forces would transform into men. He wore khaki pants, riding boots without stirrups, and held in his lap a high-crowned western hat. Standing at his side, her hand touching his hair, was the girl who had opened the door, a replica of the only friggin woman in Boyd's life. "Boyd—" said McKee, noting his glance, "that's Etoile, Maxine's daughter," and he wheeled to nod at the woman who stood at the stove, her glasses steamed over from a pot at her side. "That little fellow there is Calvin, my son's boy, and that young woman at his side is his mother." He chuckled. "Eileen," he said, "I guess you've heard me talk about Boyd?"

To head her off, Maxine said, "I guess we all have, Mr. Boyd. You people have a nice trip?"

"Sweet Jesus, did we!"

The woman on the sofa stopped cracking her knuckles. In the face of McKee there was no show of feeling.

"Etoile," said Maxine, setting the pot back on the stove, "you want to tell Lois we got a surprise for her?"

"Ha!" she replied, and they watched her cross the room, the long narrow feet in the tennis sneakers, walking in such a manner that she seemed to be losing her clothes.

As she stepped into the hall, McKee said, "See any family resemblance, Gordon?"

"You do," called the girl from the hall, "and your name is mud!"

"Eeee-toal!" said Maxine. "You hear what you're saying?"

"Just so you do!" replied the girl.

Boyd watched McKee's eyes skillfully avoid meeting his own.

"Guess your name is mud then," McKee said. "Eh, Boyd?" And he screwed up his face just the way he did the time he thought he'd caught a bee-bee in the eye. A wink. Both eyes squinting, he smiled.

McKee

When he heard the racket, McKee had wheeled and started for the door the way a dog he once owned would leave the front room when company called. When Etoile cried, "How would I know?" McKee knew the worst had happened. Only the worst hadn't happened. No, not until he reached the door. He had never seen such a look on the face of Boyd. How explain it? It was McKee's look on Boyd's face. It was McKee's role, not Boyd's, to hope for the best when the worst was happening, his jaw slack as if he still had adenoids. Stymied. That was how he looked. Never before had McKee seen him speechless.

Boyd had always looked to McKee like that man in the insurance statistics who'd get up one morning feeling a little queasy and be dead in an hour. That was why McKee had blurted out what kept him awake a night or two later, about how Boyd was like a brother to him, and stuff like that. With this tan Boyd looked almost healthy, but as Mrs. McKee liked to point out, how could you tell about the dark-skinned races with their built-in tan? If they had any teeth at all, they looked pretty white.

"You going to let them just stand there?" said Maxine. "Or is it too much to bring in a chair from the lobby?"

If there was one thing that burned McKee up it

was to go someplace, like here or a picnic, where that mailman she married might be useful, only to find he'd scooted off somewhere like a fool kid.

"Where's Bud?" he said, peering around, and then wished he hadn't. The door popped open and there he was, backing in with something. Would Boyd believe that was a quiver of arrows on his back? The contraption he had was on a metal stand, and rattled like a bag of marbles when he put it down. McKee could hardly believe his eyes. A gum-ball machine. The glass globe was as yellow as isinglass and the balls inside it were faded.

"Found it!" Bud barked, backing off to look at it. "Right there in the barbershop. Can you beat it?"

All McKee could think of, seeing him there in his mailman's suit, was that Maxine had been married to him for twenty-seven years.

"Who's got a penny?" he said, then took one from Boyd without even recognizing him as a stranger, dropped it in the slot and watched the gum ball drop into his palm. "Can you beat it?" he said, then gave the globe a shake just to hear the balls rattle. "Hear that? Dang thing is full of pennies." And he popped the gum ball into his mouth.

"Bud!" cried Maxine, and as though the sound had clapped him on the back, he spat it up. On that face that didn't look any different to McKee from the first time he saw it, he caught the look of a kid who had got into mischief just to be caught.

"Criminenty, Maxine," he said. "That's good ball gum."

McKee had the presence of mind not to turn and

look at her. Boyd had not only seen and heard him but had offered him the penny.

"Why don't we all have some?" said Eileen. "Calvin darling, you got any pennies?"

At that point McKee looked at Maxine, since somebody had to do something. If she wanted to admit that it was her husband, that was her business. The hand McKee watched her wipe across her forehead left a sooty smudge over her eyes, just as if she had used the backside of a stove lid. McKee would have liked to know how a woman like Lois could spend all day in the kitchen and look like Betty Crocker, while a woman like Maxine couldn't wipe her nose without making a smudge. As if he'd turned and gone off with it, McKee said, "Maxine, where the devil'd he get it?"

"Barber shop," Bud barked. "Anybody like a razor? Case there with a razor in it."

"Sweet Jesus," said Mrs. Boyd, "is it a friggin treasure hunt?"

All Maxine could do was wave a hand at her face, as though a fly was buzzing her.

McKee said, "The old man wake up and catch you with that machine, you better drop that bow and arrow and grab the razor."

"Bud," Maxine said, as if about to fall asleep, "you want to take it back?"

"Criminenty," he said, but he picked it up, the glass ball like a bald head over his shoulder, like something he had shot by mistake with his fool bow and arrow.

In that letter to Boyd, McKee had naturally mentioned the pride he took in his wife's family and hinted that Boyd should consider himself lucky to be part of it. Before he'd even washed his hands he'd met the boy who stuttered, then the one who swiped gum-ball machines and played Indian, and soon he'd meet, if he hadn't already, the one who thought he was part Indian and lived in a trailer with a dog that cost him nine thousand bucks. The maddest one of all, just his feet showing, was the old man asleep beside the stove, but Boyd had already met him so that wouldn't be so bad.

"You people like to wash up a bit?" McKee said, since he couldn't help noticing they were both a little dirty. What he thought was a smudge was actually a hole in the knee of Boyd's pants. Had living with those people made him loose in his habits? He'd either sat in something or his kidneys were failing.

"They probably would want to wash if there was water," said Maxine. "You men turn the water on?"

McKee remembered, the moment she said it, that was what she sent Bud off to do when he ended up swiping the gum machine. "Calvin," he said, "you know where the pipe is?" since the boy knew the place better than anybody, more or less living in it when he was a kid. He saw he did, but before he reached the door, the screen popped open. There was Colonel Ewing in what he called his mufti and the pair of riding boots he said Will Rogers had given him. He stood so straddle-legged, the dog leash in his hand, McKee could see on the stoop below him the thin yellow face of Edna, like a tobacco leaf, peering between his legs into the room. One eye was creased as if smoke curled into it. If she didn't have cancer of the lungs already, she was soon going to have it, and just hearing her cough made it hard for McKee to enjoy his cigar.

"Colonel," he said, "this is Mr. and Mrs. Boyd. Guess you're the only man who hasn't heard me talk about Boyd." To Boyd he said, "Edna and the Colonel live in this trailer about the size of a freight car. Guess it's got about everything in it but kids. Room intended for the kids got this bulldog in it. Think that's what it is." McKee didn't want to be snide about that dog, but maybe a bit of it crept into his voice. "How much life insurance you say that dog carries?" McKee said.

"His daddy carries thirty thousand, I think," said the Colonel. "Daddy's champion of his class, Mr. Boyd. But Shiloh is just a pup. Figure ten is enough till he cuts his teeth."

Eileen said, "He's just a puppy, Mr. Boyd, but the Colonel looks like him already."

If McKee didn't know her so well, he would have thought she meant to say something else. She blinked and smiled as sweet as a high-school girl.

Maxine said, "Mr. Boyd, Colonel Ewing is part Cherokee Indian. Is it on your mother's side, Colonel Ewing?"

"Yes indeedy," said the Colonel, fooling with the leash. "Mother had a touch of the dark blood in her. Will used to say—that's Will Rogers, Mr. Boyd— that the whitest man had some dark blood in him."

"Edna," said Eileen, "do you people have trouble traveling in the South?"

Edna laughed in that way she had that made McKee clear his throat. "You want to let me in, dearrrr," she said, and ducked under the arm of the Colonel. As she did, McKee could hear the bracelets rattle on her arms. She wore more of them than he'd seen on the Indians in Mexico. She saw Mrs. Boyd before she saw Boyd and just stopped dead, like a dog, and sniffed her.

"Edna," said McKee, "this is Mrs. Boyd. You remember Boyd?"

"Do I, darling! I'm the one who cleaned the pans you made all that fudge in. I'm a big girl now and live in a trailer with a man and a bulldog. Would you like a drink? There's a bar in it. Nothing he likes to do more than make you a drink."

"Sweet Jesus," said Mrs. Boyd. "What a bulldog."

McKee started to speak, but Eileen had one of her giggling fits.

Edna coughed, said, "Darling, it's not cancer. It's the glass in that foolproof filter." From her hair she removed a bone hairpin, dug it into her scalp.

"Walter—" said the Colonel (McKee had never had anybody he liked call him Walter). "Permit me. This occasion. This gathering—this congenial assembly. This—" He spread his arms and showed how much he'd been sweating. It was all McKee could do not to put out his hand and say, Spit it up.

"Clyde," said Edna, turning to him, "Mrs. Boyd wants Shiloh to make her a drink."

The Colonel held up the leash as if the dog was on

it. That military bearing Lois admired so much he
got from the corset he was wearing. McKee could
see the way it hugged him in the small of the back.
"My friends, why not—on this occasion—"
"Clyde," Edna said, "if the McKees don't like it,
we're not going to waste it. Shiloh loves it. My God,
darling, you should see him when he's tight! He's a
lover! He growls at Clyde and sleeps with me himself." She coughed.

McKee fastened his gaze on a knot in the light
cord. His eyes burned. Would Boyd ever believe
this whooping crane was the sister of Lois Scanlon?
Her mouth all teeth, yellow as corn, her scalp
chewed up where she dug at it with the hairpins. If
Boyd was not stymied, would he just stand there
and not say anything?

"Edna," said McKee, "these folks just got here.
They'd maybe like to wash and rest up a moment.
Wouldn't you, folks?"

"Sweet Jesus," said Mrs. Boyd.

"I'll just bet they would," Edna replied, "but
how can you rest up in a washroom? We got a
washroom too. One with water in it, haven't we,
Clyde?"

"Water?" said the Colonel. "In the washroom.
Strictly. In the glass—" He held up two fingers as
a measure.

"Daughter," said Boyd, "you run along and try
it. Maybe there's a jukebox."

"Clyde," said Edna. "You hear that? He thought
of it. A jukebox. I'll swear we thought of everything but a jukebox. You like TV?" She took the

girl by the arm and led her toward the door. "Mr. Boyd," she said, turning back, "you like Clyde to bring you something? Caffeine, morphine, marijuana, something like that?"

Maxine said, "Mrs. Boyd, we're going to eat soon. If I can get somebody to help me with the table . . ."

It wasn't lost on McKee, when they reached the door, the way the Colonel slipped his hand around behind her, patting the coat to see where it was she filled it out. McKee hadn't noticed till he did that, that she was wearing pants and her feet were dirty, a combination that encouraged attentions like that. Colonel Ewing, for all his military bearing, didn't strike McKee as the sort of man he liked to see married into the family where there were unmarried women around. Until the Colonel called it to his attention, McKee hadn't noticed how Etoile had developed, and how the back of her knees looked when she stooped. That was her mother's fault, dressing her in clothes that only half covered her body, as if the boys would think she was no older than she looked.

"Mrs. Boyd," said McKee, "don't forget you got to meet the rest of the family."

"I wonder what's keeping her?" said Maxine, and shuffled over to the hallway door, called, "Eeee-toal!" There was no answer.

"Eeeee-toal!" Every time she stretched it out like that, McKee was struck by what a crazy sort of name it was.

"Boyd," said McKee, "just in case you're wondering, that's not just a hog call, that's what her name is."

"She's got her father to thank for it," said Maxine. "And it's not so bad as some others he thought of."

"If he had it to do now," said McKee, "he'd probably call her Hiawatha."

"Eeeeee-toal!" she yelled. "You tell Lois we got a surprise for her?"

"I told her, muh-thurrrr. You want me to tell her what it is?"

Clearing his throat, McKee called, "Nope, guess you better not bother. She's probably taking a nap with little Gordon." Catching Boyd's eye, McKee added, "Some things have popped around here since I wrote you, Gordon. It's why you see the girls a wee bit jittery."

"I suppose you're not jittery, Mr. J. Edgar Hoover," said Maxine.

What she sometimes turned up with left McKee flabbergasted.

"Down there in Acapulco," said McKee, "doubt if you people got wind of it—"

"McKee," said Maxine, "there's no place in the world that hasn't heard of Charlie Munger. There's no place you can hide from news like that."

"Him?" said Mrs. Boyd. "Sweet Jesus, you mean he's from *here?*"

"Nope," said McKee, "not from right here. From back in Lincoln. Used to see him on the steps of the p.o. in the morning. Didn't help me with my lunch."

Maxine said, "Mr. Boyd, you mean you really haven't heard?"

"Remember Irene?" said McKee. "Used to win all the spelldowns. Well, fellow she married was one of them."

"You think all ten didn't know somebody?" Maxine said. "What's so terrible is Charlie Munger hardly knew any of them."

"What happened?" said Boyd.

"This cat up and shot ten friggin people," said Mrs. Boyd.

McKee could hear the hiss of the wet shingles he used to build the fire. It dawned on him like a light in a phone booth what she meant. He said, "Mungers, Boyd. Old Lincoln family. What you'd call respectable people."

"Darling," Eileen said, patting Calvin's knee, "your family's not respectable, so don't shoot anybody. Nobody would be at all surprised if you did."

Was there anybody like her for blurting out the truth? Hadn't they actually stopped the boy and taken away the gun he kept in the seat, just to make sure some of the people who knew him didn't shoot him on sight? McKee just wished to God she didn't have to relieve her mind in public.

"Gordon," he said, to head her off, "know what that boy said when they asked him why he did it?"

Her head in the door, Mrs. Boyd said, "He say he was a bottle baby? There's more friggin things they blame on that bottle."

Out on the stoop, Edna said, "There's even more they blame on the *other* bottle, honey. You want to come along?"

Took McKee a moment to recall what he meant to say. He had his eyes on the floor, on Boyd's shoes and the way the cuff of his pants was frazzled, but what he happened to notice was the knot in the lace of one of them. It made the lace so short on one side all he could do was tie a knot in it, and McKee could see that it had been knotted for some time. Boyd got that shoe off and on without loosening the lace. McKee had been about to say that Charlie Munger said he wanted to be somebody—but he didn't. After all, that's what Charlie Munger was. Maybe half the people in the world had heard about him. But after working at it for fifty years, Boyd had failed. He probably knew that as well as McKee, since McKee had never seen him so silent. So McKee put his eyes to the ceiling and said, "Know what he said, Gordon? Said he was tired of being pushed around. Can you beat that?"

Over on the sofa Calvin made a noise as if he might sneeze. His lower lip stuck out the way Lois's did when she was being lovey-dovey with her canary.

"Darling," Eileen said, putting her finger to his lips, "sometimes I think it's a blessing you stutter." And McKee was so sure of this he almost said amen.

"Mother," called Etoile, from the top of the stairs. "There's a strange man walking around in the yard."

McKee was facing Maxine, and he saw her hand go to her throat. It calmed him to see she was every bit as jittery as he was.

"She think it's her back yard?" said McKee. "If

a man wants to walk around the town, I guess he's free to. Still a free country in that respect, isn't it, Boyd?"

"You have to shout it at the top of your lungs?" Maxine said.

"I thought it just might interest you to know it."

"McKee," she said, "you know very well this isn't a place where people come to and walk around in. You going to ask him what he wants?"

"It's a town," said McKee. "I don't own it. I got no more business sticking out my neck and asking him his business than he has knocking on the door and asking me mine."

"Darling," said Eileen, "you want to go and see if the man is armed?" The boy pushed up, put on his hat, and in the boots that made him walk like a cripple started for the door. McKee had just time to head him off.

"If somebody's going to make a fool out of himself, guess I better do it."

He took a match from his vest, clamped his teeth on it, then walked to the door and pulled it open. In the oblong patch of light that fell on the yard stood a man. McKee couldn't have spoken if his life depended on it. The man stood with one hand behind his back, and when he brought it up front, McKee felt his hair rise. All it was, however, was a cigar.

"You excuse me," the stranger said, "you know a Mr. Thomas Scanlon?"

"Thomas Scanlon?" said McKee in a dry voice, and wagged his head as if he didn't. He turned to look at Maxine, said, "Maxine, a member of your family named Thomas?"

"You losing your mind? That's Papa. Who is it wants to see him?"

"This gentleman here," said McKee, and stepped to one side to let her see for herself.

"You excuse me, ma'am," said the stranger, "but I'm looking for Mr. Thomas Scanlon. My name is Jennings."

"Papa's asleep right now, Mr. Jennings. What is it you want?"

"I understand Mr. Scanlon knows the old-timers. I thought he just might know my father."

Maxine rolled her hands in her apron and fanned the bib at her face. "Mr. Jennings, there's times Papa thinks he knew everybody anybody ever heard of. His mind wanders. You know how old people are."

"I certainly do, ma'am, and if you'd rather I didn't stir him up—"

McKee said, "Maxine, don't you think maybe Grandpa would like to talk with him a bit? Might cheer him up to talk with somebody interested."

"I just can't imagine," said Maxine, "anybody in his right mind . . ." She stopped there.

McKee said, "Mr. Jennings, he's asleep right now, if you don't mind waiting. Tomorrow's his ninetieth birthday. Might do him good to reminisce a bit."

"You come all the way out here just for that?" Maxine said.

"I was out in the western part of the state," said

Jennings, "and thought I'd stop off on my way back."

"If you don't mind what you sit on," said Maxine, "you're welcome to sit around and wait."

"We're Lincoln people," said McKee. "We don't live out here. We just come out here for the old gentleman's birthday. It just so happened he spent most of his life right here."

"You want to let him in?" said Maxine, and McKee pushed the screen open. On the steps Mr. Jennings turned and threw away his cigar.

"No need for you to do that," said McKee. "Women in this family used to smokers."

"I'd like to know what we're not used to," Maxine said.

"Mr. Jennings," said McKee, facing the room, "this is Mr. Boyd, an old friend of the family. He and Mrs. Boyd come up from Mexico just to be with us." McKee put in the Mexico, since that was how he looked.

"We met on the train," said Boyd.

"On the train?" said McKee. "You come in on that freight?"

"You think everybody in the world drives around in a new station wagon?" said Maxine.

"What I meant is," said McKee, "could've picked you up. Had no idea you wouldn't be driving."

"We were," said Boyd, "till it stopped."

"Glad to see you get back to where the car is," said McKee.

"You have to talk about him leaving before he's so much as got here?" said Maxine. "Mr. Jennings,

I'm Mrs. Momeyer, and this is Mrs. McKee and her son, from Chadron."

"Wife of my son Gordon," said McKee, just to keep from getting things twisted. "My missus is upstairs right now with Eileen's youngest boy. 'Bout all you can see of Mr. Scanlon right now is his feet." McKee nodded toward the stove, where the old man's feet stuck out from the quilt they had covered him with. Something in the way they both stuck up, nothing else showing, made McKee a little nervous. "Car ride tends to make him pretty sleepy," he said. "Probably have to wait till he gets his coffee."

Mr. Jennings put up his hand, the palm out, and flagged it slowly from side to side. It had the same effect on McKee as one of those eye tests that made him sleepy. He felt his arms relax.

"If he waits for you men to get him his coffee, Mr. Jennings will be here forever," said Maxine. "Etoile, your father turn that water on?"

Right there in the door, where she'd been for some time, the girl said, "You better boil it before you make coffee."

"Mr. Jennings," said McKee, "this is Etoile, Mrs. Momeyer's daughter. Mr. Momeyer stepped out for a minute to turn the water on."

At the sink in the far corner, Maxine twisted the knob on one of the faucets. What came out was more like rust than water.

"*You* can drink it if you want to," said Etoile, "not me."

"Won't matter so much if we boil it," said McKee. "Might be just the thing for that percolator coffee."

He winked as Jennings and Boyd, then waited for a rise out of Maxine. None came. Had he hurt her feelings? As a rule she was tough as nails. Not often, but every now and then, McKee realized that this woman, shaped like a sack of melons, was almost ten years younger than his wife. He couldn't grasp it: all he could do was admit it.

"Maxine—" he said.

"For cryin' out loud, Muh-thurrr."

"That's what she's trying to do," said Eileen, "if you'll just let her."

And sure enough she was. Her broad back was shaking like a big bear. Whether it was better to have a woman freeze up like Lois and walk around like a poker, or break down and bawl in public like a kid, McKee didn't know. No, honest to God, he didn't know. Whatever the devil had come over the family had not gone away just because a little time passed. No, they had to wait and hang their laundry in public. They had to wait for Boyd.

Eileen said, "Calvin, honey, if your mother could cry out loud you wouldn't stutter. How would you like that?"

Etoile said, "Ha!"

Maxine stopped snuffling. McKee cleared this throat and said, "Etoile, suppose you show the gentlemen where the washroom is."

"See they get a towel. The towels are there in the carton," Maxine said, and went back to snuffling again. Was there anything like them? McKee wondered. The only place you could touch them was where they slipped on what was proper. Bawling like a kid, then breaking off to tell you where the towels were just in case some stranger might think they didn't have clean ones.

"Etoile," he said, "while you're up there, you might show the gentlemen where they're going to sleep. Mr. Jennings is welcome to spend the night if he don't mind the beds."

"There's nothing wrong with the beds," said the girl. "It's the bugs."

McKee saw Maxine lift her arms, then let them fall like she was going to faint.

"You just tell me where to get out of your way," Jennings said.

"Soon as you're washed up," said McKee, "you're welcome to join us for a bit of supper. How long'll it be, Maxine?"

She didn't reply. Like a kid standing in a corner till the other kids had hidden, she faced the stove, her broad back to the room. McKee realized he seldom saw her any other way. It was her back that he knew if she was standing at the sink when he looked in the back door, or if he sat at the table when she was at the stove. There was not room for them all to sit at her table—not to sit the way she considered proper—so they would sit and she would stand, eating off a plate she kept on the side, until she could pull up a chair for coffee and dessert. Just as if he had some say in the matter, McKee hollered, "Etoile, when you're finished up there, suppose you come down and give your mother a hand." Then he let the door close at his back before he heard what she said. Just in time. The eastbound flyer, the coach lights flickering like a film run wild in his projector, went by with a whoosh that made him dizzy and sucked at his breath.

In the silence that followed, McKee saw the moon hanging in the dead tree like a lantern: It seemed odd to him that the whoosh he heard hadn't blown it out. The tin roof of the stable was blue like a pond where the snow had melted, and the nickel glittered on the chair in the barbershop. Near the door, which was set in slantwise, McKee could see the glass ball of the gum machine, and if he could believe his eyes, Bud Momeyer was seated in the barber chair. Was it on the board they spread across the arms for kids? He sat up high like he was on a throne, the half-curtain in the window cutting him off just below the knees, like a sideshow freak without any legs.

From the trailer, where the window was down, McKee could hear the hoarse voice of Edna say, "Honey, we can put Shiloh in with us. We got beds. You can sleep right here. You been upstairs? You think it must be popcorn on the floor, but it's scads of dead flies."

Way to the east the train that had just passed whistled thin and wild.

Maxine

Not Etoile this time, not even Bud coming in with that gum machine like a small fry, but the sink, with the water running as if to keep the pipes from freezing, and her father asleep as if he'd never been removed from behind the stove. What had changed? What had changed so much as Maxine? The soft one, her father's pet, the only one of his girls he didn't say scat to, saving for her his cigar bands and the green Tuxedo tins his tobacco came in. The tin sat on the range, where her father could scratch around in it like a chicken. At the sound of it, like a mouse gnawing, Maxine would come from where she sat in the lobby just to see if his finger was getting near the bottom of the tin. The sight of that stove lid with the streaks on it where he had scratched his matches brought a lump to her throat so large she thought she would choke. Like a kid she bawled, her shoulders heaving, and the long dark lashes Bud had never noticed let the tears run down and streak her glasses like rain.

"It's not his daughter, my dear. She's not at all ashamed of him. It's not his wife. She doesn't keep an eye on him. Darling," said Eileen, "you see him look at Etoile?"

Indeed Maxine had, and when Boyd had looked at her Etoile had looked right back at him. So she said, "Eileen, doesn't everybody?" She pushed up her glasses to dab a wad of apron at her eyes.

"Darling," Eileen replied, "Mr. Boyd isn't everybody."

Two minutes after a room had emptied Eileen could tell her what people that Maxine hadn't even known were there had been thinking. Wouldn't anybody stutter who lived with a creature like that? She turned, smelling fat burning, and there framed in the door, just back from the light, like a big doll in its box, was Lois. On her head was the small feather hat that would look better on Etoile. Almost everything did. How much had she heard?

She stepped into the light and said, "There's a surprise for me?" and looked around as if she might see it.

"Etoile just went upstairs with it, dear—didn't she, Maxine?"

Simply because she had to say something, Maxine cried, "Eeeee-toal, Aunt Lois is down here now."

"There's only one room with two beds," the child yelled. "You suppose they want two beds?"

That feeling in her legs that she sometimes got on Miller & Paine's escalator led Maxine to wad up the apron, lean on the stove.

"Sweetheart," Eileen called, "don't you think you better ask him? If she's like me, she can't stand separate beds."

Cool as a cucumber, Lois said, "What a pity, my dear, you have to have them." Turning to Maxine, she said, "Are we going to need the extra leaves, Maxine?"

"Won't one do, darling? said Eileen. "She's so young and fresh she'd like to eat with the children, don't you think?"

"How many of us are there," Lois said, "with McKee's guests?"

Maxine put up her hand as if to ward off a blow, the fingers spread. "There's three of us, there's four of you, then there's Eileen and Calvin, there's Edna and Clyde, there's Mr. Jennings—"

"Do they have names, darling? I don't really think so. He calls her Daughter and she calls him Daddy. Isn't that sweet?"

"—makes fourteen, I think. Mother used to seat twelve, plus herself."

"I don't think I ever remember her sitting down," Lois said. Would Etoile, thirty years from now, hearing somebody mention *her* mother, think of her as the person in the family who never sat down? The back door—had there ever been a front door in her life?—the back door pushed in and Bud said:

"You people want to see a sight?" He put in his head, the flaps turned up on the red flannel hat he liked to wear backward, the bill at the rear. If anybody should ask her the number of her children, she could say two.

"Ask him if he knows where the table leaves are," Lois said.

"In the garage," he said, "behind the incubator."

Without rhyme or reason, seeing his face, the upper part of it like a later addition, she sometimes felt what a blessing it was to have married him. The only questions were the ones with answers in the back of Etoile's schoolbooks. The only problems were the puzzles she sometimes brought home.

"Bud," she said, "Lois means here. You remember where you and Papa put them?"

"Closet," he said, and pointed across the room at the door to the hall. His hand just stayed there, the finger wagging, as if he wanted them all to see the archery glove he had made by cutting the fingers off an old regular glove. "Hi!" he said.

Eileen said, "Mr. Boyd, you met Mr. Momeyer?"

"How are you?" said Mr. Boyd.

"You the one who used to know McKee?" said Bud.

Maxine said, "Bud." Just like that, the way she said "Mutt" when the dog was alive, and he would stop whatever he was doing and just sit. Bud just stood, and it gave her time to turn, as if nothing were at all unusual, and see Lois, just her fingers on the table, like the hostess on the Let's Bake program, smiling at Eileen as if she'd just asked her for the recipe. At her back was Mr. Boyd, as if she didn't know it, and Maxine thought she must be having the jitters from the way her head was twisted, the neck stuck out. But she wasn't. No, it just so happened that someone standing in the door like Mr. Boyd saw her face in profile, and everybody knew that Lois's profile was almost exactly the same as Etoile's. If Mr. Boyd hadn't known that before, he knew it now. She stood there like a bird dog till Eileen said:

"Lois, honey, did you people meet somewhere?"

Although her sister had it coming to her, Maxine

said, "I should think you'd know all about that, Eileen, since little Gordon has done nothing but talk about it. Mr. Boyd, what in the world did you do to that child to impress him like that?" Maxine stopped there, just the way she did when Lois used to kick her under the table.

Lois stood there as straight as the ironing board she had been advised to take her naps on. Without turning to look at Boyd, she said, "Would you say the way to impress a child is to act like a clown, Mr. Boyd?"

Before he could say a word, Bud said, "I'd sure say so. Don't think I'll ever forget Uncle Daniel. Nothing he liked to do more than play piano rolls backwards. Slow, then fast. Used to pump the piano for him. Had time of my life."

"You'll like Mr. Boyd even better, Mr. Momeyer," Lois said.

What might he have said if he could have seen more of her than her back? Maxine couldn't bring herself to look at him; she just stared at Bud, his eyes sparkling as though he could hear the piano rolls he used to play. He stood so close to the door that when it opened it tipped his hunting cap over his eyes.

"Sweet Jesus, excuse me," said Mrs. Boyd. Right behind her was Edna, holding her raincoat and a drink coated with ashes, then Colonel Ewing with that poor dumb creature with its face mashed in. If Maxine understood at all what the Colonel was saying, the dog was worth all that money because he was so ugly.

"You're just in time, darling," Eileen said. "We're talking about clowns, and who is one. Lois thinks Mr. Boyd is just a wonderful clown. Would you agree?"

Maxine had seen babies of eight or nine months who had the sober little gaze of people—usually some member of the family—clear over on the other end of life. Mrs. Boyd looked like that, with her thin pale face, and she picked the tobacco from her lips like the small boys Maxine had caught smoking in the box her piano came in.

"Daddy," she said to Mr. Boyd, "you clowning it up already?"

"Daughter, it's later than you think. I'm clowning it up before the bomb."

"Bomb?" said Edna. "What bomb?"

"The *bomb*, Sweet Jesus. He's got this friggin bomb on the brain. He won't be happy till it goes off—will you, Daddy?"

"Let there be light, Daughter. The Lord said, 'Let there be light.' "

"You call that light," Edna put in, "you can leave me in the dark, honey."

"Just before dawn," said Boyd. "That's when the breeze dies, and they do it. You owe it to yourself. Terrible as it is, it's a wonderful sight. There's this flash, then this pillar of fire goes up and up, like a rabbit's ear—" Mr. Boyd raised his eyes as if he saw it.

"In heaven's name," Maxine said.

"Daddy—" said Mrs. Boyd, putting her hand on

his arm, "it's not as late as all that. Now you just relax."

Like he saw a cat there, the Colonel's dog lunged toward the doorway. The leash was so tangled between his legs the Colonel nearly fell down. "Easy, boy," he said, "easy, easy now, boy." He braced himself as the door eased open.

Out on the stoop McKee said, "You want to call that thing off, Colonel?"

"My friend," said the Colonel. "A mere puppy. Eight months Tuesday morning. Loves children and kittens—"

"Could be," said McKee, keeping his distance.

"Clyde," said Edna, "will you call him off?"

McKee made a move, and the dog lurched at him.

"*Ahhhh*-aaaa," said the Colonel. "You are afraid. He smells it."

"Think he can," said McKee, "with that bashed-in nose?"

"Mr. Boyd—" Eileen said, and the way she had done since she had her teeth capped, ran the tip of her tongue clear around her lips.

With the wire lid handle Maxine rapped on the stove, and when they turned to look at her, she said, "As soon as one of you men put the leaves in the table, we'll eat."

The Leaves of the Table

"Take a lamp," she said. "There's no light. You know where the cupboard is under the stairs?" He took the lamp, the top of the chimney wrinkled like a piecrust, the glass chipped. The grandfather always set his coffee on it to keep it warm. Floating on the top of the oil in the bowl were beetles.

"How you figure they got there, Maxine?"

"Two leaves is enough. You so much as drop one and he'll wake up."

"Where are the children?" said Lois.

"Maybe they like each other," said Eileen. "You can't rule it out."

"On their grandfather's birthday," Lois said, "the least they might do is be present."

"Think they come out here to sit and watch him sleep?" said McKee.

"Father!" Lois said. "Father, are you hungry?"

"Lois, you wake him up, you can just sit and feed him."

"Bud, you going to get them leaves, or I have to do it myself?"

With the lamp he walked into the hall, where the moon was so bright he didn't need it. Inside the cupboard door was a milk can. What did he want with that? He put the lamp through the posts on the stairs so he wouldn't back out and kick it, then he moved the milk can so he could get at the table leaves. He needed the lamp to see. It was not there on the landing, where he had left it. Etoile sat there holding the lamp on her head.

"Smell anything, Daddy? My brains are burning."

"Holy smoke," he said. "Now you be careful."

"Ha! I just wish I had to."

"Where's Calvin?"

"In the john. He's hiding."

"Eeee-toal," her mother called, "you want to tell Mr. Jennings we're ready to eat?"

"Mr. who?" said Bud.

She pointed through the banister into the lobby. In one of the rockers at the front a man sat leaning forward, his elbows on his knees.

"He don't want to either. Who you suppose wants to?"

"Wants to what?"

"Eat, silly. I saw you out there. You shoot any Indians?"

"Don't think *you're* so smart, young lady."

"Sweet Jesus, I don't. Sweet Jesus."

"Your mother hear you say that?"

"You think I'm crazy?"

"Bud?" Maxine called. "What in the world are you doing?"

"Why don't you just say for once, Daddy?"

"Don't think she would like it."

She stood up, the lamp on her head. "I'm somebody or other, Daddy, queen of the ball."

"What you sitting in here for? You get out in that moon. Makes you blink to look at it."

"I'm dressing for the ball," and she turned slowly on the landing.

"You going to Ogallala in that toy car?"

"No, Daddy, he can only *sit* in that one."

"What kind of car you call it?"

"A blinker. You blink your lights at ones like it."

"I got to get them leaves," and he stepped into the closet to get them. When he backed out she was over in the lobby, the lamp still on her head, standing on the scales.

"This make me light headed, Mr. Jennings?"

Mr. Jennings turned in the seat to look at her. "You like a penny, miss?" and when he stood up the ashes in his lap spilled on the floor.

"What's goin' on here," said McKee at the door, "you *makin'* those table leaves?"

He stepped out of the door to let Bud walk by and they had the table opened at the middle, ready for them.

"Good as new," said McKee. "Didn't you people ever use 'em?"

"How much company you think we had back then?" said Maxine.

"Gordon," said McKee, "you remember that table on the Crete's porch. Used to play caroms on it? Think they put up to ten leaves in it at Christmastime."

"Clyde," said Edna, "just because *you* think he's a puppy, Mr. Boyd don't. Maybe he don't like that slobber."

"What you feed him," said McKee, "give him a breath like that?"

Maxine said, "Mrs. Boyd, Colonel and Mrs. Ewing have this big place in Oklahoma. Was it right on your place they found this oil, Edna?"

"I just wish to God they hadn't. You know the smell of the old oil burners? No, they burn it. Sure as we put the house somewhere else, they'll come and find oil beneath it. That's what Clyde hopes!"

"Colonel Ewing is an old friend of Will Rogers," Lois said.

"Will," he said. "Poor old Will. Will used to say he never met a man he didn't like."

"Imagine!" said Eileen. "I mean just try to. Is he the one with a touch of white blood?"

"That's the Colonel," said McKee. "Which one of them Indians is it? There's so many."

"Cherokee," said the Colonel. "Mother's side. Proud to have blood of dark race in my veins."

"My God," said Edna, "just so it's blood. Think there's probably dark blood in mine since October. They won't tell you. All I knew is my hair is not so light."

"Isn't Grandfather part Old Crow?" Eileen said.

"Bud, you and McKee want to get some chairs?"

"Mr. Jennings," said McKee, "you like to bring along what you like to sit on?"

"How many of us are there?"

"Are we counting Father?"

"You wake him up, and you can sit and feed him."

"Mrs. Boyd, since you and Mr. Boyd come from the farthest—"

"Darling, from where? I didn't catch it."

"—you can sit here. Etoile, will you tell Calvin his plate is served?"

"Not if you want him to eat it."

"Everybody met everybody?" said McKee.

"McKee, sit down."

"Mind if it's beside this pretty young woman?"

"Sweet Jesus, no."

"Mr. Boyd, don't you love it? I can hardly bear it. There anything in the world it doesn't cover?" Edna coughed.

"Not a friggin thing, madam."

"Shouldn't somebody say something? Mr. Boyd, say something."

"Ak-sar-ben," said Boyd, "spells Nebraska backwards. It's lovely country. Know it well. Game, wild fowl and snotweed abound. Traveling from east to west, one gets the impression of a verdant grassland, congenial to man, along with bones of the woolly mammoth and the dinosaur. Spaghetti made in Omaha very popular in Italy. The state capitol, perhaps finest in the nation, can be seen from a distance of thirty miles or from Fourteenth and O Street, being a matter of taste. The people of Nebraska, being conservative by nature, living close to the soil and the round of the seasons, are not swept by the tides of shifting opinion and still refer to most Negroes as coons. A predictable percentage of the women go mad, books are sold in most of the drugstores, and Mr. Charles Munger, celebrated gunman, is a native son. A restrained optimism characterizes the outlook and inlook of a pioneer people who welcome the visitor with a 'Howdy, stranger' and a friendly smile. Until a man proves himself bad he is considered good. Dust, as seen in *Life* magazine, continues to blow, and the state emblem, a stiffly pleated upper lip, symbolizes the spirit of its people resolutely carried forward into the new age."

Like he was sick, Calvin got up from the table and walked to the door with his head stuck out.

"Colonel Ewing," said Eileen, "would you say something?"

He turned to face McKee, bowed at the waist. "Ladies and gentlemen, if I may—"

"Thank you, Colonel, thank you," said Boyd. "A toast, McKee, the folks want a toast."

"Me?" said McKee. "You like to say something, Lois?"

"The children would like to leave by ten to eight," she said.

McKee squinted at the light cord. "I know Lois and me want to thank you all for coming. Especially those of you who have come a long ways—"

"A long *way* is preferred," Lois said.

"—like the Colonel here, and Boyd. It's something to give thanks for, having such old friends. I guess I should say it's a shame that some old friends aren't here with us, and we ought to be grateful for the one who still is." He sat down.

"Did you have to end on that note?" Lois said.

"I just said what come to mind."

Maxine said, "I just want to say we didn't come out here just to eat. The food is mostly warmed up. You can't cook much on an old cob stove."

"All it took her was a week," said Etoile, "working night and day."

"Eee-toal!"

"For cryin' out loud, Mother, why not admit it? What's so wrong if you just say so?"

Boyd said, "Almost everything, my dear. Your feelings would be showing."

"If you people would just eat. Etoile, shut up and eat."

"Just what you mean by that, Gordon?"

"It's okay to show a bit of leg, a bit of bosom and a bit of bottom, but the man who shows the fly of his feelings has to leave the state. Is something showing, McKee?"

"Now looky here, Gordon, just because we all don't wear our feelings on our sleeves—"

"I keep forgetting where you do wear them, McKee. Where is it?"

"I just can't tell through these friggin glasses. I can't see out, but everybody can see in. Sweet Jesus. You ever hear of such a wonderful invention?"

"Glasses, darling—what glasses?"

She tipped her head over the plate as if to lick it, and put her fingers to her eyes as if they hurt her. Something popped out and dropped on the plate.

"Sweet Jesus," said Etoile.

"My God," said Edna.

Colonel Ewing and McKee pushed their chairs back.

"Ladies and gentlemen," said Boyd. "No cause for alarm. Just a show of feelings of an unusual order."

"I swear to God I don't see a thing. Not a thing."
Edna leaned over the table to look at the plate.
"That's what's great about 'em. It's the friggin
thing you pay for. Can't see a thing."

"Eee-toal, your hair is in her food!"

"Are we going to sit and wrangle?" Lois said.
"Did we come out here just to wrangle?"

"Madam," said Boyd, "it's a wonderful sight. It's
the heat, they say, that gives off the light."

"Ha," said Etoile.

Boyd said:

> *My candle burns at both ends;*
> *It will not last the night;*
> *But, ah, my foes, and, oh, my friends—*
> *It gives a lovely light.*

"Boyd," said McKee, "I hope you didn't come
back just to stir up old feelings."

"Or is it new ones, McKee? Not the past but the
present. In the good old days we both had feelings.
How is it now? On good authority I have it that
you and Mrs. McKee couldn't be happier. You
couldn't be, so you haven't been, happier. What
scares you pissless is not the fear of death, but the
fear of exposure. The open fly of your feelings.
You know why? You might not have any. What
can one do? Keep the upper lip firmly pleated. I
see that Mrs. McKee is wearing one now, like a
veteran's poppy. How well it becomes her."

"Boyd—" said McKee.

"Seven times a week, thirty times a month, three
hundred and sixty-five times a year you couldn't

have been happier, McKee—and you weren't. Any guesses? That's just the days. Every year has three hundred and sixty-five nights. Over forty years that adds up, something like a hundred thousand couldn't-be-happier nights. My congratulations. To you both. The couldn't-be-happier pair of the year." Boyd raised his cup to McKee, then to Lois, and bowed.

"Gordon," said McKee, "I always got to remember you're at some sand pit, trying to walk on the water, or at some bullfight squirtin' pop at a bull. You like to shake up your bottle of words and squirt a string of 'em over people. Especially people you know. I don't mind your squirtin' them over me, but there's people here who don't know you as well as I do, and how you have to make a fool of yourself since you've made such a mess of your life. They might take you for as big a fool as you sound. I'd like to say to these people that I know you better, and if they have some respect for my opinion, I'd like them to like you the way I do myself." He pushed back his chair and stood up.

Lois said, "Sit down, McKee." He sat down. Boyd sang:

> *Stand up, Walter McKee.*
> *In your youth you shadowed me.*
> *All that I am or hope to be*
> *I owe to Walter J. McKee.*

"Now looky here, Boyd—"
"McKee, one question. You awake or asleep?"
McKee said nothing.

"You remember the woman who came up the stairs and asked us the question?" said Boyd. "And how we laughed? You can't be happier, McKee. You awake or asleep?"

McKee wagged his head as if it hurt him. "Gordon," he said, "maybe it's as much my fault as it is yours. Like you say. You'd never walked on that water or squirted pop at that bull if me or Mrs. McKee hadn't been there to watch you. Guess we got into the habit, the way kids will, of you showing off and me bein' there to watch you, and habits you acquire as kids tend to stick, don't you think?"

"Which one you got in mind?" said Boyd. "My habit of kissing your girls?"

"Boyd, I'm going to ask you——"

"To leave her out of this? Where else is she, McKee? Were you ever included in? That's one friggin habit that's stuck to us both, don't you think? We're included out. We're back where we came in. I'll tell you what I'll do this time, McKee. I'll let you kiss her yourself."

Lois stood up and walked toward the door as though the floor had a tip in it.

"See what I mean, McKee? Back where we came in. Think she did say nighty-night to us the first time, the smell of that goddam candied apple still on her lips."

"Bygod!" said McKee. "Bygod, now you look! You talk just as if one of us didn't have her. Bygod, when you talk like that you can talk for yourself!" He turned to leave, but he stopped when he saw Mrs. McKee in the doorway.

"Speak for himself, McKee? You like to know why he didn't? You think he knows why he didn't?"

She looked at McKee, then she looked at Boyd, then she said, "Men!" and walked into the hall. Right where she had been standing, as if he'd been hiding behind her, stood little Gordon in his flannel sleepers with the mittens. In one mittened hand he held one of the old man's pistols by the barrel. The butt of it hung like a clapper to a bell.

"McKee! McKee!" Lois called from the stairs. "McKee!"

McKee took two steps forward, then he stopped a yard or two from the boy, and said, "Lois, he's down here."

"Son," said Mr. Jennings, "what's that you got there, son?" and little Gordon, half asleep, walked over to him.

"It's a shooting iron," he said.

Jennings

Even as a boy Jennings had been frightened by what his wife had called "scenes"—the voices of women in the rooms which the voices of men had left. Here the woman had left, but her voice somehow remained in the room. When she said "Men!" Jennings had cringed as if she had included him in. Had anybody understood what had been said? Was that why Boyd could sit there, McKee could stand there, as if nothing had happened?

"A shooting iron, eh?" Jennings said. "What does it shoot?" He took the heavy pistol from the boy's limp hand. Casually, thinking he would find nothing, he cracked the barrel and saw the five shells.

"One's gone," said the boy. "Who did she shoot?" His mouth dry, Jennings shook his head.

"My God," said Eileen, "you hear that? Mr. Jennings, are they all little monsters?" With an unsteady hand Jennings shook the shells into his palm, dropped them into his pocket. "There you are, son," he said, letting him have the gun, "a safe shooting iron."

"That's the one that kills you every time," said Edna. "Where in God's name did he find it?"

"Under the pillow," he replied.

"Pillow? *Whose* pillow?"

"We're not going to talk about it now," said

Maxine. "We're worked up enough without bringing that up."

"Nope," said Etoile, "what we'll do is wait till the little darling s-h-o-o-t-s somebody."

"Mr. Jennings," said Maxine, "I swear to God you must think you're in a madhouse."

"I was born just down the line from here, Mrs. Momeyer," Jennings replied, and lifted the boy to his knee. He liked children. As a rule they liked him. Were they all little monsters? In this child, Jennings was made aware of why they built fences around playgrounds. A little animal, and a wild one, to boot. But what troubled Jennings was not so much what he felt but what he seemed to sense behind it, playing with the child the way a twister played with the wind. The havoc might be terrible, but the force behind it was impersonal. The child was not in possession of his feelings, but possessed by what he felt. What feelings possessed the little monster on his knee? What had he heard? Whom had he come down the stairs to shoot?

"Boys will be boys," said the Colonel, wagging his head. "I can well remember my own transgressions."

"Thank God I can't," said Eileen. "I'd die of mortification. Somebody once told me I ate the boogers out of my nose."

There was no comment. A potlid rattled on the stove. Jennings raised his eyes to see Maxine, as if in one room gazing through to another, staring at McKee as if she had never seen him before.

"A girl at school eats hair like a cat," said Etoile. "She's got a big hair ball in her stomach."

"If that child hears any more of such talk," said Maxine, "it's the rest of you who can sit up with him."

They turned to look at the boy seated on Jenning's knee, the pistol held across his front like a rifle.

"Will used to say—that's Will Rogers, Mr. Jennings—Will used to say that children made the best people."

"If there's one thing he don't need to be told—" said Maxine.

The boy tipped the gun—as if to get their attention—and took a long sniff of the barrel. Then he moved the gun so that it pointed at Jennings. Did Jennings look scared?

"You don't need to be scared," the boy said. "I don't shoot men, just wimmen."

"Gordon!" cried Maxine.

"You shoot *any* woman, son, or just the ones you know?" said Boyd.

"Will you people stop goading him on?" said Maxine. "Mr. Jennings, you want me to take him?" She came forward and put her hands on the boy, but he grabbed the gun and pointed it at her. With the palm of her hand she slapped him sharply across the face.

"I will not stand for that, you hear?"

Jennings doubted that the boy did. He tried with all his might to pull the trigger. "*Bang!*" he screamed. "You're dead!" With her other hand Maxine slapped him hard across the mouth. He sucked in his lip as if to see if he still had it, then set his mouth in a line that made him look years older. Jennings recognized the face as that of Mrs. McKee.

"My baby! My baby!" Eileen cried, and leaned over to throw her arms around him. The boy sat stiff, like a wooden doll, his hands gripping the gun.

"It's a tantrum," said Etoile. "You throw water on him."

Eileen said, "Maxine, stop your bawling. If he thought it would make you bawl he'd stop breathing. Mr. Jennings, my child specializes in holding his breath."

Dipping his fingers into his water glass, Colonel Ewing leaned forward and sprinkled his face with water. "Son," he said, "stop that!"

"Try slapping him on the back," said Boyd.

Tipping the glass, the Colonel wet the boy's face as if sprinkling clothes. On his scarlet cheeks the drops of water looked like beads of sweat. Jennings pushed up, the boy in his arms, his small blue hands gripping the pistol, and carrying him like a big stuffed doll, made for the door.

"Nothing would please him more," cried Eileen, "than to die knowing we all killed him."

As he went through the door Jennings was thinking about himself. He had used the child as an excuse to get out of the room before another scene. Half trotting, as if he carried something that had to be dropped far from the house, he lumbered up the grassless bank to the tracks. The moon was rising.

It seemed to emerge, like a balloon, from the stable and cast a pale green light on the objects behind it.

"That's where I'm going," said the boy, and Jennings glanced at him, saw the moon in his eyes. The prospect of it, the moon crawling with small fry, made Jennings weary; he lowered the boy to the ground. Like a department-store rabbit, in his flannel sleepers, he scooted down the bank and picked up a small object.

"What you got there?" said Jennings, but his hand clamped shut on it. At his side, gripped by the barrel, the boy held the shooting iron. "You won't need that shooting iron on the moon," Jennings said, and walked down the bank to take it from him.

"There's nothing there to shoot?"

"Nothing but yourself," Jennings replied.

The figure of a man blocked off the light in the doorway. "How's everything out there, Doc?" said McKee. "Okay?"

"Say no," said the boy.

"We're getting a breath of fresh air," said Jennings.

"Take your time, Doc. No rush. When he's got that breath of fresh air, his Uncle Walter will tell him a story."

"What story?"

"How about the choo-choo that went chuff-chuff?"

"He thinks I believe anything I hear," the boy said to Jennings. Then, to McKee, "Mr. Jennings is going to tell me a story."

"Is that so?" said McKee. "Well, it better be a good one."

"Is it a good one?" the boy asked.

Moonlight, like a thin fall of snow, lay on the plain, the limbs of the lone tree, the galvanized roofs and corners of the buildings, and the nickel-plated trim on the barber chair. Two bottle stoppers burned like candles in the mirror. Did Jennings have a story? A good one?

"How about the man who knew Santa Claus?" he said.

"What you take me for?" he said. "A girl?"

"Kid," he said, "that's my story." Through the open door to the kitchen he could see Maxine fanning her face with her apron. They stood there, upright on their moon shadows, and Jennings felt he had been through it all before. Where? The men's room of the Paxton Hotel. His father had taken him there to wash his hands. He had turned from the bowl and said, "Kid, I'd like you to—" then, hearing what he had said, he had stopped and wiped his hands on the towel. But it was still there. On that day one boy had died, another had been born. He turned slowly as if looking for a place to get off his feet. A glint down the tracks to the west proved to be Mr. Momeyer with his bow and arrow, crossing the field between the hotel and the cattle loader. In the wall of the hotel, when he raised his eyes, he noticed the face at the rear window. Using the blind cord, someone was tapping on the lower pane.

"Psst, darling. You hear me?"

"Just pretend we don't," said the boy.

The pane raised from the sill, and a voice said, "Mr. Jennings?"

"Yes, ma'am?"

"I'm not dressed to come down. Would you be so kind as to bring him upstairs?"

"Mr. Jennings believes in Santa Claus!" cried the boy.

"I think that's very fortunate indeed," said Mrs. McKee.

"You like him right now, ma'am?" said Jennings.

"If you'll bring him to the front door, I'll let you in. I'll come down and let you in." Her face withdrew, but when she stood against the lamplight Jennings could see the hat on her head.

As Jennings stooped for the boy he said, "You're like Uncle Walter—" But he didn't go on, since Mrs. McKee, like a phantom, was beckoning to them in the doorway. Over her dress she wore a man's bathrobe, the belt lapped around her. On her head, as if she had forgotten it, was the hat.

"My baby!" she said, reaching for him. "Where is it?"

"Where's what?" he replied, and hung on to Jennings.

"You know very well," she said; then to Jennings, "Mr. Jennings, did he come to you with something?"

"Say no!" he said.

Jennings was spared a look at her face. The narrow brim of the hat cast a shadow to a point below her lips, her chin protuding like an egg. The night was warm, but she gripped the robe tight at her throat.

"Mr. Jennings," she said, "may I trouble you for Father's gun?"

Jennings hesitated, then he said, "Yes, ma'am," and held the boy with one arm while he groped for the pistol. Holding it by the barrel, he passed it to her. "It's all right now, ma'am. It's not loaded."

"It's not?" she said.

"I got the bullets right here," said Jennings, and put a hand to his pocket.

"I got one too," said the boy. "You can have mine, Grandma." He held out to her his small tight fist. Into the palm of her hand he dropped the shell he had picked up.

"Thank you, darling," she said, and with the gun gripped at her front she went up the stairs to the landing.

"Grandma!" yelled the boy.

A step above the landing she turned and said, "Tell Mr. Jennings to tell you his story, darling. Your Grandfather Scanlon has believed in Santa Claus all his life."

Boyd

That maverick uncle on whom he had never set eyes: the one gassed in the war, the one who slept with his eyes wide open, who wore his hat like Napoleon, sidewise, who always wore blue serge with grass-stained elbows, his pockets full of Cracker Jack prizes for children, on his feet a pair of unlaced hook-and-eye shoes, in his vest gold coins and ten-penny nails, and across the back and the seat of his pants the pattern of bench slats, some of them freshly painted. Every family had one in the photo album—but here, in Jennings, was one in the flesh. "I was born just down the line," he had said.

McKee said, "Doc, why don't you put that boy down? He'll ride you like a horse if you let him. What's this story about? This one of those stories for kids of all ages?" He snorted.

"I had no intention—" Jennings said. For a moment his vest seemed to hang loose on his paunch. The boy stood between his legs now, his hands on his thighs, the tail of his coonskin hat sweeping Jennings' front.

"It's about Santa Claus. He knows him," said the boy. He slapped his little hands on Jennings' thigh.

"I don't doubt that he does," said McKee, "but I'd never tell that story to certain little scoffers."

"What's a scoffer?"

"That's what you are," said McKee.

"Never you mind him," said Maxine. "You're not a scoffer. It's McKee who's a scoffer."

"I'm not ashamed to say," said McKee, "—and Boyd'll bear me out—I guess I believed in Santa Claus till it came my turn to be one." He winked at Boyd, who replied:

"McKee is the true believer. When McKee dies, Santa Claus dies."

There was a moment of silence, then Eileen said, "Amen."

Maxine said, "Are you going to tell this story, McKee, or is Mr. Jennings going to tell it?"

"Mr. Jennings is the man who knew him," said McKee. "Not me."

They turned to face Jennings. He said, "Nobody has to believe this story."

"What you call it?" said McKee.

"The Man Who Thought He Was Santa Claus," Jennings replied.

"I wish Papa could hear it," Maxine said. "You think we could wake up Papa?"

"There's only one story I ever heard him listen to," said McKee, "and we've all heard it."

"I just wish I could hear *this* one," said Eileen. "You think we might let him tell it?"

Boyd said, "The kid and me are all ears—as you can see for yourself."

Rising from the table, Colonel Ewing said, "Ten to nine. If you'll please excuse me. Shiloh likes his walk regular as clockwork." He stood winding his watch.

"That's his dog, Mr. Jennings," Mrs. Ewing said. "If he don't get his walk, he gets insomnia. You know what it's like to live with a dog with insomnia?"

"Pretty doggone awful, I bet," said McKee, and snorted.

At the door the Colonel said, "You folks mind if I let him run a little?"

"Think he can," said McKee, "on them broken legs?"

Maxine said, "Mr. Jennings, is that boy asleep?" He sagged between Jennings' knees, his head lolling backward, the tail of his coonskin hat around his neck like a fur piece.

"I'm *not*," he said. The eyes rocked open like a doll's, closed again.

"He just got tired of waiting for that story. He just got tired of listening to McKee talk."

"If the idea's to put him to sleep," said McKee, "can't say I don't do that."

Pushing on her knees as if they hurt her, Maxine rocked to her feet. "Mr. Jennings," she said, "you'll excuse me," and she started toward the hall door, one foot dragging.

"Now look here," said McKee. "Maxine, now look—"

Framed in the door, where she could brace her arms, Maxine stopped. "McKee, you know why you can't shut up? Lois isn't here, so you got to talk. If Lois was here you wouldn't say any more than Calvin has all night." McKee did not speak. "You'll please excuse him, Mr. Jennings," she said. "I've known him a long time, and he's not as big a fool as he sounds."

She wheeled slowly, as if the floor were uneven, then went off.

Eileen said, "Give us this day our daily bread. You go on saying that, and one day it happens."

The boy was getting sleepy. Jennings shifted his weight so that his legs folded across his thigh. The boy's head, cushioned on the hat, lay on the slope of his chest.

Mrs. Boyd said, "No bedtime story?"

Boyd said, "How about Wake Before Bomb?"

"*Ha!*" said the voice, and for a moment Boyd did not believe that it came from Calvin. A Sears-Roebuck catalogue from many years back lay across his knees, open at the saddle section. He looked around as if for Etoile.

"Darling," said his mother, "you going to talk all night?"

McKee said, "Mr. Jennings, you know this Santa Claus personally?"

Jennings wagged his head slowly, careful not to disturb the boy.

"Wonder if we knew the same man?" said Boyd. "Happy childhood days spent eating licorice and idly pissing into narrow-necked bottles or hiding in closets where underclothes of females *zieht ihn hinan*. Authority on women seen through dining-car windows and caliber of man as indicated by his luggage. Early manhood wore green visor with leather band that left ridge on his forehead, and used indelible pencils that left stain like a birthmark on his lower lip. Liked to wear black-sateen cuffs to protect his sleeves, detachable collars to protect his shirts, preoccupied air to protect him from members of opposite sex. Hooked detachable collar, tie dangling, over mirror or bedpost every night, tie untied to save wear and tear on knot."

"Boyd," said McKee, "you know there's men who still do that?"

"McKee, they still have those chutes on the side of the schoolhouse we used to slide down with a piece of bread paper? A fat-assed kid like yourself needed two of them. They still clean the erasers out on that fire escape? Brick wall where we used to slap them almost white, bricks fuzzy with the lint. Remember how we used to open that window just to sneak into the annex and use the scales? You couldn't keep your hands out of the box of tongue depressors, I forget why. While you were swiping them I'd sneak into the ladies lounge and look for hairpins. If a comb was there I'd look for strands of red hair. Mrs. Healy's, you know, but I suspect she dyed it. Story was she went to St. Louis every Christmas and slept with the young harvest hands for nothing. God, how I wanted to be one. Were you ever a harvest hand, McKee?"

"Don't you people mind," said the girl. "His friggin feelings are hurt. He's the one who has them."

"It's not my feelings, Daughter, it's my vanity. I'm Santa Claus, but Jennings has the patent. You know how he looks without the whiskers? The snot-stiff mittens, the frozen rubber boots, the moth-eaten suit, the flannel-coated barrel candy, the sled, the chocolate reindeer, the bag of goodies? You know how he looks seated on the bed, snowing dandruff on the rug?"

"Yes sir, Mr. Boyd," said Jennings, "I do."

"I was afraid of that," said Boyd. "Let's skip it."

Calvin looked up from the catalogue and stared at a spot on the wall as a dog would. The boy on Jennings' lap sleepily screwed a finger into one ear.

"You hear that, honey?" said Edna. "I swear to God more people than dogs can hear it."

"One of them inaudible whistles?" said McKee.

"I swear to God that's what it is for Shiloh." She raised her arms over her head just to hear the bracelets slide like curtain rings. "I'm tired. You people find the less you do the tireder you get? Clyde says why don't I rest in the trailer. Can't you see it? If I'm not there to watch him he drops right off at the wheel."

Eileen said, "If you children are *going* to Ogallala—"

"I want to hear about the bomb," Etoile replied.

"I don't," said the girl. "I've heard enough about it."

"Let Mr. Boyd tell us about it, darling. You have all night to read Calvin's mind."

Etoile pushed back her chair. "You know what, *darling?*" she said. "I've read it. If anything is going to happen he's got to read *mine*."

She popped up, her back so straight her hair hung free of her shoulders. No sound but the pad of her catlike feet as she left the room. What led Boyd to turn, as if tapped on the shoulder, and see the pleased eyes of McKee fastened on him? Just like the early model? Was that it? One of McKee's eyes flicked, sharing with Boyd—as he had shared forty years earlier—the taste of beauty on a summer porch.

"Calvin, darling," said Eileen, "why don't you look under 'Women' in the index? They must have something that reads their minds, don't you think?"

Boyd faced Jennings, the child sprawled like a sacrifice across his knees, his lips pursed in the manner of a man who would not be upset by what he hears. At his side, the catalogue in his lap, Calvin gazed through the door where the girl had disappeared. An expression? That would come later. The face had been invented by poster artists faced with the promises that men lived by. Had Boyd once had such a face himself? Calvin's lips puckered as if to check the gibber; something like firelight seemed to flicker, light his eyes. He did not look at Boyd or McKee or into the corner at the old man, but across the room where a shadow loomed on the wall. Mrs. McKee, the lamp held like a torch, stood in the door.

"You want to order something that reads minds for Mr. Boyd, Calvin? He knows us all so well he might as well know what we're thinking." She raised the lamp as if to throw its light on them all, but most of it fell on her own face.

"Don't move!" cried Eileen. "Let me guess!"

"Hold on!" yelled McKee, pushing up.

"My God, it's tipping!" cried Eileen.

And so it was, in Boyd's direction, the oil in the

base holding its level as the wick lapped at it like a tongue.

"Hold it—" hollered Boyd, not in time for the chimney, which toppled off and rolled like a glass across the table, but in time for Lois, who had tripped on the robe, to fall flat against him and stiffen like a corpse when he propped her back on her feet. McKee was there beside him, his mouth open, but the voice Boyd heard came from another quarter.

"Samantha," the old man barked, "that you, Samantha?" and he rose from the shadows as from a grave, his jaw slack, his gaze on the door to the hall. Etoile, a bonnet framing her face, her bust squeezed high, her waist narrow, stood smiling as if the taste of candied apple sweetened her lips. On the draft from the hall did Boyd smell divinity fudge? Would the taste of it—when Calvin kissed her— come off on his lips? She gave Boyd the look the vamp gave the bashful fellow in the movies, her eyes pleased with the curve of her own bust.

"Eee-toal," cried Lois, "do you know how you look?"

"I just hope to God that Calvin does, my dear," Eileen said, then turned to McKee. "McKee darling, can the children elope in your car?"

McKee

"Lois," he said, "you let me carry him. You run along."

He wagged his hand at her as if shooing chickens, and her own went up as if she felt a wind about to blow off her hat. Or was it her head? Had she ever heard talk as full of wind as that? If McKee thought for one moment that the rest of them understood any more of it than he did, he would go and put his head in that bucket of sand at the foot of the stairs. He just relied on the fact that Lois— in more ways than one like her father—never heard much of anything she didn't want to hear. She got the pitch like a piano tuner and just turned you off. On the other hand, she always seemed to hear what McKee lacked the nerve to say himself. What was that she had said? *Men!* Just as if McKee had been yelling at her. Since McKee had brought Boyd over at her own invitation to play pinochle and eat divinity fudge, she was inclined to mean both of them when she said "you." McKee might as well have kissed her, since he took most of the blame for it.

"You run along now—" he said, shooing at her, and when she went, he knew she wasn't normal. Had she heard more of that talk than McKee? If she had, he would hear it all later. One thing he did hear was that Boyd had the habit of kissing McKee's girls. Now why did he say "girls"? McKee had had just one girl in his life. But from now on he'd get credit for all the ones he hadn't had. She never believed a word Boyd said unless he said something like that.

"Doc," he said to Jennings, "now you let me take him," and stooped to slip his hands under the child's arms.

Was it like Eileen said? Did the boy get heavier when he was full of sleep? Sleepy as he was, just as McKee raised him up, the boy gave him sharp kicks on both legs. It wasn't that McKee's legs just happened to be there; the kicks were sharp and practiced as a good pro football player's. McKee could not control the impulse to shake him a little, and did. So far he steadfastly refused to admit what was plain as the nose on his face—that he had a spoiled brat of a grandson he didn't like, who had his mother and his grandmother tied around his little finger and half the family scared to death that he might kill himself if he didn't get his way. McKee almost wished that he would. He was a smart little bugger, and soaped up McKee the way he did everybody, giving him a big kiss just before he swiped the money out of his pants. McKee had caught him red-handed, his arm in up to the elbow, his tight little fist knotted around the sweaty coins. He had come into the bedroom wearing his sleepers with the mittens, but he had slipped off one mitten so he could grab more of the money. When McKee popped his head up from the pillow and caught him, the boy just stared right back: it was McKee who flinched. How did the little rascal know that it was

just between the two of them? That McKee
wouldn't dare tell his mother, his grandmother or
anybody else? The only person McKee could tell
was Boyd, who had swiped money like that himself
for the pop and Hershey bars they guzzled under
the Cretes' porch. The idea gave him the willies.
Were they going to have another wild one in the
family?

"Say goodnight to everybody," said McKee.
"Say sleep tight," which was one way of making
sure he wouldn't.

"My baby!" said his mother. "My sweet little
monster," and she pulled up his nightshirt to kiss
him on his bottom. How did people expect to raise
a sensible child when they acted like that?

"Say nighty-night to everybody," said McKee,
and Boyd said, "Happy shut-eye, Crockett."

"You still squirt pop at bulls?" said the kid.

"Sweet Jesus," said Mrs. Boyd, "when was this?"

"Say nighty-night to Aunt Edna," said McKee,
and scooted off. Until he got into the hall he didn't
know if the kid was quiet because he was sleepy or
was having another tantrum and holding his breath.
He was sleepy. His breath was warm on McKee's
neck. The moon was so bright there was almost
more light at the front of the lobby than in the
kitchen, and McKee stopped, as if he felt warm in
it. He had been married at the front of the lobby
and felt about it, after forty years, the way he did
about the light-tan shoes he couldn't wear or bear
to throw away. One day, like most of his old rub-
bers, he would see them on the feet of one of those

men who sold Legion poppies and shoelaces on the
steps of the p.o. Mrs. McKee always seemed to
know the man they would fit.

A car, a car without lights, moving like an appari-
tion down the moonlit street, made the goose flesh
rise on McKee's uncovered arms. Then he saw it
was Calvin, Calvin and Etoile, on their way to Ogallala. Were they a likely pair? "Walter," Eileen had
said, "he's more of a talker than his father. He can
nod his head." McKee's eyes had been on her face
when Maxine blurted out that he was talkative only
when Lois was not in the room. Eileen had winked
and smiled. Was it *with* him or *at* him? The car
turned at the stable, slowing up for the crossing, and
not until then, because of the dust, did he see the
dog, Shiloh, galumping along at the rear. McKee
felt a pang of sympathy for the mutt. What he
wanted to do, like most mutts, was get out and run
around like a normal dog, slobber up a little gar-
bage, chase a car or two, instead of sitting in a trailer
and wearing his prize ribbons. Where was the Colonel? Near the lone tree, holding the leash. McKee
could see that he was blowing on the whistle that
human beings were unable to hear but Shiloh could.
Who was to tell? Could you put a mutt on the carpet for something like that? McKee watched the
car, the dog trailing, rock across the tracks and
drop out of sight. The only sound he heard was
there in the lobby, on the stairs. Up on the landing,
her nightgown like a tent she had put her head
through, was Maxine.

"You seen Bud?" she said.

"That's one thing I've been spared," said McKee. He felt ashamed the moment he said it. Wasn't she the one who had to live with him?

"There's no use my trying to sleep," she said, "until I know they're back and in bed." But she had more than Etoile on her mind. Was it McKee? Something was in the look she gave him.

"Maxine, you better go to bed."

"I don't think she cares about the stutter," she said, "but I think she expects him to say enough to ask her. It's her pride. She's got Lois's pride."

McKee opened his mouth to say that wasn't all she had from Lois, but it would only make matters worse. The only thing Maxine had got out of her marriage was a child that nobody thought was hers and legs that would hardly get her up and down the stairs. The boy moved his head so he could eavesdrop with both ears.

"You want to take him to Lois?" said McKee. "She won't settle down till she gets him." He let the boy slide down his front to the steps. "Ever see this boy walk in his sleep, Maxine?"

Just to get away from McKee he did, the four or five steps to where Maxine grabbed him. McKee hadn't noticed till the boy moved into the dark the luminous buttons on his sleepers, so he could see to unbutton himself in the dark. It made McKee wonder how it was *he* had ever grown up. McKee had to find his own fly buttons in the dark, and often as not in the dead of winter, make a run for the privy through eight or ten inches of snow. He could tell, the way Maxine stooped to lift him, that she had one of her migraines, and if he wanted any breakfast, he would have to get up and make it himself.

"I'll be here in the lobby," he said, unwrapping a cigar, "if anybody wants me."

Maxine did not reply. That boy on her hip, her arm hooked around him, she went up the stairs one step at a time to where McKee could see, in its rack on the wall, the fire hose like a collapsed accordion. He turned to the door and scratched his match on the frosted glass. Through the pane he could see, as if snow was falling, the row of buildings with their tipped false fronts, almost as pretty, from where he saw them, as a Christmas card. Over the half-curtain in the barbershop window he could see the mirror, like a hole in the wall, and reflected in the mirror a hat he didn't remember being in the shop. It took him almost a minute before he saw the head under it. Bud Momeyer was back in the seat of the barber chair. This time he had pumped himself up and cranked the chair around to face the street. To see him sitting down, Bud looked about the same size as anybody, if not a little larger when he was wearing a hat with the ear muffs pinned up. McKee could make out the bow he held across his lap.

The day after his marriage McKee had stepped over to the shop for a shave. Even back then the town was skidding, but the farmers came in for a haircut, and there had been two waiting while McKee sat in the chair. One had a boy with a boil on his neck that he wanted lanced. The boy's mother and his sisters stayed in the buggy tied up at the front. Cold as it was, they seemed to feel that women didn't belong in a barbershop. They were sitting up so high they could watch McKee, stretched out horizontal with his toes up like a man one of those vaudeville magicians was about to saw in half. Up on the wall, tipped so he could see it, was a picture of the Lone Tree baseball team, which had never managed to have more than seven men. The barber, seated with his legs crossed, had been the one who covered two bases. Three of the men stood with their arms folded, their fists turned under to bulge out their biceps, and a dog named Victor, their mascot, sat wearing the catcher's mask. They had beaten teams with the full nine men fairly regularly. Kurt Javits, a Bohemian from Schuyler, had several times pitched a ball so fast the catcher hadn't seen it till it tore a hole in the chicken wire.

"McKee," said Maxine, from the top of the stairs, "you want to ask Mrs. Boyd if she would like a lamp?"

He didn't. He said, "This moon is so bright nobody needs one. It's fooling around with old lamps like that that starts your fires." That did it. Both Maxine and Lois were scared almost silly by the idea of the place burning down beneath them.

She wouldn't let him off that easy, so she said, "McKee, who's watching Papa?"

"The Lord must be," said McKee, "since he's been around for almost a century. If he should happen to want anything, don't worry but what we'd all know about it."

She didn't bite at that, and McKee entered the lobby, which was full of light like a fishbowl, and looked around. Five or six solid oak rockers sat at the front. A brass spittoon, the sides dented where the old man rested his feet on it, sat on an old fireboard, protection in case he missed the spittoon, which he often did. McKee could almost read the headlines of the newspaper on one of the chairs. He moved closer with that in mind when he heard the clack of heels in the hallway, and looking around for someplace to hide, saw the desk. The counter stood chest-high, with the registery on it, but on the left was a hole the clerk could duck in and out of. McKee ducked in and let himself down on the swivel seat—just in time.

On the floor of the lobby McKee could see Boyd's shadow, the oval frame of the door around it, but he couldn't tell if he was looking in or out. The habit he had noticed at the bull ring, the way Boyd drummed his nails on his pants leg, in the lobby sounded like mice in the wastebasket.

McKee leaned forward to catch what was said, but at the door to the kitchen Eileen called, "Maxine, you want me to bring you the alarm?"

Did she hear that? Through the grill that let warm kitchen air into the upstairs hall came her voice. "Eileen, just wind it. I got one. He'll be up before daylight, the way he's been sleeping. He'll take that stove-lid handle and hit it on the pipes till he gets something to eat."

What was it McKee heard? A fly buzzing? Was it the Colonel's inaudible whistle? As if he had ears like a rabbit, McKee felt his head twist around. Through the floor, through the soles of his shoes, he felt something like the tickle on the sidewalk when he roller-skated, or the feeling in his legs when he got up to pee at night. He heard no whistle. The train seized the building, shook it and then left.

"Where the hell is everybody?" he heard the Colonel ask.

"I think she's in the trailer, taking in the Jack Paar show," said Eileen.

"Shiloh," said the Colonel. "Shiloh. He's missing."

"Don't you think it's the moon, Colonel Ewing? Don't you think he may think he's a dog or something? Mr. Jennings, do you ever feel the call of the wild?"

"Not especially, ma'am," he said, "but I know people who do."

Calvin

When the old man hollered "Samantha! Samantha!" Calvin had his head within a foot of the window, where he could hear everything but couldn't see so much. The curtain veiled the room like a piece of cheesecloth, and the girl in the door, her face framed in the bonnet, might well have had hair as black as a mule's hide since none of it showed. He only knew it was Etoile when her braces glinted as she smiled. He just wished she was there at the window to see the rear of the character, his bald spot showing, she seemed to think was so great from the front. What had he said? That McKee was scared pissless. Whether he was or not, he should have punched him in the nose. Calvin would if Etoile would just take her eyes off him. He raised his hand, then brought it down flat on the broad side of the trailer, the sheet of metal vibrating as if it were flapped by the wind. He heard the dog dig a hole as he scratched for footing, then the snap of the chain as he lunged toward the wall.

The kitchen door suddenly opened and a voice said, "For chrissakes, what's the racket?" It didn't sound like the Colonel, but that's who it was. He came out on the stoop and said, "Down, boy! Quiet, boy! Down, down, Shiloh baby!"

The dog roared.

"Darling!" cried Calvin's mother, pushing by

him. "You fall, darling? That thing scare you? He should hang a lantern on it. Etoile, my baby—" she kissed her—"just don't keep us all up for nothing. You stop and eat somewhere. Here's money, baby—"

They got in the car, but before he had the keys in the ignition, Etoile said, "Sweet Jesus, is she flat-chested. Not at all his type." He sat there. "Are we going to wrangle?" she said. "Let's sit here and see if we got any feelings. You have. You got a veteran's poppy for a lip." She took the keys from him and found the ignition, started the car. "You know what scares *him* you-know-what, darling?" She put her knee against his own, rubbed it. "When I looked right at him I thought his eyes would pop out."

"I—I—I—I—" Calvin said, and shut the motor off. Since McKee hadn't clobbered Boyd, Calvin would. He reached for the door.

"No, silly. He didn't *do* anything. I did."

Calvin just sat a moment, then leaned forward and switched on the ignition.

"Darling, what does friggin *really* mean? She's got matches from Harold's Club. Where is that? She does the same with her hair as Debbie, but when I asked her what she thought of Eddie, she said 'Ugh.' Can you say 'Ugh'?"

Calvin watched Mr. Momeyer, with his bow and arrow, come out of the stable and walk along the road, one shoulder lifted as if he was wearing his mailbag.

"You just happen to notice they both had dirty feet? He was the one hitchhiking. It was her who picked him up. It's her initials on the bag. P. B. L. You see her expression when she blows out smoke? Like Miss Larkin hanging head down on the rings. Darling, if the habits we acquire as kiddies are going to stick, will I have to get Mr. Boyd to kiss me? Sweet Jesus. Who was Samantha? Somebody must have kissed her."

He kept his unblinking eyes on the road. He got over the tracks, then south to the highway before he noticed he didn't have the lights on. "I thought you were saving the battery," she said. Going west, toward Ogallala, he hardly noticed the cars coming up behind him, their lights dim in the moonlight, and he stepped on the gas when one of them started to pass. When the siren went off, right at his elbow, it gave him such a start he stopped a little too fast. The tires of the police car shrieked as it pulled off the road. When the dust had settled, Calvin could see him, one of those big guys, with the straddle-legged stance, standing off as though he thought Calvin meant to run over him. He hitched up his guns before he moved in to read the license. When he came back with the ticket, he leaned on the door, pulling off one of his gloves very slowly.

"Nice night for a ride," he said, "ain't it?"

Calvin could taste the dust on his lips when he licked them.

"Cat got your tongue, bud?"

"No," Etoile said, "I got it."

All Calvin could do when the trooper looked at him was look back.

"I don't mean that the way you think," she said.

"I mean we're just married." From the bag at her side she took out a sign, showed it to him:

JUST MARRIED

dim lights

"Now ain't that sweet," said the trooper, and used it to back the pad on which he wrote out the summons. He gave them both to her and said, "You bring that along with you. The judge'll love it."

Calvin's eyes burned as if someone had thrown salt into them. He stared down the road where the lights of the cars seemed to be streaked with rain, the blinker on the trooper's car revolving like an airport light. As he drove off, one of the wheels threw gravel back on the windshield and the hood.

"Darling," she said, patting his knee like his mother, "just don't be surprised if I ham it up a little"; then she ran the window down, put her head on the door and bawled. All the women in the family, the women in his life, broke down and bawled. His mother bawled with a big smile on her lips, as if all those new porcelain caps hurt her, the tears running down the white powder on her face into her mouth. On his mother's side, his grandmother wept with the same sour smile, the handkerchiefs she stuffed into her apron pockets wet as diapers. Mrs. Greeley, who had done the baby-sitting when Calvin was the baby, had sobbed like an organ when she sang the hymns that put him to sleep. Calvin did not bawl, that being, along with an interest in horses, what distinguished the males from the females in his family. Like his father, he sat quiet, the car rocking like a boat when a van went by. Until she got her braces, he could tell if Etoile was about to cry, but they changed her mouth so that her lips didn't tremble the same way. One of the long narrow feet that his mother said she ought to wear gloves on instead of shoes lay on the seat beside him, the toes all together like a family of nursing mice. He sat quiet until she stopped, then he cupped one hand over her toes and let the car go along with one wheel off the pavement, as if the tire was flat.

The only man with mules who would let Calvin have them was Mr. Laird, over near Olney, which was just a little more than eighteen miles from Lone Tree. That was quite a trip for a girl in a wagon, so Calvin agreed to settle for a buggy. Mr. Laird had one with rubber tires but no top. He agreed to rent Calvin the mules because he knew Mr. Scanlon personally and knew why for a surprise on his birthday it had to be mules. Calvin promised to walk them, not run them, and leave the car as warranty just in case anything might happen. To avoid complicating things for Mr. Laird he didn't mention that his cousin Etoile would be going, since he hadn't been too sure of that himself. All he had said to her was that it might be nice to take a buggy ride. He figured if they left Olney about midnight they would be in Lone Tree about four, and if nothing went wrong, back in Olney by eight o'clock. It was as simple as that, but hard to explain, a stuttered word at a time, to a girl like Etoile, so he put it off till she could get the pitch herself. She liked horses.

It remained to be seen what she thought of mules.

East of Olney at a drive-in, she had a butterscotch sundae covered with salted peanuts while he had a cheeseburger and a cup of black coffee to keep him awake. She left her foot on the seat, wiggling her toes like fingers when the ice cream chilled her braces. In Olney he found the mules tethered in the yard, and Mr. Laird in his house watching a basketball game on TV. When he saw Etoile, he seemed friendlier and said he would have had the mules hitched up if he had known what they were up to. He was so sure of what they were up to he put two saddle blankets under the seat just in case, as he said, it turned a bit cold. Along with a feed bag for the mules, he loaned them a Thermos they could fill with coffee and lanterns to hang at the front and the rear. The lead mule was Mike, a hat between his ears, and Mr. Laird asked Calvin to walk him on the shoulder since he had a game leg. Calvin said he would, and then Mr. Laird said, "Now you kids be careful—at least with them mules and the old man."

Etoile sat up as if the crack in the seat had pinched her.

"The old *who?*" she said, since Calvin hadn't got around to mentioning it.

"I don't mean to be disrespectful," said Mr. Laird. "Known Mr. Scanlon for years. Just mean he's an old-timer."

When Etoile turned to Calvin, her eyes were like holes in her head.

"You kids have fun now!" Mr. Laird said, and

when she yelled "Ha!" both mules almost bolted. She almost fell out of the seat, not so much from the jolt as from one of her crazy fits of laughing, upsetting the mules so much Calvin had to stand up and work at them. He could hear Mr. Laird yelling directions, and he was still out in front, looking like a gas pump, when Calvin looked back from the rise at the tracks. He waved, but Mr. Laird didn't wave back.

Was it the buggy or the mules? Whenever he looked back he could see the wheel tracks tangled like mop strings over half the road, as if the mules spent most of their time zigzagging. The mule with the hat pulled to the left as if one wheel on the buggy were cockeyed, and reining him in made the bit sore in his mouth. Calvin had handled horses all of his life and cantered his father's mares from the ranch clear to Chadron without a touch of soreness in his hands or his back—but they were horses, not mules. He hadn't thought to wear gloves, and after four or five miles both of his hands were blistered. In the muscles of his legs, braced on the buckboard, he was sure he had cramps. Getting off the highway to spare the mules had sounded great back in Olney, but after five miles of gravel his teeth were loose in his head. He kept his eyes on the mules just to keep them off of Etoile, her feet tucked under the seat, since the tails of both mules swept the buckboard like wire brooms. There wasn't a mile some dog wasn't barking at them. Was it the moon? He could hear them baying like wolves. Near Minden, seeing the light in a farmhouse made him almost bawl to be home in bed or anywhere but under the moon with Etoile and that pair of mules. A Diesel whistle frightened them both so bad he had to pull them off the road like a runaway team, their eyes rolling and their jack-rabbit ears flapping up and down. Five miles from Lone Tree he didn't feel much of anything. That was not a good sign, and he pulled off the road into a school-yard with a pump at the front, but his legs would hardly hold him when he jumped to the ground. He had a pail in the buggy, but he went to the pump, his hand so sore he could hardly work it, and after what seemed forever got a little water in the crown of his hat. He wanted that himself, but with Etoile watching he brought it back to the mule with the hat, and held it up for him to drink. Was he sick? He blew what little he got on his muzzle into Calvin's face.

"Ha!" she cried, the only sound she had made in more than three hours. He went back to the pump, got some fresh water in his hat, then walked back to the buggy and offered it to her. He hadn't really looked at her until that moment. Her face was in shadow, but the moonlight made a halo around her bonnet—what would his grandfather cry to see her now? He stood there, watching her grip his hat with white hands, then turn it like a pail to spill on his upturned face. He didn't speak. Through a film of water he gazed at her.

"You're nuttier than Grandpa!" she cried. "You're both dead, but he knows it!" And then she turned, got up on the seat and sailed his hat over the roof of the schoolhouse, the wet rim gleaming like a flying saucer in the moonlight.

"My hat!" he yelled, without a gibber, and ran for it, going around the building and into the moon shadow just as the hat sailed into the bank across the road. He didn't see the strip of sagging barbed wire and sprawled face down into the ditch, where he heard the clop-clop of the mules at his back. At a wild and crazy gallop they came out of the school-yard, the girl standing up, whipping them with the reins. The mule with the hat, one leg over the traces, had his neck stuck out like a jack rabbit, with the lantern swinging like a clapper between his legs. They came right at him, the buggy careening, and with his legs thrown high to miss the swinging whif-fletree, he went up between them. In a tangle of harness and reins he got a grip on the mule's neck and ears. In weeds so high they were sweeping the buckboard they came to a stop, the lame mule bray-ing, but the seat of the buggy was empty when he looked back. He went along the road, hollering Eee-toal, a word that had always given him trouble, to where he saw her sprawled in the waist-deep grass, her bonnet gone, her hair wild, and one leg out, the shoe gone, the foot white. When she put up her arms, he hugged her so hard she cried, "Sweet Jesus." With both hands she took a firm grip on his ears. "This time I want to know what happens. If anybody asks you, just remember I got your tongue." And she drew his face down to her own.

Maxine

Were they talking? Unmistakably she heard something about Lindbergh and the buckle of a belt thump on the floor. In the morning, if he was like Bud, he would first put on his pants and shoes, then drop his pants to the floor when he stood up, straddle-legged, and put on his shirt. Why was something as unimportant as that such a strain? Maxine would lie there so tense her feet would ache the way they did in a dentist's chair, and she would almost groan with relief when Bud finally left the room. That chain, the chain for his keys, rubbing on his pants leg, sliding through his fingers, catching on the doorknob when he went into the bathroom, was like she had one end of it between her teeth. And every day of the year except Sundays he would leave the socks he had worn under the bed after first using the tops to clean between his toes. But thank heavens he didn't wait till a family reunion to wash their linen in public, although it hardly mattered, since *their* linen was clean enough. A little dirt here and there gave people something to talk about.

In Lois's sink she had seen McKee's shorts soaking in Chlorox, they were stained so badly, and in the bathroom cabinet two or three remedies for piles. Thank God he didn't have that, whatever it was. What they had might not be love, but it was comforting. The night she slipped and broke three ribs in the tub Bud had never once let on, although she almost drowned him, what a horrible sight she must have been. His arms wouldn't go around her, and because of the soap he couldn't get a good grip on her, and she was like cut-up pieces of chicken in a plastic bag. Out of pity for him, as well as herself, she had slobbered and bawled like a baby, but thank God it was him, since he thought she was crying because she was hurt.

What made her think of that Bohemian boy back in Schuyler? He had asked her to play house in a piano box with him, and not until he let the lid down did she know what he meant. He had taken every advantage of her she would let him have. He had bitten her in several places, and she had bitten him. It had been the one thing—she liked to tell herself—she did not want to happen to Etoile, but if that didn't happen to her, then what else would? Of that order. Of being taken advantage of. There was such a short time when lack of advantage meant anything.

Lois had been seventeen, if Maxine had been nine, when Walter McKee, who had his own egg route, began to do more than just stop at the back door with his eggs. If it was cold, he would step in for some coffee, or in the summer for a piece of cake or candy, and just sit at the table while the rest of them ate and talked. He was quiet and well-mannered and always willing to run errands for Uncle Roy. At that time Lois had been in her first year of college and generally recognized as quite a beauty, with young men driving over from as far as Kansas State to visit her. Uncle Roy just assumed that McKee was a nice local boy who liked to be friendly, but not in any way that had to be taken seriously. He was just handy to have around when the girls had a picnic or a lawn party, since he liked nothing more than to let Lois pin an apron on him and help eat up whatever the others had left. How she used to make fun of the way he talked about his friend Boyd. Alice Morple had been the one to suggest that if he was all McKee described, why in the world didn't he bring him around? Maxine had not been there when Lois got herself kissed—she had gone to the neighbors' to make room for Alice Morple—but she heard about it even before she got to sleep. Alice walked over that night to tell her something extraordinary had happened, and Maxine had just assumed somebody had been compromised. At the time the idea just thrilled her to death, and she could hardly think of it without blushing, but never, not once, did she know what a *compromise* really was. Did anyone ever speak of being compromised today? What would Etoile say if she heard of it? She would say *Ha!*

When Bud's father had his first stroke, Maxine went to Aurora to help his mother take care of things, and they were still living in the house where Bud had been born and raised. His room looked almost the way he had left it, with an airplane model hanging from the ceiling, looking like flypaper it was so spotted with flies. His father was a small wiry man with forty dollars a month from the telephone company, and his mother had the feeling Maxine had never learned how to cook. Every morning, although she was in her eighties, she was up ahead of her to make the oatmeal and recommend that only sour milk and Clabber Girl baking powder made good hotcakes. It led Maxine to wonder if anybody ever lived long enough to catch up with the old folks who never got over the feeling that everybody else was still a child. Night after night, lying in the sagging hollow that seven children had worn into the mattress, Maxine could hear Mrs. Momeyer go over everything that had happened from morning to evening, as if she had planned it with that in mind. What she had said to Maxine, what Maxine said to her, how she used more soap than was necessary, and how surprised she was that a person like Maxine bought sliced bread. Then when she was quiet, he would sandwich in everything that had happened to him, which was usually between the water sprinkler on the side of the house and the tire with the dead hollyhocks at the front: how baked the ground was or how wet; who had borrowed the lawn mower and almost ruined it; and how the lout who now did it hardly took the trouble to cut all the grass. He was so old and feeble he would drop off to sleep with the blade of his jackknife half open, but every day enough happened to fill his head with talk. The night was hardly long enough to get in what happened to them during the day. Never so much as a mention of Lee Roy, who had driven half the family crazy, but who had come along so late he hardly figured in their lives. Neither the bomb nor Lee Roy nor the Munger murders proved to be as important as a crack in the hose or as interesting as the temperature in the shade. When Maxine came home to lie beside Bud, who fell asleep when his head touched the pillow, she hadn't felt relieved— she had felt cheated, so cheated of life she could almost bawl. It hardly mattered how little had happened if by just going to bed she could live it over, especially with something like Etoile to talk about. Love? It seemed to have nothing to do with love. When Mr. Momeyer died and they took him away, Mrs. Momeyer would not be much of a problem if they could just put something in the bed that would listen to her. That would prove she had been alive during the day. How did a person know, when they were young, that how they felt when they were old was what was important? One day, and it wouldn't be too long, Etoile would have to keep her long feet under the table or have thirty-five dollars to spend for the only shoes that would fit. And if she spent half the day at the sink she would soon come to wish that her legs were shorter so there wouldn't be so many varicose veins to show.

On the pillow, Maxine's head wagged with shame. Would she rather be Mrs. Momeyer, or Mrs. Walter McKee? Just supposing her child should come to her and say, "Mother, should it be McKee or Boyd?"—what would she say? Knowing what a mess Boyd would make of his life? She could see Boyd, but she could *not* see him, like McKee, never noticing the feet that his wife walked on, but putting cork floors in his house so it would be easier on them. McKee would never take her feet and kiss them on the bottoms so she almost swooned giggling, but he would work and slave to keep them in fine shoes and looking nice. Was it a choice between men or between shoes? The kind Lois now had to walk on or the kind Maxine had to stand on, most of her weight on the arms she propped on the sink.

What had Alice Morple said? Maxine, nobody ever rushed Lois off her feet. Nobody. And she meant what she said. It had not been between Boyd and McKee so much as between two kinds of feet. And the kind Etoile had were going to be even worse.

That would be Maxine's answer if the child was ever crazy enough to ask her. Would she be, in twenty years, on or off her feet? "There's your poor Aunt Lois," she would say, "just scared to death she'll grow old and look it, and there's your mother, so old and worn out she's no longer scared." That should settle it. But would it? There was a stubborn streak in Etoile. People said what a pity that Calvin stuttered, with his looks, and maybe eighty thousand head of cattle, but if he didn't stutter, if he talked for himself and had no more to say than his father, there might have been no need to get them off alone and hope for the best. "My dear," Eileen said, "just so *she* thinks he's thinking." Maxine sometimes wondered if she had no shame. When Lois suggested that the babies of some cousins might not be normal, Eileen replied that was what she hoped. Hadn't Mrs. Munger testified that her little monster was a normal baby in every respect? Then Eileen had said, "Besides, darling, maybe they just won't have any babies. Can you imagine *any*body having more fun?" Even to recall it made Maxine's face hot. Almost everybody, unless it was Lois, knew that little Gordon had come along so late simply because his mother got tired of birth control. "I simply got tired," she said to Maxine, who did a little nursing for her, "getting out of bed right when I enjoyed being in it the most." She might say anything to anybody, but she said almost everything to Maxine, usually by long distance, pre-paid, from the ranch. When the phone rang in the morning, it was usually her. Some of the things she said Maxine forgot as she heard them, just in order to go on being at peace with herself. "Dar-ling, if I had your bust I'd either be pregnant all the time or wet-nursing." Maxine had scarcely thought she had a bust, except when the bra straps made a crease in her shoulders or Mr. Lockwood, the bread man, sometimes glanced at her broad front. Mrs. Boyd was like Eileen as she was when Gordon first set eyes on her. Older than Gordon, not even pretty, looking like a boy when you saw her on horseback with her hair pushed up into a wad under her hat. He came with a line crew, putting poles on their ranch, just about as handsome and as shy as Calvin, and Eileen just happened to be there because they had sent her home from this school in Boston. She saw him on Tuesday, and Friday she married him. The same day Lois had mailed a can of cookies Gordon could share with the boys on the line crew she got the telegram saying he was married, but not to who. Lois had gone to bed, and McKee had been fit to be tied till he visited the family and saw the twenty thousand Herefords her father gave the kids just to get them, as he said, started. Lois had never cared much for Eileen, who was wearing split skirts with hip-length stockings the first time she set eyes on her. She liked to wear her blouses unbuttoned, there being so little reason why she shouldn't, and sometimes she carried Kleenex in the cups of her brassières. Etoile was mad about her, but Maxine had never seen Etoile sit and stare at anybody the way she sat and stared at Mrs. Boyd. Was it the way she talked? Maxine could hardly follow what she said. She had the nervous habit, like Eileen, of sweeping up her hair as if her neck was hot and looking right at you as if you were not looking at her. Why did Mr. Boyd, as if Maxine had nudged him, crook his head around and give her a wink, as if there was something between them and nobody else? Was there? It made her head swim at the time. Had she ever seen Etoile's eyes so wide as when her Aunt Lois set eyes on Mrs. Boyd, and she knew she was seeing the loose type of woman she had only read about? Living in sin just the way she would like to live herself.

Why was it Maxine felt so little upset? There they were across the hall, so near she could hear their voices if she put her mind to it. She raised her head to see the white bar of moonlight under their door. From the sock on the floor she withdrew the clock, saw where the bent hour hand pointed and that her father was now in his ninetieth year.

Aloud she said, "Sweet Jesus." For no particular reason, and hardly caring why.

Boyd

He watched her feet in the golden sandals go up the stairs to the turn on the landing, a spot on the heel bright as a coin where the strap rubbed. He could not see her face when she said,

"What are you all so friggin scared of, Daddy?"

"Kithophobia, Daughter. Fear of one's own kind."

"Sweet Jesus, you think they really are?"

"That's another friggin habit that just stuck, don't you think?" ·

"Yours did. Is that why you didn't ask her?"

"Could be, Daughter. Might have hurt my feelings if she'd turned me down."

He heard the sandals slap down the hall. *"Bygod"* McKee had said. "Now you look. You talk like one of us didn't have her." One of them didn't? Did that explain forty years of silence, as well as talk? Just forty years ago Boyd had mailed a letter enclosing a blank piece of paper. Speechless. For the first and last time in his life. Clever, very clever, and while waiting for an answer he had heard from McKee that God's loveliest creature had agreed to share his life. Would Boyd be the best man? My God, wasn't he? The irony of it seemed to justify his loss. Awake Before Bomb? Not so you would notice it. Perhaps the one talent he had was the talent for sleep.

He walked into the lobby, and with the heel of

his hand wiped a clear spot in the window. Strewn with shadowy pits and weedy mounds, the plain looked as if recently bombed. Something alive, seemingly headless, crawled from the pit and ran off as if crippled. A dog? A studded collar gleamed at his neck. The head was there, the face bashed in as if from a head-on collision. Like an animal slough-ing up water, it sucked for air. Boyd watched it break, puppy-fashion, into a lumbering frolic, then stop, the huge tongue dangling like a piece of raw ham. Head down, like a carpet sweeper, it disap-peared into one of the pits. Boyd turned, then eased himself into a hardwood lobby rocker—pushed himself up to remove what was on the seat.

A newspaper. Folded with the headlines up. Peace? No, larger than peace, it had to be war. He spread it out on the floor and read

LINDBERGH OVER ATLANTIC

Last night? Last year? The story beneath it was dated May 20, New York. May 20 when? Under the banner of the Kansas City *Star* he saw that the year was 1927. Lindbergh was over the Atlantic. There was a snapshot of him in his helmet, the Lone Eagle gaze fixed on Paris where in four or five hours it was said he would be.

Had he made it? Why was it Boyd did not smile? Why did it seem, there in the moonlit lobby, almost as good a question as ever? Lindbergh had to be somewhere. Over the Atlantic was where he be-longed. There in Lone Tree the future still hung in balance, the moonlit plain was like the stormy Atlantic, something to be crossed, a stage in a journey, with the gold fields the great good place at the end. Lone Tree, like the *Spirit of St. Louis,* was up there in the wild blue yonder, the cuckoo-land between the end of your dreams and wherever you are from. For the old man asleep behind the stove in the kitchen, Lindberg was still up there.

Anybody else? Boyd turned his head as if he might see. On the lobby scales, his shoes off, getting his honest weight, which would be considerable, Boyd could see the face of Jennings reflected in the mirror. Like trout on the scales were his white-heeled-and-toed socks. His coin dropped, and at the sound of the chime he disappeared as if through a trap door.

"That you, McKee?" Maxine called at the top of the stairs.

"No, ma'am. Just Jennings."

"I wonder if you'd bring me an aspirin, Mr. Jennings?"

One of the boards in the hall cracked like a branch as Jennings went off. At Boyd's back, behind the desk in the lobby, he heard a drawn-out squeak like a door opening. Through the gate in the desk he watched a chair turn clockwise, then the bowl of a hat, like a large ash tray, with the sweat of McKee's balding head darkening the crown.

That you, McKee? Boyd asked himself, and nodded his head. Good citizen McKee, of Polk, Nebraska, enjoying the blessings of a family reunion by sneaking off for a smoke and a little privacy. Where did he find it, now that the privy was an elegant part of the house? Or did he need it, now that he couldn't be happier? From what window did he spy, cigar in hand, on God's loveliest creature as she raked the yard, her pear-shaped bottom spreading like a delta when she stooped for leaves? How long, for Citizen McKee, had Lindbergh been over the Atlantic? How long for Morgenstern Boyd, the self-unmade man? His story was already written.

At the top of the stairs a voice called, "McKee—"

He did not reply.

"McKee—" Lois repeated. "Just don't come to me when the horse is stolen."

That was all. Boyd could hear the bolt slip in the door.

Maxine said, "Mrs. Boyd, that moonlight keep you awake? I'd just as soon lie awake in the light as the dark."

"Do people live out here?"

"You get used to almost anything, Mrs. Boyd."

"You can say that again. Sweet Jesus."

On the wall that he faced, emerging as he stared, was a railroad map of the state, crisscrossed by the chicken-track railroad lines. Someone had punched a hole, for reassurance, at Lone Tree. What did it mark? A fossil bed, a burial site of dinosaurs? Above the desk where McKee was concealed a clock had stopped at 11:37. Had time stopped at that moment here in Lone Tree? Lindbergh suspended over the Atlantic, the old man suspended in his covered wagon, and McKee in a state wherein he couldn't be happier. Lone Tree, that place where the dreams crossed, a point in time rather than in space, a hole in the map where the artifacts were stored. Hardwood rockers, a brass spittoon, a pair of lobby scales, a stopped clock, and in a rack on the stairs fifty feet of cracked fire hose. All in varying states of repair, but giving honest weight, no springs, at the moment when Lindberg was over the Atlantic, and time had stopped.

Was it the view through the window that brought it to mind? The elderly woman who wore pinned to her dress a piece of metal the size of a dog tag, who had written after the name of Boyd:

WAKE BEFORE BOMB

How did one go about it? Was it, indeed, advisable? If the clock had stopped, if the dreams had crossed, and if one couldn't be happier—only unhappier—why wake? Why shoot the Lone Eagle down? He picked up the paper, folded it in such a manner that the headlines were exposed, and as he pushed up from the chair, knowing it would startle him, said, "Nighty-night, McKee."

"Night, Boyd," McKee replied, as if slapped on the back, then exhaled the air he had been holding.

At the top of the stairs, light from the room lay across the hall where the doors stood open; in the room at the front where the door was closed, moonlight filtered through the panes of colored glass in the transom. He walked down the hall to where a draft, cool on his face, came from the room where the clothes lay in a pool on the floor. Dark, the bottoms dirty, her feet stuck out from the end of the sheet.

"Wake Before Bomb, Daughter! Lindbergh's over the Atlantic!" and he held up the paper, flagged it at her.

"Over what?" she said, and raised on her elbow as if to see.

"Over the Atlantic," said Boyd.

"Sweet Jesus, where you think *you* are?" and when Boyd did not reply: "That's where you all are, the whole friggin boatload," and he stood there, gripping the paper, the light so strong in his face it made him blink.

"I mean that's where we *all* are, Daddy," she said, moving over, her hand patting the bed. When he remained standing, she added, "It's been a long day. Now you come lie down."

Lois

Only the rooms at the front had transoms, with pieces of what her mother called church glass, rectangular in shape, blue, green and red to match the panel in the window overlooking the street. While she was still a child, working the lever on the transom, one of the pieces had dropped into the hall, and she and her sisters had thought they would use the broken chips to look at an eclipse of the moon—in case there was one. There hadn't been, and the hole remained, like a piece of clear glass in the transom. Through it she could hear, as if she put her ear to the hole, the voice of Boyd.

"Wake Before Bomb! Lindbergh's over the Atlantic," he said in that eager boyish way that could be in such a short time so tiresome. Had either of them ever gotten off that porch? What had he said? "I'll tell you what I'll do. I'll let you kiss her yourself." Did either of them think he'd ever had her? She hadn't known Boyd as a child, but she was certain he brought in caterpillars to frighten little girls and was one of the first to suggest spinning the bottle. More than the kiss, what he liked was the effect. This little girl he *did* have understood him so well it was impossible to say why she had married him. Or had she? Wasn't that just the latest of his tiresome stunts? To get them all together, then startle them with his child bride? So different from, and yet in so many ways like, her father: living by himself so he could believe the stories about himself. People were always looking for complicated reasons to explain a person like Boyd, when a simple explanation would probably do. They simply hadn't grown up. They were still little boys at heart. They would live if they could arrange it in rooms full of other people's clothes which they would slip on, then run downstairs and startle the grownups. And if they happened to live long enough, like her father, what was childish about them would be said to be a virtue, and the family could be proud of what they had been privately ashamed of for years. A ninety-year-old boy, her father was now a historical monument.

Just before Christmas people from the museum at the University sent a man over with apparatus that recorded in his own voice all the nonsense he had been talking for years, so that there might never be an end to it. He was part of a collection that included ox shoes, strips of harness eaten by grasshoppers and their own copy of the Montgomery Ward catalogue. She hadn't complained, because the same people had taken the muzzle-loading rifle that she would have paid to get out of the house. "Mrs. McKee," Mr. Longacre had said, "if anything of interest turns up—" and it had. They not only took it off her hands but put it in the case with a card beneath it, so that her father could be taken over on Sunday afternoons to see how important he was. Never once did he ask what such things were doing under glass. Such a fuss had been made about his age and tall stories that he probably saw himself propped like a wooden Indian in the corner with his squirrel rifle and Davy Crockett hat. If President Eisenhower asked him to come to Washington and receive a gold medal or a plaque, it would never cross her father's mind to ask why. He agreed with what he heard, and if he didn't hear it, he thought of it himself.

But all he wanted—all any of them wanted—was history of a certain order, like the scalps hanging in the room across the hall from her father's things. Did anybody ask about the wife of the man whose scalp it was? Did anybody ask—after he was scalped —who had taken care of his family? She would like that little ninny to take down on his tape what it was like to have a father who had never been more than a piece of history. Who wore, from the time she could remember, that silly drayman's hat on his head, with the badge that made him think he had some position of some kind. There had never been a baggage wagon, with the hotel right there on the tracks, yet her father kept for years a horse named Belle just in case he might need a wagon, and the horse did nothing but graze around the tree all day and then eat oats and kick the stall boards all night. Her mother said the horse went crazy like all of them. Lois couldn't remember her father ever having harnessed her up.

And when they talked about the wonderful life of her father she would like to tell them about Mr. Bickel, dangling on the wires where a train had tossed him, with Mr. Foley's two dogs licking the blood off the ditch grass beneath. She would like to mention the case of Mr. Hawley, the salesman from Sioux City who slept in the lobby with his bare face on the platform of the lobby scales. Weighing his brains, as he himself liked to say. When her mother got him up in the morning the pattern of the scales would be on his face like a waffle iron, with sometimes a letter or two of the word in the center of it. He was a nice man, he loved children, and he saved for them for weeks at a time the spools he used to demonstrate the Singer sewing machines. She would like to put on the tape when they asked her for intimate details about her father how he loved to hone like a barber the blade of his knife on his plate, and use the prong of his fork to open the hole in the can of milk. It didn't matter if the hole was open or not. All the forks had their prongs bent, just the way all the plates had sandpaper edges since he had made them into honing stones for his knives. The clock that woke them all up every morning he would take from the stove, wind like a toy, set the alarm, then leave in the room where their mother slept. One of the bells had been lost before Lois was born, and as it ran down, it made the sound of a fly trapped in a bottle, the way they were all trapped in his life. The last straw being they were girls, all four of them, with nothing to do day and night but wash and dry their own dishes, wash and dry their own laundry, and wash and dry their own bed sheets, since traveling men no longer stopped in Lone Tree.

What kept her mother, all those years, from going mad? She just closed her eyes to it, the way she drew the blinds at the kitchen windows, and worked all day at the sink, humming hymns to herself and facing the calendars. She couldn't bear to look out in any direction and see nothing but the empty plain, or after it had snowed or rained a little, the tangle of buggy tracks in the road. In the winter the rails shining like sleigh tracks and in the spring the snow first melting on the manure pile that Belle always kept fresh. The kitchen, where they all lived, steaming with the wash that would freeze on the line if they hung it out, her father's change of underwear drying over the back of one of the lobby chairs. Long underwear, summer and winter, so that she never once saw more of her father than the skin at his wrists or the whiteness of his neck when he took off his shirt. When she read about the Pole and people locked in the ice and Commander Byrd at Little America, she knew just as well as the explorers what it was like. No, she knew better. None of *them* had been born and raised in it. Nevertheless, hadn't they all done pretty well? Violet dead, but in her sleep, Edna married to all those oil wells, and Maxine—well, Maxine had Etoile, as if to make the best out of the worst situation.

Although Lois had been partial to Etoile as a child, when she was gawky and would sit staring at her, the likeness didn't show till her teens: a little more full-bodied due to the way they fed and cared for children nowadays, and more relaxed. She was not without talent (there was the year she made pastel drawings of puppies and kittens), but Lois didn't like the dreamy, lazy way she mooned around. Maxine didn't care so long as she was occupied. Just to keep her occupied Lois would pick her up when she went shopping and they would have a soda at Miller & Paine's, then go buy her a purse or hat or something that was smart. Her mother had the worst possible mail-order taste. People who didn't know the family very well just naturally assumed Etoile was *her* daughter. It had been fun for them both to see how she looked in some of the dresses, more than thirty years old, that Lois had never thrown away. Hipless things with flowers pinned to the shoulder in which the child looked like what McKee called a vamp. For most of one spring she practically lived in Lois's closet, so that she smelled, as Maxine said, of nothing but camphor and moth balls. McKee had the jolt of his life, he said, when he came in from the garage and found Etoile there at the door wearing one of Lois's old dresses and hats. Something unheard of, McKee had actually asked her to stop play-acting and go take it off. It happened to be a dress that dated from the summer when everything had happened—or when nothing had happened, depending on how you felt. The organdy print had taffy stains on it that would never come off.

In the bed at her side she felt little Gordon stir, and put her hand out to touch him. "You asleep or awake?"

"I got to you-know," he said.

How did she know that was a lie?

"You can you-know in the potty," she said. "You're not going down the hall at this time of night." He smacked his lips, a sign that he was mad.

"Potties are for babies," he said. He didn't say girls, but that was what he meant.

"Your great grandfather used a potty," she said, remembering too late how he had used it.

"He used it as a hat!" said the boy. "He didn't use it for you-know-what."

That terrible story, how her father had found *his* father propped up in bed, mad as a coot, with the flowered nightpot balanced on his head, all the ashes, cigars and filth it contained spilled down his front into his lap. Whether one believed the story or not, her father always gave the impression that he thought it a fine way to go—as he said—and would do it himself.

"Gordon—" she began, but he cut her off by rolling out of bed and running to the window. She had drawn the blinds so the room would be dark enough to sleep in, and she could see him between the blind and the light, his right hand dipped into the crotch of his pajamas, standing straddle-legged just like McKee. "Gordon!" she said, in a different voice, since he knew very well what he was doing. One reason little boys liked to play with themselves was that they didn't like to play with little girls. In Mexico, where he did it just to annoy her, she had blurted out, "All right, just play with yourself and see what happens when you grow up."

"What will happen?" he had said. Interested.

"You will learn soon enough," she said, "and

when you do don't come whimpering to me."

"Will I be like Bud?" he had said, and she had been speechless.

He turned from the window at the front. "Is there nothing on the moon to shoot, Grandma?"

She let her arm fall back across her eyes. She knew that he was standing there, thumb-sucking, his eyes on the moon and not even listening, yet he could ask her questions that would keep her awake all night. Did one know one's own children or people one had lived with all one's life? Just before locking up the house she had run around emptying the wastepaper baskets, since she had read somewhere that fires seemed to start there all by themselves. In McKee's she had found his newspaper, as usual. Out in the yard at the incinerator, she had stooped to hold a match to one corner and saw that parts of the page had been clipped out. What parts? It proved to be the obituary page. She had asked Maxine to save her that paper in order to see who had died, but it had not been anybody in particular. Just two men about McKee's own age. After that she checked to see what he had clipped out. In that chair she had bought him to relax his heart he would stretch out every evening and read little more than the obituary notices, then clip some of them out. She would have said nobody gave it less concern than McKee, and there he was, almost obsessed with it.

"Darling," she said, for no particular reason, and slipped out of the bed to go and stand beside the boy. Was it the thought of Santa Claus that made

the plain seem covered with snow? The light daz-
zled, gleaming on the tin roofs, the broken bottles
along the tracks, and it seemed to be trapped like
spun sugar in the boy's silken hair.

"Isn't it beautiful, darling?" she said, controlling
an impulse to hug him, and he wagged his sober
little head, said,

"Sweet Jesus, you bet."

With the greatest effort she controlled the impulse to grab and shake him. Were they little mon-
keys? Mimicking everything they heard? Would
she now be hearing that awful "Sweet Jesus" for
the rest of the year? She just stood there, she did
not touch him or dip her hand into his hair as he
expected, and sensing that *he* might be losing something—he came to her. First his arm crooked about
her legs, then his head inclined on her thigh, turning so that she felt the warmth of his breath. If she
had any pride at all, she would reject him, but his
beauty made her helpless. What did she care about
the evil in his little heart? The long twisted lashes
of his eyes still made some people think he was a
girl if they saw him in his nightgown, or any of
those pictures showing just his head. Did he know
what he was doing? Much more than McKee ever
did. On how many occasions, rolling his sleepy
head, he had given her a bite on the breast or the
lips, and at the same time such a look as the serpent
must have given Adam, sucking in his lower lip as
if to taste the forbidden fruit. He knew exactly
how to make her suffer like those lovers in the
oriental operas where they screamed, swooned,

took draughts of poison or fell on knives. How she used to smile at such goings on.

She let her hand drop to his head, the knobs at the back that gave the barbers such trouble, and without speaking, his head on her hip, she drew the blind on the moonlight, then stooped and kissed him. He tasted, as she knew he would, of the licorice cigarettes she had warned him not to eat.

McKee

McKee had sat for what almost seemed forever in the swivel chair without rollers, gazing at the chipped green-and-gold scene painted on the door of the office safe. A crouching Indian maiden bathed herself in a mountain waterfall. Behind it loomed a snow-capped peak, and on the shore, where it seemed to be evening, a young warrior was returning from the hunt. Perhaps the moonlight made it look better than it really was. Except for the Lone Wolf in his room at home behind a sheet of glass that made it hard to look at, McKee had never looked at a work of art so carefully before. The waterfall, chipped as it was and worn away where they leaned on the safe to dial it, seemed as real to McKee as—if not wetter than—those beer ads showing the mountain water the beer was made of pouring right at you over the rocks. On the right-hand corner, scratched into the paint, were the numerals McKee took for the combination, but he had no desire to open that door, only to look at it. More doors had already been opened than he'd ever be able to shut.

Above the safe hung a mirror so flecked and tarnished McKee had first thought it was some sort of picture. Part of the moonlit lobby was darkly reflected in it. In Polk, McKee had sat right behind a black boy who had been in the same grade for three years, but in different seats, because he couldn't seem to learn fractions. He made crayon drawings of wild horses in moonlit scenes. These horses were the most lifelike creatures McKee had ever seen. He just sat and drew horses, by the hour, the way McKee did pen exercises, and the top of his desk was a drawing of Custer's Last Stand. Even his color, in McKee's opinion, wouldn't stop a talent like that, and for years he had expected to hear about him. He looked for his horses when he glanced through the *Saturday Evening Post*. His name was La Rue Gater, so they naturally called him Alley, but McKee never saw that name once he had left the school. What had happened? Something people referred to as luck. Had McKee had it? Had a person like Boyd lacked enough of it? McKee had given this problem some thought since an old friend who had been reasonably lucky, hale and hearty with everything to live for had been in one of those planes that fell into the Grand Canyon, his life snuffed out. McKee had a post card from him the day he left. "See you on Monday," he had said, but little did he know. Did anybody? That was the point. Those scientific fellows who knew everything calculated that what happened just couldn't happen. It was like two gnats, as McKee had read somewhere, colliding with each other over the state of Texas. It was just that unlikely, and yet it had happened. What they call an accident.

Until that event McKee had taken the word in his stride, like most people. Then he began to notice how often it turned up. Every day of his life the

papers were full of it. In more cases than he cared
to remember what was described as an accident was
the most important event of a man's life. Loss of
an eye, or a hand, or his wife and his kids, or his
own life. An accident? The word had got to be for
McKee like those they used in invisible advertising;
he didn't know he was seeing it, but it was there all
the time. People took it for granted like the weather
because of something called insurance. If you had
it, that is, the accident made sense. It didn't explain
what had happened, but it paid you for what *had*
happened. McKee had bought a policy to protect
his loved ones in case something might happen to
him, as if the policy would keep something worse
from happening to them. All those children and
grandchildren the policy promised to put through
college and protect from worry and starvation
might be dead the next day in a highway accident.
What troubled McKee even worse was the way they
determined what a loss was worth. One man's eye
was worth fifteen hundred dollars, no matter what
it was he saw through it; whereas one that people
liked to look at was said to be worth several hundred
thousand. What about the eye that hadn't been
insured at all? Over in McCook a grade-school
bus had gone off the road and killed fourteen of
them, and only one turned out to be insured. Did
it mean that thirteen of the children weren't worth
anything? And then Charlie Munger. If he had
raised his gun and leveled it at McKee, which
McKee could well imagine him doing, would the
death of McKee have been an accident? If it was,

then McKee would like to know if there was anything in this world, except insurance policies, that
claimed to make any sense out of life.

In *Life* magazine McKee had seen a picture of a
crowd of people, blurred and faceless, into which a
racing car, like a man-eating shark, had suddenly
dived as if to gobble them alive. That was how it
looked, just the tail fin showing, but in the air over
the heads of the crowd one could see the shoes that
had been on some of the feet. Shot up there like
popcorn, and horrible as it was, McKee found himself wondering what the insurance representative
had made of it. In the old days the pastor or the
priest came around; now this fellow did.

McKee slowly wheeled in the swivel chair, as if
to put such facts behind him. He no more than had
when Boyd called out, "Nighty-night, McKee!"
and McKee replied, "Night, Boyd," as if they had
been sitting in the lobby together. The words
popped right out as if Boyd had given him a clap on
the back. How did he know the squeak in that chair
was McKee? But it was so much like him McKee
hardly knew if he was mad or not. When Boyd
knew he was slipping, first thing he did was trip
the other fellow up. McKee would never forget
that time in New York when they had found Boyd
living up in this attic with the hairpins on the floor
and the pair of silk stockings on the doorknob to
the john. There was nothing in the attic but these
two card tables, one of them with a typewriter on
it, the other with a coffeepot and a piece of dirty
flannel cloth. It looked like a pot holder, but what

it happened to be was a ball player's pocket that Boyd had once torn off Ty Cobb's pants. "I'm putting it in a book," Boyd had said when asked. "Small limited edition. Each book will have a piece of Ty Cobb's pocket and Gordon Boyd's ass." That was how he could turn your advantage against you, and when he said, "Nighty-night, McKee," it was because he had felt himself slipping all evening, and at one point he had almost fallen on his face. When Mrs. McKee tripped and fell in his arms, McKee thought Boyd would be next. But was it Mrs. McKee propped on his arms or was it the girl, Etoile, who looked so much like her it often gave McKee a start? Was it the one he had kissed or the one he hadn't who scared him like that?

McKee would like to ask him—when things quieted down—if he happened to remember Irene Merkel, a girl who was quicker on fractions than he had been. If he did, then McKee would just mention that she had been a passenger in that airplane where a kid who wanted to blow up his mother had planted a bomb. Irene Merkel, the brightest girl in Polk, married and the mother of three fine children, snuffed out along with twenty-five other people this kid had never known. What was the connection? McKee would like to hear what he had to say. And maybe one thing more if he bit on that one; McKee had a clipping in his wallet mentioning the fact that the Polk grade school had been torn down. Thought of it the moment Boyd mentioned the fire escape where they used to come out and clean the erasers. The way Boyd described it you could see that he thought it was still there. Likely to be forever. McKee didn't have the heart to tell him that the building was gone. Worse than gone. A used-car lot was now in its place. When he saw the clipping, McKee had driven over and stood dumfounded on the corner, watching the paper banners flap in the wind above rows of used cars. Gone. Every single brick of it. The cinder-covered yard, the trees along the walk with the bark worn off where they swung around them, the fire escape, the nurse's room in the annex where Boyd looked for Mrs. Healy's bone hairpins and McKee would swipe a pocketful of the pine tongue depressors he whittled down for his airplane models. In his mind's eye McKee could see it all, but nowhere else. The black stockings on the girls who stepped out on the fire escape to clean the erasers, and the bloomers of the girls who hung by their knees, letting their hair sweep the grass edging the sidewalk. One thing after another, like going through a box of slides, came to his mind. The box of green chalk kept by Mrs. Partridge because white chalk seemed to make her sneeze, but the green chalk left a smear on her nose where she stroked the bruise made by her glasses. In Mrs. Partridge's class it was Boyd's small voice that gave the pledge to the flag, and his hand, powdered with chalk dust, that McKee could see plainly on the bricks of the wall that was no longer there.

Forgetting where he was, McKee pushed up from the chair and thumped his head. Back in the seat, he took off his hat and examined the crown. Where it was dented, cobwebs. He rocked back in the chair and peered over his head at a pigeonhole rack for mail and keys. There were no keys, but in one of the slots were several pieces of mail. McKee could make out the corner of a calendar, rolled up in a tube. Who was crazy enough to send the old man a calendar? He tipped forward to see if the stamp was one that might appeal to little Gordon, flicking at the corner of the tube with the rim of his hat. Two of the letters in the slot dropped into his lap. The writing was faded, but he could plainly see the two-cent stamps. When could you mail a sealed letter for two cents? In the *Reader's Digest* McKee had read of letters lost for forty years that one day turned up. Just like that. Wouldn't it give a man a jolt? What if it said, "Come home, all is forgiven," just forty years too late? He held one of the letters into the moonlight and strained to read the writing. The ink had faded. He fished in his pockets for a match. The letter in his lap, the flame cupped in his hand, the name was even more familiar than the writing.

MISS LOIS SCANLON
LONE TREE
NEBR.

That's what it said. In the top left corner before the flame went out he saw the signature of Boyd. The match head went on glowing until McKee, crouched above it as if to protect it, felt that disturbance that just might be his heart. Came on him when he stooped to tie his shoes, buttoned the flap on little Gordon or strained at the stool. Rocking back, McKee noticed how the pressed-tin ceiling seemed to have a roll in it, and certain he might be dying, he relaxed. He lay back with his head on the counter, his feet propped on the safe. In his hand he gripped the letter, and he thought of himself not at all—no, his thought was where, in the event of his death, the letter should be found. The pigeonhole, three feet overhead, was out of his reach. If found on his body—what, in God's name, might it contain? He struck another match—did he intend to burn it? No, just to peer at the date on the postmark. May something or other, 1920. That was the month McKee had written to Boyd, announcing his great good fortune, and Boyd, which was not his custom, had answered him. In the dark corner of his mind where he buried bones and piled ashes, a matchlike flame flickered for a moment, then went out. But it was light enough for McKee to see:

> *It isn't often that a plain simple young man wins the hand of the only creature on God's green earth. Let me know if the arm and leg go along with it.*
>
> *Yr. friend*
> GORDON

McKee had burned that letter piece by piece in the flame of one of his egg incubators, recognizing in it a young man deranged by jealousy. He destroyed it to protect Boyd from himself. But what, in God's name, had he written to her?

McKee sat there, the letter in his lap, gazing at

the Indian maiden splashed with mountain water, indifferent to the fact that he might be a dying man. He was in one of those planes, cruising over the canyon, and a stranger had approached him with a letter on which was written *To whom it may concern*—nothing more. Was it better to open the letter and know in advance what you were in for, or to slip it in your pocket, where, with other effects, it might be found? On the inside of his coat, where he slipped the letter, he found a fresh cellophane pack of cigars, and with the patience he always seemed to lack, carefully opened it. The smell of the wrapper seemed to revive him; with the last match in the pack he lit the cigar, and on the cover read, as he had a thousand times,

CLOSE COVER BEFORE STRIKING MATCH

Had he ever? No, he never had.

Boyd

Someone taller than Boyd had slept with his feet through the bars at the foot, his toes rubbing the wall, and the knob on the post was green where he had hung his coat. The same man perhaps had stood on the bed and used a newspaper to kill the mosquitoes, the streaks crisscrossing on the ceiling wallpaper. A piece of the window, the tuck in the curtain like a cobweb in the moonlight, looked in the bureau mirror as bright as a hole opening on the sky. Up there, as in a deep freeze, the *Spirit of St. Louis* was suspended, a star of Bethlehem over the stable of Lone Tree. In this manger the dreams were crossed. The child who thought he was Davy Crockett, the man who thought he was Buffalo Bill, the one who thought he was Santa Claus, and the fellow who merely thought, and thought, and thought. Morgenstern Boyd, the man who still had everything to live for, since everything worth living for had eluded him.

He could hear her finger nervously twisting a strand of hair. On that hand her ring, the one she still wore, a girl's ring with the cheap red stones that once brightened the dashboards of the sporty cars. The whole friggin business of the good old days she liked to believe were lost and gone forever, like Irwin, were there on her finger in a ring that would not slip off. How did she feel back home? "Tired. I never got enough sleep." How did Boyd feel? Asleep. Had he ever been awake? "Gordon," McKee had said, "habits you acquire as kids tend to stick, don't you think?" Walter McKee with his spaced front teeth, his licorice-dirty face, his Sherwin-Williams paint hat resting on his ears, had the habit of peeing in the dust under porches and spying on Boyd, with his tapeworm, his talent for farting and his habit of walking on air, water or anything else guaranteed not to support him, before the bugging eyes of McKee. "There's people here who don't know you as well as I do and how you have to make a fool of yourself since you've made such a mess of your life." Amen. A sound like hymnbooks closing, and Boyd had raised his eyes to see pity, like an illness, on the face of Maxine, and wonder, like a drug, on the face of her daughter, a white goddess with green eyes and a golden smile. Helen in the tent of a stuttering Achilles. Was the potion love or pity?

"You sound different," she said, "when you know people are listening. You think they are?"

"I thought you were," he replied. "How do I sound now?"

"When his feelings were hurt, Irwin would get out of bed and try to sleep in his friggin Eames chair. He loved that chair. It hurt him worse than I did."

"It's beginning to hurt me too," said Boyd. "You told me that once."

"Were you in the war? Irwin was in the war where he met this cat who opened the freight cars full of gassed people. Know what he found? Most of them making love. Irwin said copulating in order to spare my feelings. He didn't want me to think that what we were doing was the same as being scared to death and copulating. This cat told him they were all the sort of people who would have died rather than admit it. If they hadn't been gassed, they would have died of shame. They had to be sure they'd never see each other or they wouldn't have made love."

Boyd had raised on his elbow to look at her face.

"Irwin used to say he couldn't tell what I was thinking unless it was dark. Is it too friggin light?"

"What you're saying," said Boyd, "is not what you're thinking."

Over his shoulder she looked at the moonlight. "That poor friggin girl," she said, "in all that goddam light with one just like you."

"She's a lucky girl," said Boyd, "and I envy him."

"I know," she said. "If you had it to do over, you still wouldn't do it. Not in the moonlight. Sweet Jesus, how friggin dark would it have to get? You and Irwin in the corner talking about the good old lays." She rocked her head from side to side on the pillow. "What's that bird? The one who isn't with it?"

"The dodo?"

She shook her head. "The dodo wasn't. This one isn't right now."

"The whooping crane," he said, "isn't with it much."

"I dig them," she said. "Sweet Jesus. You think I

dig them because they're so friggin hopeless, or so full of hope?"

The blind puffed from the window, and Boyd lay there, his eyes closed, as he had once stretched on a trestle and let twelve freight cars back over him. Not to eat, not for love, but because Sancho McKee, knee-deep in creek water, stood directly beneath bearing witness to the deed as done. Cinders from the locomotive had sprinkled his hair. In McKee's pocket, doorknob green, was the watch with the compass in the stem-wind, held in trust in case Boyd should come to an untimely end. Had he? To write a book on that subject Boyd had gone to Mexico. *Hope and Hopelessness*, or the friggin schizoid life of Morgenstern Boyd. A character named Kopfman had shaped, like a dream of hopelessness—but not quite. The green stain of hope had rubbed off on his companion Morgenstern. The characters showed a tendency to merge that was troubling. Who was speaking? Who was living or dying? It was hard to tell. Did Boyd dig them because they were so friggin hopeless, or so full of hope?

"Daughter," he said, "would you like to hear the story of my life?"

"Didn't I hear it? The friggin self-unmade man, and all that jazz?"

"I have the text before me, Daughter. If what you dig is something hopeless . . ."

"How hopeless can you get, Big Daddy?"

"Should I read?" She did not reply. On the ceiling, as if some small fry below played with the moonlight with a pocket mirror, a light danced.

"In the middle of life Morgenstern stood waiting his turn at a knothole provided for those who watch other men work. The scaffolding over his head collapsed, trapping three other idlers besides himself, one dying on the spot, another suffering only minor injuries. Morgenstern and the young man who stood ahead of him at the knothole occupied adjoining beds in the accident ward. The young man, Hyman Kopfman, was given a fifty-fifty chance to live. Morgenstern, being twenty years older and only half alive to begin with, was expected to hang on only until complications set in. They nearly always set in in a man of his type. In the locker at the foot of his bed was the suit in which he had been delivered, as the doctor said, like a sack of crushed ice. It had been cleaned and pressed, just as if he would live to wear it again.

"Hyman Kopfman was a small rabbit-faced young man of foreign extraction, as he said himself. At an early age he had been brought to America. With three brothers and a club-footed elder sister who did typing, he lived in an apartment six flights up from the street. A small detail, but important, since Hyman Kopfman seldom got to the street. His health was frail. Both his lungs and his heart were weak. He passed the day in the apartment, wearing the chestful of clothes his father had left them and his mother couldn't bring herself to throw out. They dated from the turn of the century, if it could be said to have turned in Vienna. French braces, pearl-gray spats, celluloid cuffs and collars, and a silver-headed cane concealing a sword in the shaft. If Hyman had worn such things in the street, which happened to be a tough one, the boys would have taken him into an alley and left him stripped. But up in that apartment it was all right. His mother did sewing, and Hyman Kopfman could sit at her side holding the material, with a row of the straight pins in his mouth. Frail and sickly as he was, something hard to explain made him likable. His father had it, but only his mother knew what it was. Hopelessness. It was this that made him lovable.

"That was his story, but Morgenstern got awfully tired of some parts of it. Kopfman talked about himself as if he were somebody else. He was apt to repeat certain things time and time again. He would sit in bed, his head in his hands, like a man contemplating a crystal ball, seeing within it the things he talked about. Morgenstern saw little about him that was lovable. His skin was a pale doughy color, and his blood count was so bad that when he got excited his gums would bleed. Thin streaks of red, like veins in marble, would show on his chalky teeth. With a tongue like a piece of flannel he would lick them off. His eyes were large, almost goatlike, and there were times Morgenstern would have sworn they gave off light, like certain fish. The pupils dilated peculiarly. In spite of all that, and considerable dandruff which flecked the collar of his pajamas, there was something appealing about his hopelessness. Take the way he passed the time calculating what he would do with one leg and ten thousand dollars, or twenty thousand and no legs at all. It took something like talent. One that Morgenstern, for instance, lacked.

"For example, Hyman Kopfman had only one foot but he sent out both of his shoes to be polished; at some expense he had the heels and soles replaced. In the metal locker at the foot of his bed hung the pin-stripe suit, as if any day he might slip it on again. It was strange behavior for a person with one leg. Not that he wanted very much from life—no, hardly more than most people had. All he really seemed to want was the empty sort of life Morgenstern had lived. To have slept with a woman, fought in a war, won or lost something in a raffle —to have had memories, that is, to look back to. Somehow Hyman Kopfman had picked up the notion that life was hardly worth living, but it was no consolation, since he had lived so little of it. He had picked up the tab, so to speak, without the fun. He always used the word 'fun' since he thought that was what Morgenstern had had.

"His idea of life being what it was, Morgenstern found it hard to understand why he hadn't reached out and put his hands on it. But he hadn't. No, and it led to bitterness. Who did he blame his troubles on? America. Yes, he said, back in Vienna he would have taken life as it came, but what was America if it wasn't promises? And what were promises if a man couldn't live it up? Where any man might win the jackpot or be president of something, the man who didn't had this fever in his blood. It was this, he seemed to think, that was killing him. The collapse of the scaffolding on his head had been the climax, nothing more, of Hyman Kopfman's dream of America. In the long run what did it do but fall on you.

"It did Morgenstern no good to reason with him. Hyman Kopfman's gums would bleed, his eyes would dilate in their peculiar manner, and he would long for what he called the good old days. What had been good about them? Well, it was hard to say. He had passed his time at a window, as he later did at a knothole. Right below this window was a private park. There were gravel paths, shady trees, benches to sit on and flowers to smell. That was important. The flowers could be smelled but not seen. It just so happened that the people who used this park were blind. From Hyman Kopfman's window, however, it was hard to notice this. The only thing that seemed unusual was how quiet it was. Nobody laughed. Nor were the loud voices of children heard. No one came to this park to fly a kite or bounce a ball or skip a rope or play a game of hide-and-seek behind the trees. There was no need, of course, to hide from anyone. You could be right there in the open and remain unseen. There were always flowers, since nobody picked them, there were always birds, since nobody killed them, and one day Hyman Kopfman, wearing the pearl-colored spats, the striped banker's pants and the celluloid cuffs, stepped into the garden and walked about with his silver cane. Nobody raised an eyebrow when he passed, or noticed whether or not his gums seemed to bleed. Life had never been so pleasant, in Hyman Kopfman's opinion, than the spring he passed as a blind man, seated on a bench or tapping his cane along the gravel paths. Then one day—"

"Daddy, you hear something?"

"—it was toward evening. He sat in his customary arbor, lifting a scab with a pair of nail tweezers, when the man across the path sucked air with a hiss through his teeth. Hyman Kopfman caught the birdlike glint in one eye. He wore a skullcap, and fastened to his cane was a hook to which a tin cup was attached. Kopfman had dropped a coin into it as he had left."

He paused there. Was she listening?

"You through, Daddy?"

"Be patient, Daughter. We are as good as through with poor Kopfman. The case of Morgenstern, however, is even more strange. The week that Hyman Kopfman took a turn for the worse, Morgenstern took a turn for the better. He had been failing. For no apparent reason he began to improve. Now that poor Kopfman's pulse grew weaker, that of Morgenstern grew stronger. He sat propped up in bed with the look of a man who would soon be up. Here you had Morgenstern, with nothing to live for, day by day getting better, and Hyman Kopfman, who hungered for life, daily getting worse. Not wanting to live, apparently, was still not wanting to die. You might say that Morgenstern waxed better in spite of himself.

"Not that Kopfman took this reversal lying down. He snickered openly the day that Morgenstern stood on his feet. He never tired of making slurring remarks. He referred to Morgenstern's arms as chicken wings. He called attention to his imminent pregnancy. Nor did Morgenstern's wide bottom, where so much of his top seemed to have settled as if it had melted, escape Hyman Kopfman's critical eye. All it seemed to do, however, was speed Morgenstern's recovery and hasten Kopfman's pitiful end. It became a contest of sorts as to whether Morgenstern would get back on his feet before Hyman Kopfman lost another limb or managed to die. In this curious battle, however, Kopfman's greater will power showed to his advantage, and he deteriorated faster than Morgenstern was able to improve. He managed to die so quietly that Morgenstern didn't know about it till morning, when he woke up and saw that Kopfman was not in the bed. That afternoon, the day before his release, Morgenstern suffered a relapse, and two days later he was moved on a stretcher to the hopeless ward. How explain it? Had what killed Kopfman kept Morgenstern alive? He had been coming along just great—"

Did she rise on her elbow to speak or to look at his face? Her own was cheese-green in the moonlight, one strand of her hair twisted. "I got news for you, Daddy—" she said, but Boyd never heard it. The explosion seemed to be in the window where she put out her head like a target, and said, "Sweet Jesus, that the bomb?"

Boyd was there, his head beside her, just in time to see the team, the buggy lurching, careen around the corner as if being chased by a pair of ghosts, one a little crippled, the other like Cupid, with a quiver of arrows on his back. Down the hall at their back the voice of McKee cried "Lois! Lois!" just as Colonel Ewing, one hand to his heart, rose from behind the railroad embankment and blew a long silent blast at the face of the moon.

Lois

Sometimes her mother, who feared nothing, would wake from her sleep when the curtains stirred and sit bolt upright, sniffing the air for smoke. What was there, Lois had wondered, that frightened her in the scent of smoke? The smell of it was always there, trapped in the rooms or in the folds of the yellow curtains, and it was never necessary to sit up in bed and sniff for it. But her mother did. And nothing would persuade her to stop. In the cool of the night, as if a voice had spoken, up she would sit, sniff the air like a hound, then roll from the bed and pad around the halls looking for the fire. As children they had all believed she was scared to death she might find it; but now Lois knew differently. Her mother left the bed in search of it. Just the way her daughter, lying rigid as a plank, lay awake half the night waiting for something to happen, while her husband patted her shoulder and assured her that nothing would. But it was not the smoke that awakened her mother any more than fear of darkness awakened her daughter. No, the smoke and the darkness were merely as big and vague as their terror—not that something might happen, but after waiting so long it might not.

Trapped in the hotel, her mother had waited all her life for smoke to become fire, just as Lois had

waited for the masked killer to reveal himself. Then
she would do what she had put off doing, what they
had all put off doing until nothing they did made
any sense. That crazy boy had reached that point
when he just turned on his heel and started shooting
people: if she feared him—and she did—it was because she understood him so well. The way little
Gordon in one of his tantrums would run wild
around the house shooting off his cap pistols and
meaning every word of it when he said, "Bang!
Bang! You're dead!" Oh, she understood it so well
that she felt bewitched as she had this morning,
when her father came in for his breakfast, and some
hand other than her own seemed to crack the eggs
in the skillet and not, one after the other, over his
head. It was not an impulse which she was able to
resist, she was simply no longer clear about the
orders she followed. If she did not break the eggs
over her father's head or pour coffee down the
back of McKee's shirt collar, it was because she had
imagined doing it for so long it was as good as done.
What she wanted was something more expressive
than that. That was what that young delinquent in
his simple-minded way had stumbled on: one way
to impress on people how he felt was just to murder
them. The one advantage that Gordon Boyd had
had over them all from the very beginning was
that he *might* do something—or that he might not.
That had brought him back here with that young
woman just to see the shocked expressions on their
faces, as he had managed just a few months before
by squirting pop into the bull's face, and as he

would always manage, since all they did was sit around and wait for what he might do next.

She did not awake—as she said later—and make her way like a sleepwalker to the window. On the contrary, she had never been so wide awake. Who else had heard the creak of that buggy crossing the tracks? A sound she knew from her childhood, through this same window, when the Jewel's Tea wagon would rock on the tracks, the bell would tinkle, and her mother would say, "Tell him your mother will be down in a minute," since she might be ironing in her slip when he arrived. Then she would buy coffee and spices, whether they were needed or not, just to have somebody to talk to about the weather or Halley's comet or the end of the world that people in Chapman had sold their shops to be ready for. From beneath her pillow, where she had hidden it, she withdrew the pistol with its single cartridge and came to the window where the curtains were pinned back. Nothing. Had her father's madness caught up with her? A faint clopping, like the background sounds of little Gordon's TV programs, led her to stick her head out of the window just as the heads appeared. Mules, almost the color of their shadows, one with a hat propped between his ears, walked from the door of the stable—or was it from behind it? Hitched to a buggy, the wheels turning so slowly the spokes cast a blur of shadows, with one figure on the buckboard and another seated at the rear. The mules turned, coming toward her, before she saw that there were four feet on the buckboard, although the wide-brimmed hat seemed to shade only one head. Behind them Bud, seated on the tailboard, one arrow glinting in the quiver on his back. What time was it? She drew in her head to look at her watch. A quarter past twelve or just about three? She put out her head to let them know that not all their elders were asleep just as the mules and the buggy passed below. In the shadow of the buckboard, a white object caught her eye. A sack?

"You kids sure it's a dog?" Bud said. Otherwise she might not have known it was that ridiculous beast.

She watched Calvin turn on the buckboard, the girl's arms still around his neck, and whistle softly, the one thing he could do.

What came over her? Her doctor would probably say something or other had triggered the release of all her pent-up fears. McKee would probably think the events of the evening had stirred her up a little and she had been sleepwalking. What did she think? She had never been so wide awake. *That* was the trouble. If the only way to leave an impression was to do something crazy like Boyd, she would do it —she would leave them with one they would never forget. In order to properly grip the pistol she had to rest the barrel on the window, and while she was groping with both hands for the trigger it went off. The kick shook it from her hands and it fell to the floor, bruising her foot, but she felt nothing with the explosion ringing in her ears. As if the pupils of her eyes had widened, she saw the mules rear, the one with the hat looking like a horse on a circus poster, then each got four feet on the ground and went off. She saw the girl, sprawled on the seat, gripping the iron rail of the buckboard just as the mules went around the corner and along the tracks. She did not see Calvin. No, she only heard his voice. He was screaming "Whoa!" without the slightest gibber on the *whhhhh*. Did she hear, or imagine she heard, the hoarse bark of her father? Dust, just the taste of it, like the scent of smoke in the curtains, rose from where the team kicked it up, one wheel of the buggy plowing a furrow so deep the soil looked dark.

"Lois!" she heard McKee calling. "Oh, Lois!" It calmed her to hear how excited he was himself. She stood at the window, her gaze across the room to where the child with eyes like lanterns gazed at her with fear and admiration for the first time in his life.

"Lie there till Grandmother tells you to move," she said, and stooped for the gun. The child did not scream or scoot for the door, but sat there as she opened the door and faced McKee. She could not see his face, and he was so winded he couldn't speak. She stepped back—his breath made her wonder how he breathed it himself—and said, "You realize you might have killed yourself."

His head, with the hat loose on it, pumped up and down.

"There's no need to worry," she said, "we just assumed it wasn't loaded," and placed the gun on the night table. When he didn't speak, she said, "Has something happened?"

"He's dead, Lois," he said. Her hand went for the first time to her head, the veil on her hat. What in the world did he see in her face that led him to blurt: "Not *him*, Lois. Your father. Your papa," and put his hand to the elbow of her right arm. "Easy now," he said, "easy, easy now," and stood in the door, his back to the room, while she turned to put something on.

"Grandma," said the child, "which one did you shoot?"

Jennings

Through the dazzle of moonlight like a TV screen, Jennings could see Colonel Ewing blowing on the whistle that only Shiloh could hear. Was that the call of the wild? Not for Shiloh. Jennings caught the prickle of it in his own ears. The Colonel's cheeks, full of soundless wind, made Jennings think of some Pied Piper who had come to whistle out the dead. It gave him the feeling the place was inhabited. At any moment now the shop doors might open, the place come to life. In the weeds beside the stable the water sprinkler was painted with the message: VISIT THE LYRIC TONITE. And why not? If the call was wild enough maybe some of them would.

"Mr. Jennings," said Eileen, "if Grandfather shouts at you, shout right back. If he starts to tell you his story, you tell him yours."

"Yes, ma'am," said Jennings; he watched her pour a cup of coffee and with it held like a lamp, step into the hall. He could see better with the light off than on. In the dark corner, like a part of the stove, the face of the old man who had believed in Santa Claus all his life gleamed like a pot. A sound like a rocking potlid escaped from his mouth. Was the old man a true believer? Like McKee? When he died, would Santa Claus die?

In Omaha Jennings had an apartment facing the

restaurant where he did most of his eating, a park where he did his loafing and a neighborhood theater that specialized in double-feature westerns. In the movie he kept himself up to date on the Wild West. In the summer the lobby doors stood open and gusts of music, shouts for help and the crackle of whips or gunfire would come into the room where Jennings dozed or slept. Other tenants complained of the racket and the blinking of the lights on the walls and on the ceiling, but without it Jennings found it hard to sleep. A dozer rather than a sleeper, he liked to know that life was going on around him and justice was being done, even though he himself slept. The crackle of gunfire was reassuring, fit into some part of the Wild West dream he was having, and as a rule only silence, which was ominous, woke him up.

The restaurant, open all night, featured pyramids of grapefruit and bananas in the window and a machine that sounded a gong when each guest took his check. Late at night, if his sleep was fitful, Jennings would raise on his elbow at the sound of the gong to see who it was had entered the restaurant. Lonely men, as a rule, who would order coffee, then stir it with a spoon until it was cold. These men contrived to keep a table, or a post, or one of the carts, or part of the counter between them and anybody else. It took some doing, and sometimes they would stand rather than share one of the marble tables. Propped on his elbow, Jennings would observe in how many cunning ways they avoided contact, how they would delay their trips to the men's room, go right or left toward the exit, postpone their second cup of coffee until they were alone at the counter, like cats coming down to a water hole. Did Jennings find it strange? Not exactly. He was gazing down at himself. Since he ate there often, he knew the boys at the counter, referred to them as Roy and Lem, and sometimes chatted with the cashier as he bought and lit his cigar. What was it that drew men toward the light, the warmth and comfort of a cup of coffee, but made it even darker where they lived with themselves? The elbow Jennings leaned on, like his mind, would go to sleep.

Early in December, the previous winter, Jennings had been awakened by a bell that sounded like a railroad-crossing gong. Below his window on the restaurant corner was a Santa Claus. He wore the red suit, the tasseled hat; a tattered beard was twisted in a wire, and on his feet was a pair of three-buckle overshoes. They were so large and so loose that he shifted from foot to foot within them, hardly disturbing the cake of snow on the street. A brass school bell with a wooden handle, hung like a lantern from his mittened hand and tolled like a switch engine idle in the yards. From a cord around his neck he wore a toy drum with a hole in the side for coins; a sign on the drum read:

HELP THE NEEDY

On his way to breakfast Jennings had paused to grope for a coin in his pocket just as an old man, a bum, slipped between him and Santa Claus, pushed his face over the drum and croaked, "That you, Conley?" then shuffled off without waiting for an answer.

Jennings had dropped his coin into the drum and glanced in passing at the shaggy cotton brows over the faded, watery eyes.

"And may the Lord bless you," the voice said, whether that of Conley or somebody else. On the icy crust of one soiled mitten he wiped his runny nose.

In the early evening he was still there, but at ten to nine, peering from his window, Jennings saw him go along, with the bell by the clapper, making his way through the crowd at Douglas Street. He slowed down to accept proffered coins, chuck the chins of small children, then disappear through the swinging doors of the big department store on the corner. In the morning the tolling of his bell woke Jennings up.

On his way to breakfast Jennings dropped another coin and received the Lord's blessing. Did it improve the food? He ate more of it. In the evening from his window, he watched him go up Douglas, bell by the clapper, through the same crowded swinging doors of the department store. He did not come out. Not as Santa Claus. Did he reappear as Conley after a change of clothes?

The problem interested Jennings professionally, and the following night at five to nine he was on the corner when Santa entered the store. He took note of his lean figure, his shuffling walk. He stayed at the entrance till the store closed and the watchman

locked up the building, but no one resembling Santa
Claus came out.

The following evening, as he entered, Jennings
trailed along behind him to the toy department,
where he seemed to feel at home. Seated in a sled
drawn by reindeer, his HELP THE NEEDY drum in
his lap, he sorted out the day's take in coins and
shared the pennies with some of the small fry. He
was still there, part of the scene, when Jennings
took the elevator to the street.

Then in February, while he waited for a cab in
the snow near the Union Station, a bum put out a
mittened hand into which Jennings dropped a coin.
"May the Lord bless you," the fellow croaked, and
Jennings almost cried out, "That you, Conley?"

The mittened hand at his side seemed to grip the
clapper of a heavy bell. But Jennings had not tagged
along to see where he spent the night. In that flop-
house over in one corner would he have seen the
bearded face that looked familiar and wondered
where it was he had heard the hearty laugh? From
some dark corner of the room might have come
the query, "That you, Jennings?" as if he was one
of those big fellows, fond of children, his pockets
full of balloons and barrel candy, wearing a red
flannel suit himself.

A sound, almost a whinny, came from the corner
behind the stove, as if the steam in one of the pots
had wobbled the lid. When Jennings looked he saw
nothing but the soles of the old man's shoes. Then
his head appeared: for a moment he gulped for air
like a fish. Was he answering a call, or breathing his

last? He exhaled the air he had gulped, and his head dropped from sight like a swimmer's.

The screen door opened, and the Colonel's head, the whistle dangling, peered into the room. "It's worth five hundred to me," he said, "to recover that pup." To whom? He did not seem aware of Jennings. "Anybody who knows shit from Shinola knows that dog's worth money," he said. As if Jennings didn't, he pulled back his head, let the screen close. With the whistle in his mouth he blew a long, silent blast.

Through the window Jennings saw the poster peeling on the wall of the stable, where the headless woman, swinging on the trapeze, seemed to come alive. Pale as the moon's shadow, Mr. Momeyer stood below as if to catch her, part of the scene the Lord had intended him for: a clown dressed as a huntsman, his quiver of arrows on his back, about to shoot down the lady on the flying trapeze. In the unearthly light he looked like part of the poster, his face torn away. Behind him, as if laughing at him, a monkey wearing a toy hat pedaled away on the wheelless bicycle. The sight affected Jennings strangely, like those walls exposed where a building was being salvaged, and one could see the wallpaper where hands had soiled it and pictures had hung. Sometimes the plumbing, like the white stitching in a suit of overalls, diagramed the walls like a blueprint, showing how the people had lived and where they had died. Jennings gazed at the poster, as if any minute the rest of the woman would emerge or the head of the lion in the lower corner might roar. Mr. Momeyer, as if stalking something, moved through the weeds behind the stable, and a moment later Jennings saw him cross the tracks.

Ghostly in the moonlight, he saw the mules, then the buggy, rise from the far side of the embankment, the two figures on the buckboard with their heads under one hat. On the tailboard at the rear, legs dangling, sat Mr. Momeyer with his quiver and red hunting cap. That was all Jennings saw: mules and buggy dropped down the slope and disappeared behind the stable. Not inclined to spy on a pair of youngsters, Jennings didn't look again until Mr. Momeyer, right there beneath the window, said, "You kids sure this is a dog?" Then the shot rang out. Jennings ducked, naturally. He threw up one arm to cover his head just as Calvin yelled, "Whoa, whoa!" and all hell broke loose. When he glanced up a cloud of dust was where the team had been, and through the door at the rear he saw the buggy, then Calvin, pass. Jennings had popped up to do something when he saw Mr. Scanlon rise from behind the stove and start for the door.

"That you, Samuels?" he croaked. Jennings opened his mouth to give him an answer, but none came forth. No, he wasn't Samuels—but who was he? Santa Claus, perhaps? Or "That you, Conley?" Whoever Conley might be, Jennings had the feeling he would speak for himself. When confronted by "That you, Samuels?" he would push up his beard and bark, "No!" Did every man wear another man's outfit and walk around in another man's shoes

until the voice cried out "That you, Jennings?" and
he knew who he was?

Raising on his elbow, Jennings peered through the
moonlight and said, "That you, Scanlon?" just as
the old man dropped as if through a hole in the floor.
Hardly a sound, no more noise than if a suit of
clothes had slipped off a hanger, and the man who
had worn them had vanished into thin air.

McKee

At the crack of the gun he rose an inch or two, as if he had been stuck. Time and again McKee had asked himself what he would do when he faced a killer, and time and again he had feared the worst. But he needn't have. He found himself doing just what Mrs. McKee expected, which was just what he had been doing all his life. He was up without a thought for himself, crossing the moonlit lobby to where he tripped on the lobby scales and sprawled on his face. In that position he heard a voice crying "Whoa" and what sounded like scuffling in the kitchen. He might have lain there safe, but he didn't. He got up and yelled "Coming!" just in case his luck would be better if they knew it was him. At the kitchen door, facing the moonlight that streamed in through the back door, he saw Jennings, his suspenders hanging between his legs like a harness, bent over the figure sprawled on the floor. Had Jennings shot him? Should McKee leap forward and seize him? In his underwear he looked like a broad-backed polar bear. What did McKee do?

"Doc," he said, simply, "somebody shoot him?" and without turning Jennings replied, "Mr. McKee, you like to give me a hand?"

McKee was there, bent over feet that might have belonged to anybody till he got his hands on them,

like wheelbarrow handles, and knew they were old
man Scanlon's. There had been times he had to be
lifted out of the bed. He and Mrs. McKee could do
it, since he weighed no more than clothes on a
hanger, with just enough to him to keep the pieces
from falling apart. Was he alive? That was often
hard to tell when he felt his best. McKee took his
legs, Jennings his top, and they went around the
table, the oilcloth shiny where something had spilled
on it, and laid him out on the sofa like parts of a kite.
Right at the last minute McKee almost dropped him.
The legs were stiff.

"He shoot at somebody *else?*" said McKee, and
watched Jennings strike a match, hold it to the lamp
Mrs. McKee had dropped on the floor. It had no
chimney, the flame smoked, but there was more light
than McKee wanted, or Jennings needed, to see that
the old man was dead. "Think he's a goner, Doc?"
he said, since something about it seemed to escape
him. A man dead? One he knew? One who had been
in the family forever? Through the window he
stood facing, the piece of frayed curtain like a veil
around it, he saw the blank, open-mouthed face of
Bud, the lamp flame in his eyes. That adenoidal stare.
McKee had seen it somewhere before. On Boyd.
Snorfeling like that bulldog when he breathed.

"I'm afraid he's a goner," Jennings said. To keep
the flame from smoking he turned it down to a slit
in the lamp.

"Let me get Mrs. McKee," said McKee, and knew
the moment he said it what had been missing from
the old man's kicking off like that. She hadn't been

there. He would feel it when he saw her and broke the news.

He called her name to prepare her for it, and he was up on the landing before it crossed his mind that it must have been Boyd. Boyd depressed by the ruin he had made of his life. Wouldn't it be like him just to come back here and do something like that? The last word, somehow he always had it, and with that wild streak in him you couldn't put it past him. Not him. Not once it had crossed his mind.

"Lois!" he hollered, "Lois!" But not till she opened the door did he realize he might have killed himself running up those stairs.

"There's no need to worry," she said, letting him see the pistol on the lamp table. "We just assumed it wasn't loaded, but we're both all right." That's what she said, but he saw her hand, as if something had struck her, go to the hat that was still on her head and gaze at him just the way she did when she had passed out at the bullfight.

McKee said, "Not him, Lois. Your father. Your papa," and put out his hand to steady her arm. It was as stiff to his touch as the bony leg of the old man.

Then they turned and saw Maxine, like something in a sideshow, draped in whatever it was she slept in, holding in her hand one of Bud's socks with something heavy in the toe.

Without blinking an eye, Lois said, "It's Papa. You want to put something on before you come down?" Then Lois slipped past her, but McKee had to wait till she gave him more room. To include her in, McKee said, "We're going to need some coffee,

Maxine," since the old man had been her papa too. The lower hall was so dark McKee thought the moon had gone down or clouded over, but it was just Jennings in the kitchen door blocking the light. He had slipped on his shirt but not his collar, and seemed to have forgotten about his suspenders, since they hung down in loops around his knees. Why in the world should that make McKee think of Santa Claus? To ease the blow, Jennings said, "Mrs. Mc-Kee, I'm afraid—" then he stepped back to let her by. Without so much as a tremor she crossed to the sofa and put her hand on the old man's forehead. "Father?" she said, as if he was listening, since she never took McKee's word for something important.

"I'm afraid he's passed on, Mrs. McKee," Jennings said, and McKee was grateful: coming from him she was more likely to believe it. The way she did for McKee when he dozed off on the porch, she pulled the old man's pants legs down so they covered his garters, and smoothed his shirt where it pulled out of his pants. It made McKee wonder if she really thought he was dead.

"Not all of us are so fortunate as to go in our sleep," she said.

Did she think he had? McKee could hear Jennings take in air like holding a bladder under water, but that was all. He took it in, he didn't let it out. "That's right, ma'am," he said, which was true enough and didn't make him a liar.

"Matter of fact," said McKee, to reassure her, "I thought he'd dropped off this evening. Didn't you, Doc?"

"Mr. *Jennings*," she said, "didn't you, Mr. *Jennings*."

Jennings thought she was speaking to him, and said, "Why yes, I guess I did, Mrs. McKee. While you people were upstairs, he had trouble with his breathing a time or two."

"You got to hand it to him, though," said McKee. "Today's the thirty-first. He hung on till he was ninety."

She didn't comment on that, and he and Jennings watched her take a piece of the sheet which Maxine had put on the couch and put it over her father, tucking in the ends the way she did to keep the sun off her new porch furniture. Not until she did that was McKee sure he was dead. No air. No, he wouldn't need more of it. In McKee's mind popped that awful story that the old man never tired of telling, of how they ran wagons across the fresh graves to throw the Indians off the scent. They would dig up the corpse just for the boots it might have on.

The screen door opened, and before he stepped in Bud took off his hat. He wiped it off like a kid would, then stood just inside the door with his feet together like the flag was passing by. McKee felt his eyes water. Was it grief or shame? His own hat remained on his head. Fifteen minutes after a death in the family, McKee felt it in his loins, what the Bible called his withers, simply because the one knucklehead in the family took off his hat.

Maxine came in, a towel around her head as if her hair were up in curlers, and McKee knew what she would say before she said it.

"You people sure he's gone? You know how he sleeps sometimes."

"We can be thankful," Lois replied, "that he went so quietly."

Maxine turned to look at McKee, then Bud. "Bud," she said, "what was that infernal racket?"

"Mean the runaway team?"

"The runaway what?"

"Infernal racket," said Bud, "scared the team. Went off with the buggy to the west." He turned and pointed.

"Went off with who?" Maxine said. "Bud, you crazy?"

"That child of yours," said Lois, "is sometimes too clever for her own good."

"That child of mine? I suppose she was alone in the buggy?"

"If it was clever, we know who thought of it," said Lois.

Maxine wiped the towel from her head and held it to her face. She looked up and said, "I swear to God—" but there she stopped at what she saw in the door. Colonel Ewing, with Shiloh's leash in his hand. Hadn't he gone to bed? He didn't look it. He put his face to the screen, said, "Mind my asking what the hell is going on around here?"

"There's been a death in the family, Mr. Ewing," Lois said. "Father died in his sleep."

"Jesus Christ!" said the Colonel. He just stood there.

Maxine cried, "McKee, will you do something?" and McKee did. He turned to look for Jennings and saw Boyd standing in the door to the hall. He was wearing a T-shirt with a hole near the belt, and looking just the way he had looked in New York, only worse. How long had he been there? Long enough to watch them all make fools of themselves?

"Gordon," he said, "there's been a death in the family."

"I know," he said. "It died while we slept."

What did he mean by that? Did he think it was the time for one of his jokes?

"If one doesn't have a family, I suppose one doesn't feel it," Lois said.

Right at his back, her nightgown so thin he thought she might have come down without it, he could see Eileen against the lobby moonlight. She said, "What died in our sleep? Did I miss something?"

"You missed the bomb, my dear," Boyd replied. "The past is dead, long live the past."

"You men!" said Maxine, and started for the door with one foot dragging, as though it were asleep. She had the screen open before McKee could head her off.

"Hold on," he said, but he didn't need to. What did she see? Coming in from the west, in the weeds along the tracks, he could see a team of mules, from the way their ears looked, with Etoile limping behind them, holding the reins. Right behind her was Calvin with what looked like a sack on his back.

"Something new in a buggy ride?" said McKee, since he felt the need to say something, but neither Maxine nor the Colonel, at her elbow, laughed. Was it the mules or the kids that looked so tired? They came along pretty slow, with Etoile limping, to where McKee could see the hat on one mule's head, and from the neck of the other a sign hung dangling on a cord.

"I swear to God—!" Maxine said, then raised the skirt of her apron to her face as if to hide behind it.

"Excuse me," said the Colonel, squeezing by, and dropped down a step below McKee, where he stopped as if he found it hard to get a full breath. McKee thought it was that instead of what he saw that made him moan "Oh my God!" and let himself down as if his heart had failed him. McKee would have sworn they had another funeral on their hands. He looked up to see Calvin, right near the trailer, let the sack he was carrying slide off his shoulder, holding on to it by what turned out to be a dog's rear legs. If that was what you could call the pins Shiloh had to get around on. "Oh my God, my God!" the Colonel moaned, and from the trailer Edna called:

"Oh Clyde, that you Clyde?"

He didn't let out a peep. The way he sagged, McKee thought he was a goner. He could see the ring on his neck from that whistle on its cord and the dark streaks in the back of his shirt he took to be sweat.

"Clyde?" Edna hollered. "You all right, Clyde?"

"For cryin' out loud!" Etoile yelled. "Don't anybody care who just got married!"

"My babies, my babies!" Eileen cried, and in that thing that didn't cover her at all, pushed by McKee and ran barefooted into the yard. She hugged and kissed Etoile, then Calvin, then she almost hugged and kissed Edna who was standing there looking at the dead dog.

McKee hadn't noticed until then one arrow sticking in the thick neck of Shiloh, and another, without the feathers, sticking in his ribs.

"My God, Clyde," Edna said, "the insurance cover something like that?"

Maxine

Sometime between two and three o'clock Maxine had just stopped waiting and begun to worry, the way she did when letting fudge come to a boil. Every ten or twenty minutes she would look at the clock and more than likely shake it, thinking it had stopped, since the hour hand scarcely seemed to have moved. Lying on her back, she could hear a whining sound which she had thought to be in the bedsprings, but proved to be the cars on the highway a mile away. The Youngbloods, who asked Etoile to baby-sit on Fridays, had a dog, Puddles, who they claimed could tell their car from anybody else's just from the way it sounded far down the road. Everybody of course had a remarkable dog, but the more Maxine listened to the sounds on the highway the more she was sure the dog was right. He was listening for *one* car like she was, with snow tires or a loose muffler, and all the other cars simply didn't count. The new McKee station wagon seemed to run without a motor, but Maxine knew, like the Youngblood dog, the sound it made when it turned into the yard. Bud had never fixed the driveway, since they had been waiting for twenty-three years for the city to put in the sidewalk, and Maxine could tell, if she was down in the basement, if it was Bud, McKee, or Mr. Lockwood with his milk wagon from the way it moved in and out of the ditch. She had been tempted to tell Mrs. Youngblood—who mentioned her dog every time she called—that what he did was not so much, since she could do it herself. It was really a sign of how little you knew, instead of how much. Her father dead, her daughter lame, limping in behind a team of runaway mules, her husband, with his bow and arrow, the killer of a dog worth more money than he was. Maxine stood in the door feeling no pain whatsoever, not even in her feet. Was it the new-type aspirin? Or what they called battle fatigue? Roger Lampson had come home with it from Korea, and hour on end, week on week, he sat on the rear porch stoop swatting flies.

The dog Shiloh, with his bashed-in face, one arrow in his neck and another in his ribs, made her think of nothing so much as the horrible new funny valentines. Was there nothing as it should be in this world? Etoile so beautiful people could eat her, but with feet she could hardly walk on, and Calvin so handsome it made girls swoon, but with those pebbles in his mouth. Unless it was Bud, coming in with that gum-ball machine and that red hunting cap on his head. She couldn't imagine him any better—or any worse.

Behind her Lois said, "Before we call anybody, just so we are agreed as to what happened."

"Does anybody have the faintest idea?" said Eileen.

"Father passed away quietly, in his sleep."

"Before we call anybody," said McKee, "we got to connect that phone we disconnected last summer."

Lois said, "Perhaps Omaha. If we're not going to have it all over Lincoln how we brought him out here just to tire him—"

"Omaha?" said Eileen. "Is he dead, or just dying?"

"Doc," said McKee, "you got any suggestions?"

"If you'll excuse me," Mr. Jennings said, "but Omaha and Lincoln—"

"I get it, Doc," said McKee. "Lois, we got to get him somewhere a lot sooner than Omaha or Lincoln. First, that is."

"Know what he'd like?" said Bud. "Know what he'd like the most?" Before Maxine could turn and stop him he said, "What he'd like is to be buried right here in Lone Tree. Right out there under it."

"Bud—" she said.

Lois said, "I believe it's Sunday. Do they do business on Sunday?"

"You die on it, guess they're glad to," said McKee. "Eh, Doc?"

Jennings said, "Mrs. McKee, if I remember correctly, there's a funeral home in Ogallala."

"Think Ogallala," said McKee, "is only eighteen or twenty miles—"

"Ha!" said Etoile.

McKee said, "It's ten to five. We can drive over in about twenty minutes. No use going over till there's some chance of finding 'em up."

"Think it'll take longer than that," said Bud.

"Might in that Hupmobile," said McKee, "but the Buick'll do it in about twenty minutes."

"Would if it was here," said Bud. "Don't happen

to be here. Pair of tired mules take a little longer than that."

Maxine saw McKee lid his eyes as if they hurt.

"I suppose you forgot," she said, "that Calvin and Etoile took the Buick?"

"Took it, sure," said McKee. "Didn't they bring it back?" He turned from the door to look at Etoile, her ankle so swollen it looked like the McLeod child's clubfoot.

"Darling," said Eileen, "you children remember where you left it?"

"In Olney," she replied. "We swapped it for the mules, Uncle Walter."

At the screen Edna cried, "Anybody got some aspirin? We got snakebite kits, but no aspirin."

Maxine walked right around in a circle, like a chicken with its head cut off.

"Mrs. Momeyer," said Mr. Jennings, "it's in the box of Kleenex."

"If it's too much trouble, never mind," said Edna. "Clyde'll live, if somebody don't shoot him."

Maxine actually felt the sweat on her forehead might be blood. "Don't you feel any shame!" she cried. "Papa lying dead there on the sofa and there's nothing on your mind but a dog's life insurance."

"There's plenty on my mind," Edna replied, "and I guess I'm more ashamed of it than you are. There's sadder things to have on your hands than a poor dead dog." She was gone.

"Sweet Jesus," said Mrs. Boyd, "look at that friggin sky."

Everybody in the room but Maxine turned to look

at it. She could see the red of it in their faces, cool as it was, every one of them sweaty.

Leaning forward, McKee said, "Now what the devil's he up to?"

Through the curtained window Maxine could see Calvin and the mules at the front of the stable, and as he led them out, just the front of the wagon with its canvas top. Through the holes in the canvas she could see the red morning sky. In that covered wagon her father had been born. So long ago she'd rather not remember, his children had played in it.

"Hey!" said Bud, and she waited for Etoile to say, *straw's cheaper.* "Hey, didn't that used to be a dead wagon, Maxine?"

Maxine made an effort to lift her arms, let them flap at her sides.

"Matter of fact," said McKee, "think it was. Forget who died in it."

Rubbing her palms together, Lois said, "I wash my hands, Mr. Jennings," and started for the hall door.

Was it the sight of her back, flat as an ironing board? Whatever it was that swept over people swept over Maxine. "Honest to God, Lois," she cried, "will you do it and get it done with!" bringing the stove-lid handle down on the table with a bang. Lois stiffened like a piece of it had hit her. She went so rigid that for a moment Maxine thought she might fall over backward, but she didn't, she kept going, since it was Boyd who would have had to catch her. Nobody said a word till they heard her feet on the stairs.

"Look at that, will you," said McKee, nodding his head at the window. But Maxine just wished to God the blind had been drawn. She saw the mules, first the one with the hat, the JUST MARRIED sign dangling like a license, then Calvin, high on the seat, his boots braced on the buckboard, looking as pleased as her father leading the Fourth of July parade. Had Etoile just *married* something like that? With her father dead, was it all to start over again?

"Sweet Jesus," said Mrs. Boyd, "you people come out here in something like that?"

It was McKee, clearing his throat, who said, "Guess some people did, didn't they, Maxine?"

Why didn't *she*, once and for all, say it and get it done with? There would never be an end to some things until the women in the family had more say in the matter, and maybe they would have it if a woman like Maxine would just speak up. She wadded up the apron in her hands, said, "I'm afraid they did, Mrs. Boyd," and looking straight at McKee, "I just wish to God they never had."

McKee

"One of you men," Maxine said, meaning McKee, "build me a fire and I'll make you some coffee."

Wanting coffee, McKee built it, using the fruit crate she had brought the food along in, a picture of oranges the size of grapefruit on one end. The smell and crackle of the pine kindling made him rub his hands and shift from one foot to the other. "For heaven's sake," said Maxine, "you cold?" No, McKee wasn't cold. He was just ashamed to admit— with the old man dead—he felt so good. Was it the smell of the coffee? The sound of frying eggs? He stood at the screen, as he hadn't in thirty years, and watched the light spread out on the plain. He'd been up at sunrise, but he hadn't really seen one since he was a kid delivering his eggs. Maxine had been a stick-legged girl with braids that she chewed on the ends of. Lois had been—well, Lois had been pretty much the same. When things got a little out of hand she would go off till they had quieted down. "When you people have control of yourselves," she would say, "just let me know," and go to her room. That much hadn't changed—she was up in her room right now. How much really had? They had all grown old with trouble in their legs, their hearts or their heads, but Boyd still tended to get out of control, Mrs. McKee still retired to her room, and Maxine still

fried an egg you couldn't dent with a fork. She
would go on frying them like that to the end of her
days. Since he couldn't stand the eggs, why did her
doing that please him? He turned and let his hand
rest on her shoulder, as broad and sloped as a mare's
haunch, nodded his head at the stove and said, "You
call that a fried egg?" It was a joke between them
how she cooked an egg. Maxine had never been
much for looks, first like a bean pole, then a sack of
potatoes, but McKee would no more think of josh-
ing with Lois, his hand on her shoulder, than slipping
it between the bars of a cage at the zoo. When he
happened to put his hand on Lois, steering her between the tables in a restaurant, she would twitch
just a bit like a horse shedding flies, and then check
to see if something was showing, as if McKee had
put his hand there to cover it up.

"You want to make yourself useful, McKee?" she
said, which was the way she liked to banter with
him.

"Coffee?" he said. "You think it'll pour?" which
was the way he liked to banter with her. He used a
towel to get a grip on the handle, then he turned to
see Boyd and Mrs. Boyd standing near the door,
holding hands like a pair of kids. Somewhere in Mexico, up a street they had gone, McKee had seen two
old men go along holding hands. "Lois," he had said,
"look at that, will you," but she wouldn't. No, he
couldn't persuade her, since she seemed to feel there
was something wrong in it. McKee could dimly recall, when he was a kid, being told by somebody, he
didn't know who, to stop holding hands since it was

not done by little boys. Had it been with Boyd? Had McKee pulled his hand away first? He thought of that, pouring the coffee, and the next thing he thought of was the letter in his pocket.

"McKee!" called Maxine. "You see what you're doing?"

McKee sopped up what he had spilled with the towel, then he turned to see Boyd, still wearing that T-shirt, trying to get the snag out of Mrs. Boyd's zipper, holding up her pigtail like a horse's tail off the buckboard. He could just as well forget about that letter, but he couldn't remember how long it had been since he had known something Boyd didn't know or had something Boyd wanted.

"Gordon," he said, " 'fore I forget it, thought I'd better ask you if you want this letter mailed."

Boyd turned and said, "What letter?" McKee let him wait while he fished it from his pocket.

"Been some time," he said, holding it up. "Thought you might feel different about it now."

"About what?" said Boyd. McKee noticed his Adam's apple when he swallowed.

"Maybe I just better mail it," said McKee, wishing that he hadn't brought it up. Once he had an advantage, he didn't seem to know what to do with it. He tapped the letter on his palm the way lawyers did important papers.

Leaning over his shoulder, Maxine said, "A two-cent stamp? Who in the world put that on a letter?"

"Two was enough back then," said McKee, "wasn't it, Gordon?"

For just long enough for McKee to feel it, Boyd

hesitated, the letter there between them, the same look on his face McKee had seen the night before. Boyd stymied. Boyd actually not so sure of himself. "Stamp's probably worth money now, Gordon," he said. "Why don't you steam it off and give it to Etoile? She collects stamps."

At that Boyd took it, the envelope so thin McKee could see right through it when he held it to the light. Was there nothing in it? There was, since Mc-Kee could see the corner of it when Boyd tore off the stamp, bowed to Etoile and said, "My dear, two cents for your thoughts."

Before Etoile could even open her mouth, Maxine had clamped a wad of apron over her face. "I don't want to know *your* thoughts," she said, "or anybody else's," then turned and grabbed the letter Boyd was holding, raised the lid on the stove, and tossed it on what was left of the fire.

McKee was so dumfounded he just blinked.

"I'll be goddamned," said Mrs. Boyd.

"Mother—" said Etoile.

"Don't you mother me, you hear? If you're married, you act like it. If you don't know how to act, why then I'll show you." Did she know she was holding that stove-lid handle over Etoile's head? The girl ducked, and Maxine gathered up her apron as if she was going to weep—but she didn't. No, she mopped her face with it, then she let it fall like she was unveiling a monument, and McKee would swear to God that was how she looked. Like the one to long-suffering motherhood in the Hastings park.

"I'm sick and tired of hearing you people talk," she said. "Will you please shut up?"

McKee put up his hand as if he felt cobwebs tickling his face. He let it drop, then looked around the room from face to face, from Eileen to Jennings, and they all looked shamefaced and sheepish, like McKee felt. Through the screen he saw the mules, Calvin's feet on the buckboard, and up through a hole in the tattered canvas the beaming face of Bud, as though he had been swallowed by a whale. In the voice of a train announcer, he said:

"All aboard for Cheyenne, Laramie, and the gold fields." All McKee could do was stare at his grinning face.

"Like me to give you a hand?" Jennings said to McKee, and made clear what he meant by moving over to the sofa. He slipped his hands under the top end of the sheet. When McKee took the legs, and they didn't bend, he almost dropped him.

"Like to hold that screen, Boyd?" he said, and Boyd hustled over quick enough to do it, McKee's left arm rubbing on his paunch as he squeezed past. Made him think as he felt for the steps, trying not to think of what he was doing, of how it took something crazy, good or bad, to pull a roomful of people together. He took it slow, the way he used to do it with a case of eggs. The fact the old man weighed almost nothing was what bothered him.

"Easy does it, you men," said Bud, and at any other time McKee would have let him have it. The tailboard was down, but the floor was so high Mc-

Kee had to wait till Bud could help him. He took McKee's end, then said, "Which way you think he'd like to ride?"

All McKee could think of was how people would surprise you, even people like Bud.

"Since we're going west," Jennings said, "think he might like to face forward," and McKee wagged his head as if that struck him as full of sense. Up where the canvas had the fewest holes they lowered him to a piece of crib mattress McKee recognized as once his own. He raised his head with the intention of inquiring about that just in time to see the trailer, as though the brakes had slipped, glide from where the Colonel had parked it. They had all the room in the world in that trailer, but McKee would dig the grave before he'd ask him for help.

"Hey!" he yelled. "Hey, Colonel," but the trailer just kept coming till he saw the Chrysler at the front of it, the Colonel at the wheel. He didn't look well. He didn't look well at all. Leaning across his chest, her head on the wheel, McKee could see the face of Edna.

"We're going to Grand Island, Walter," she called. "There's an office of Clyde's insurance company in Grand Island. Nobody's going to believe it if they don't see it with their own eyes."

McKee just about called out, "See what?" then he remembered in time. He could hear her coughing till she ran the window up. He watched the trailer stop at the tracks, where the Colonel put his head out to look and listen, and McKee saw the light of morning on his purple face. Did he look like a man who had lost something his insurance wouldn't cover? Did McKee? On his own face he felt little more than a film of sweat. He waited till the trailer, like a streetcar, came between him and the rising sun, feeling the coolness of its shade on his face.

"Got room for two more?" Boyd said, and there he was, on the stoop, with his missus. Did McKee care any more if they were married or not? Boyd had slipped on his shirt, leaving the tails out, with his coat folded over one arm, and it dawned on McKee he was probably wearing the only clothes he had. Did he need money? Why didn't McKee speak up? He could write a check, right there in the wagon, for enough to set a man up in business, if you could imagine setting Boyd up in anything.

McKee glanced around, saw Jennings, said, "How about you, Doc?"

"Will you stop calling him Doc," Maxine said. "He's got a name like all of us."

She turned to look at Jennings, who said, "Yes ma'am, Mrs. Momeyer, the name is Jennings."

"Sweet Jesus," the girl said, "I've been up this late, but never this early." Hadn't she slept? Or was it those things she wore on her eyes? Not a pretty girl at all, and when he stopped to think, when Mc-Kee stopped to think of how Lois once was—well, when he stopped to think of that he couldn't help but marvel how times had changed.

"There's not much choice of seats," he said. "You people like the buckboard or the tailboard?"

"Nobody's going to sit on that tailboard, McKee. Do you hear?"

McKee heard, settling his eyes on the pair of cushions in Eileen's sports car.

"Eileen," he called, "it be all right if we borrow that car seat?"

"Help yourself, darling, it's what people do whenever I park it."

Maxine said, "Mrs. Boyd, why don't you wait? A ride like that will jar your teeth out."

An arm around her shoulders, Boyd said, "Mrs. Momeyer, she is dying to know what it was like in the days beyond recall—"

"I just wish to God they were," Maxine said. "You don't need the ride. You like me to tell you?"

As if he thought Daughter might change her mind, Boyd put his hands to her waist, hoisted her to the tailboard. McKee gave him a hand as he climbed aboard himself. Through the tunnel of canvas he could see Jennings humped on the buckboard, as if he belonged there, just as Calvin made a loop in the reins and slapped the mules. The yard had looked smooth as a carpet till the wheels began to move. To keep from falling, McKee took a seat on the tailboard. What the devil led him to glance at the sky? Up there was Lois, her head out of the bathroom window. The hat was still on it, and her glasses were slipping down her nose.

"Lois!" he hollered. "Your glasses!" since they were apt to slip when she stooped over.

"Just remember, McKee—" she replied just as one of the mules let out a hee-haw, as if he had heard what she said. Was it the rocking wagon that tipped

McKee's hat over his eyes? When he looked back, the head against the sky was gone. Bud stood on the stoop, his back turned to Maxine so she could loosen the strap on his quiver, like a kid who had got himself tangled up in something. Then the wall of the hotel, the MAIL POUCH sign peeling, moved in between them and the rest of the town, like an old-style curtain between the movies and the vaudeville. Had one just rung down on something? McKee counted the windows, five of them to a floor, the screens rusted, the cracked blinds drawn on rooms with empty beds and trapped dead flies. One window was let down an inch or two at the top. That blind was up. He could see the hole poked in the screen. Back in the thirties there had been some complaint that the old man shot at people when they made the track crossing, but nothing serious, since he didn't manage to hit anyone. They just heard the report or saw the flash of the powder at night. Now they wouldn't, not at that window, and it dawned on McKee, as it hadn't before, that something he had taken for granted in the world was no more. Tomorrow it would be different. Could anybody say in just what way? When he had a question, one of the kind to which he really wanted an answer, the only person he ever thought of was Boyd. He glanced at him there on the car seat, one arm running along the sideboard so the girl could lean her head back. Her eyes were closed. Had she already seen too much? Boyd needed a shave worse than McKee did; on his forehead was a smudge about the same color as the nail polish on the girl's toes. A bit of cigarette paper was stuck to her lips. What had McKee meant to ask him?

As if he felt him looking, Boyd said, "Well, Daughter, you see where I'm from?" McKee saw her smile without opening her eyes.

"Don't let him fool you," said McKee. "He's not from here at all. He's from Polk."

"Where's Polk?" she said.

"Polk's at least eighty miles down the line," said McKee.

"Polk's different, Daddy?" she said, rocking her head on his arm.

"Home of the hero," said Boyd. "Morgenstern Boyd, pop-squirter, water-walker and friggin bore. First and last of the completely self-unmade men."

To shut him off McKee said, "Polk's a town of twenty-seven hundred people. She'd like Polk, wouldn't she, Gordon?"

"Four express trains stop there daily," said Boyd.

"Don't you let him josh you," said McKee. "You get him to show you around a bit. Might surprise him to see how it's looking up. Eastern capital is waking up to the fact that Polk is just off the center of the country, best place in the world for light industries serving both coasts. All around Polk, if not right in it, they're springing up. Roads the way they are, live in Polk, work somewhere else. Mr. Eldredge of Corn Exchange National said there never was a time better than the present for the small-loan risk to a man with eyes in his head. Take Polk. Right now it's quiet, but any day now the roof might blow off. All those people now living in trailers might decide to build homes. Population curve's on the rise all over the state. Right at this minute a man and his wife could make a good thing with one of these new motels. Air-conditioned. Only stop between North Platte and Omaha. Happened to mention that," said McKee, lying through his hat, "when I was talking to Mr. Eldredge, who said he'd be glad to see right man got the necessary cash." Wagging his head, McKee added, "Mrs. Boyd, maybe you're the one to get him to come back."

"Back?" she said, opening her eyes. "Daddy, you ever been away?"

McKee wondered whose leg she was pulling, his own or Boyd's.

"Hang on, you folks," Jennings called, and McKee could see they were rising toward the tracks. The harness creaked: he could hear the mules dig in on the slope. The pitch of the road was so sharp he took a grip on the board to keep from sliding: rocking on the tracks, the ribs over his head cracked like they would snap. How the devil did men ever cross the country in a wagon like it? He turned to look at the body wrapped up in the sheet. Had he ever gone anywhere? Not that McKee had ever heard. Yet he felt for him a certain affection, now that he was dead. If somebody had offered him the ride, he would have gone. He glanced back just in time to see the top floor of the hotel, with the uncurtained window, the top branches of the tree like bleached cattle horns, just before the weeds growing along the track bed cut it off.

"Now you see it, now you don't," said the girl. "Sweet Jesus."

"Nevertheless," said Boyd, "You know it's still there."

"What's that?" said McKee, and leaned forward as if he might see. Somebody new to the country had planted a field of wheat, as if he thought it might rain, and at this time of year it was green as a carpet of grass. One day they'd run water along the ditch and make Lone Tree like it was around Polk, with the clover in flower and the smell of it so strong it would go to his head. Had it already? A queer thought crossed McKee's mind. Was it the sniff of that clover and the sight of that wheat—was it this that disturbed the old man's sleep? Was it this that led him to get up and die in the night? The last man in Lone Tree didn't want to smell clover, or see the wheat wave or the corn flower, or hear that the last of the dust had blown itself out. No, he really didn't.

Did McKee? Along the tracks, where the town would appear as if the bank dropped a notch to reveal it, the first wavy ripple of heat rose from the cinders and blurred the sky. If the smell of clover had killed the old man, it had been in his dream. Aloud McKee said, "It's going to be a hot one," and turned to see why they paid him no heed. The old man was past caring. The two on the car seat were asleep.